What Others Have Said about Dan Diggles

"[Dan's] teaching is thoughtful, caring, kind, generous, carefully clarified, and inspiring. He is one of the most highly complimented instructors with whom I've ever had the pleasure of working. While there are many of us who think we know something of acting, there are but a few who really teach it well. Dan is one of those."

—Gary Sullivan, Department Chairman,
Wagner College Theatre Department, Staten Island, NY

"Dan's dedication to teaching is clearly evident when one observes his class. He has been one of the most sought after instructors in the department because he continues to challenge the student."

—Bill Bordeaux, Professor of Theatre,
Marymount Manhattan College, New York, NY

"Dan Diggles is an outstanding teacher of improvisation. . . . [His] technique and style are unmatched. . . . He knows his subject matter inside and out and, as a successful working actor and improv artist, he serves as a role model to his students."

—Laura Huntsmann, Education Director,
The McCarter Theatre, Princeton, NJ

"Dan's particular style of improv involves three fundamental rules which teach useful life lessons for anyone who needs to collaborate. [His] constant encouragement and positive outlook are invaluable enhancements to the entertaining and useful content of his classes. . . . it will be our good fortune to incorporate many of Dan's unique approaches to improvisation into our future course work."

—*Allen Kennedy, Senior Teacher,*
The Dalton School, New York, NY

"Dan possesses the incredible capacity to ignite and enthuse, all the while teaching both the necessary skills of drama and the invaluable skills of survival. His teaching carries with it the experience, wisdom and caring that are so particular to him. . . . Repeatedly, Dan proves that learning can also be fun."

—*Ron DeMaio, Director, Student Television Arts Company,*
Herricks High School, New Hyde Park, NY

improv for actors

improv
for
dan diggles
actors

**ALLWORTH
PRESS**
NEW YORK

07 06 05 04 03   5   4   3   2   1

Published by Allworth Press
An imprint of Allworth Communications, Inc.
10 East 23rd Street, New York, NY 10010

Cover design by Derek Bacchus

Page composition/typography by Integra Software Services Pvt. Ltd.,
Pondicherry, India

ISBN: 1-58115-325-2

Library of Congress Cataloging-in-Publication Data
Diggles, Dan.
    Improv for actors/Dan Diggles.
      p.   cm.
Includes index.
    ISBN 1-58115-325-2 (pbk.)
    1. Improvisation (Acting)   I. Title.

PN2071.I5D54 2004
792.02′8—dc22

                                                  2003024693

Printed in Canada

Table of Contents

Part I
Introduction to Improv

Chapter

[1] The Three Rules

There are three rules to good improvisation. If you follow them, whatever your background—whether you've had any training as a performer or not—you will be an excellent improviser. The rules are:

- *Say the first thing that comes into your head.*
- *Say, "Yes! And . . ." to all of your partner's offers.*
- *Make your partner look good.*

Simple as these rules sound, you're probably going to find, as most people do, that they are antithetical to everything life has taught you. And that you have to bend the spine of your will to accomplish them.

Theater and improvisation are communal art forms. Both require not only spontaneity (*Say the first thing that comes into your head*), but also a sharing of offers (*Say "Yes! And . . ." to all of your partner's offers*), and generous, mutual support (*Make your partner look good*). It is these last two rules in particular that mark the difference between solo art forms, like writing, sculpting, and painting, and the communal forms like acting, dance, etc. When we say "Yes! And . . ."

to our partners offers and when we make our partners look good quickly and unconditionally, we create something that is bigger than all the participants. Just as important, we become more and more of the best of ourselves in the presence of others who not only encourage and support us, but also take delight in what we reveal.

Audiences know this. They long for it. And they will flock to watch you play by these rules.

Education

In her book *If You Want to Write*, Brenda Ueland writes:

> The only good teachers for you are those friends who love you, who think you are interesting, or very important, or wonderfully funny; whose attitude is:
>
> "Tell me more. Tell me all you can. I want to understand more about everything you feel and know and all the changes inside and out of you. Let more come out."
>
> "And if you have no such friend—and you want to write-well then you must imagine one."

The approach this book takes to improvisation is based on this attitude. The Latin root for the word "education" is "e-duco," meaning "to lead out." This is what any good teacher does for his pupils. He doesn't impose himself on his pupils, but exposes them to wisdom he's accumulated, hoping that each student will "try it on" and adapt the wisdom to uncover more of *himself.* And by this definition, this is what all participants in a communal art form do for each other. They educate, or e-duco, each other. They encourage their partners to, as Brenda Ueland says, "Let more come out."

When this happens in an improvisation, the scene takes off. A good sign of a good improv is when you see two performers surprised by what has just happened, grinning at a creation that seemed out of their control because each one was both giving (*Say the first thing that comes into your head*) and accepting (*Say, "Yes! And . . ."* to all of your partner's offers) so rapidly and unconditionally that there was no time for fear or censorship, simply mutual delight in what was happening.

"Am I a Good Improviser?"

When students ask me "Am I a good improviser?" my immediate response is, "Do people want to play with you?" If people don't want to play with them, it not only implies that they aren't particularly good improvisers, but I gently suggest they might consider changing their major. There are any number of solo art forms that are equally rewarding. If people *do* want to play with them, however, they are not only good improvisers . . . they will only get better. People seek out people with whom they enjoy playing. This increases your opportunity to grow. And just as important . . . people *hire* people with whom they enjoy playing.

Purpose of This Book

This book is a practical approach to learning these three rules. It is designed to strengthen specific improvisational skills that are useful not only for an improviser, but that readily translate to scripted theater and all communal art forms.

In the next three chapters the three rules are discussed. They are followed by a chapter on "Status," an exceptionally powerful concept for bringing improvisations and all scripted scenes alive. Next is a class-by-class breakdown with specific exercises and games for learning the rules and applying status work, each class building on the other.

How to Use This Book

This course can be used in a variety of ways. It evolved over twelve years of teaching improvisation to theater students and, as such, can be used as a class plan in a theater curriculum. If so, students should become familiar with part I, chapters 1–4, as soon as possible, which explain the three rules. (They can read part I, chapter 5, on Status when it's introduced later in the course.) Throughout the early exercises, students are continually invited as "observers" to give examples of all three rules after each exercise. The sooner they're familiar with these chapters and the thought behind these rules, the more effective these observations are and the more immediate their application in subsequent scenes.

This book can also be used to help start an improvisation company. There are many sources for improvisational games that your group can play, games that are useful for building skills as well as performing (see Appendix 6). But my experience as an improviser has been that as these three rules go, so goes the company. Use them as the foundation for all your work. And use this book as a resource. As you're forming your company, have everyone read the introductory chapters. Then, follow the course up to and including the "I Love You Scenes" with Expertise. These sections include exercises that are not only great for learning the rules, they're also excellent performance games as well, as you begin to build your repertory. And with all the exercises, before each couple begins a new scene, have them give examples of each rule from the previous scene.

At that point, you can introduce improvisational games you've heard about or read about. But continue with the observations. And then come back to the course, alternating outside games with the course chapters, etc.

Finally, this book can be used as introductory material to any improvisation workshop or workshop that involves team building of any kind. I have used many of the exercises in corporate situations where creativity was encouraged and cooperation required. My experience has been that most people quickly cancel other people's suggestions because they are too frightened to voice their own and are, therefore, afraid of being "overwhelmed" by someone else's. This can be either a personal issue or one of job security, but the results are the same: "creativity" meetings that gradually hiccup to a standstill. These exercises, the playfulness they engender, and the trust that follows, usher group participants rapidly and safely into the sort of creative team behavior that encourages saying the first thing that comes into their heads, "Yes! And . . ."-ing their teammates offers, and making their partners look good.

Play

I'd like to say one more thing before closing this introduction about the value of "play" in this course. Adults frequently misunderstand the purpose of play. Most think of it as something children do to fill their time until they're mature enough to accept adult responsibilities.

In fact, play is something that children do to help them grow, to stretch their limits as they investigate how well they can work with the world around them. When children are having fun, they push their limits. I remember facing monkey bars when I was in kindergarten. They scared me. I know that if my father had yelled at me, "Go climb on the monkey bars!" I would have. But once his back was turned, I never would have done it again.

But I was bored, curious, and could see that my friends weren't getting hurt. Most importantly, I wanted to play with my friends . . . and they wanted to play with me. So I tried the monkey bars and liked what I was doing. And then we got into a sort of a "King of the Monkey People" game. You were cooler the higher you climbed. I was having a ball, and climbed higher and higher, stretching my limits. And uncovering more of the "best of Dan" in the process. (I'll come back to this idea of "the best of yourself" in chapter 2).

Now theater students taking several courses at once are often overwhelmed by the number of new skills they feel they're being forced to learn. I know I almost left graduate school during my final semester. As I explained to the faculty, I felt I was no longer "entertaining" or "communicating" anything, but was learning how to prepare work for teachers just well enough so that at least it looked prepared . . . only to have it torn apart. It was no longer fun. I felt unskilled and inadequate. And I found that bartending, my evening job, was bringing me more satisfaction than any of my theater classes. I made great drinks, pleased customers, and made money.

Yet skills-training is essential. Without it, your performances are blurry and you'll find a career as an artist ordinary and dull.

I demonstrate how essential skills are by telling the class that I'm now going to portray the part of an angry character. I place a chair facing away from them, sit with my back to them; think about something that really makes me angry, and sit still for about twenty seconds. Then stand up and ask them if they got it. "But I *felt* angry!" I tell them. It makes no difference. Without the skills required to physically and vocally project your intentions efficiently to an audience that can number in the hundreds, it doesn't matter how you feel.

There is this style of acting called "realism" or "naturalism" that most actors will use throughout their stage and movie careers. It shouldn't be confused with "being real." It is a *style* that you use to communicate the playwright's intentions efficiently while *looking* like you're simply being real. It starts with basic skills like facing downstage and projecting your voice to the back of the house. Think about it: You're doing an intimate love scene that takes place in a library where people are supposed to be quiet, and yet you're projecting your voice well enough to be heard throughout the auditorium. And if you're doing it well, no one in the auditorium thinks it's weird that you're talking so loud in a library. They just think you're being real.

There is a famous painting by Magritte of a pipe filled with tobacco, and the caption below it is "Ceci n'est pas un pipe." or "This is not a pipe." People stand in front of it, as I did, confused. Finally somebody asked me what I thought it was. I said, "A pipe." He replied, "If it's a pipe, smoke it." Of course it isn't a pipe. It's a representation of a pipe. Just as a movie isn't real, it's light and colors projected on a screen. However, the audience is *eager* to be deceived into believing it's real, just as I stood in front of that painting, impatiently insisting that it was a pipe. In acting, "realism" isn't being real. Act naturally and your performance would never communicate throughout an auditorium. "Realism" is a set of skills that solve this issue and yet give an audience the *illusion* of reality; just as the Magritte painting gives the illusion of a pipe.

You drill these skills until they become instinctive, just as a ballet dancer drills the five positions or a singer shapes vowels over and over. And these are just the beginning. The skills required in acting are just as numerous and sophisticated as those required in carrying on a successful love relationship: you keep learning, keep refining, and keep improving.

If you think this is daunting, keep in mind that you already perform a skill of *extraordinarily* intricate sophistication every day, a skill that you've been working on since childhood, and that you accomplish with amazing efficiency and without thinking about it. You speak English. You weren't born doing this. And the language with all its vocabulary, subject/verb agreements, odd plurals, and so on, is very difficult to learn. Yet you face someone, you feel something; you open your mouth and instead of "Aaagaarrrr," out comes this amazing string of interdependent words balanced with syntax and grammar while you place that feeling in another brain. There's an even more amazing thing you do: I'm making an arbitrary arrangement of black squiggles on this white page, and you're looking at these patterns and reading my mind. Reading is a highly sophisticated skill—a miracle in fact—and you do it effortlessly every day.

And I think you'd agree: It's worth the effort.

The skills required for all art forms are equally sophisticated. And the more sophisticated you become, the better you communicate, the more color and variety you can add to what you do, *and* the more validating and delightful it is for you. The greater your "bag of tricks," the more fun you have.

However, as I mentioned before, learning all these skills can become a deadening experience. I became an actor originally for the same reason I suspect that everyone else does: I liked to show off. People paid attention when I did, and consequently I could make my presence felt in the world. After three years of graduate school, however, this spark was being snuffed.

This is why a sense of "play" is so important, and a reason why a class in improvisation where a playful atmosphere is maintained is so vital to one's growth as an artist. Yes, all artists must appreciate how important structure and organization is to healthy development. But a piano teacher once told me to spend at least 10 percent of my practice time goofing around. Otherwise, he told me, I'd lose touch with what made me want to play the piano in the first place. Then what difference would it make *how* much structure I'm capable of? (All serious dancers should goof around. It will become *their* choreography.)

Develop this sense of play and maintain it throughout your career as a performer. In *A Practical Handbook for the Actor*—a marvelous and succinct book on acting technique—the writers say that one of the nine criteria for choosing a good objective is that it must be fun to pursue. "Getting her to change her mind" is one objective. "Getting this bimbo to wake up and smell the coffee!" is similar, but my voice changes even as I'm saying it, my body is invaded with an energy, and it's a lot more fun to pursue.

Improvisation can put you back in touch with the obvious, "average" you, the unique voice in the arts that you already are, the best of you. It can be scary because, in a world full of rules, there are no rules for "you." Improvisation's power is that it makes this journey fun.

Chapter

[2] Say the First Thing That Comes into Your Head

There is a vitality, a life force, an energy, a quickening that is translated through you into action, and because there is only one of you in all of time, this expression is unique. And if you block it, it will never exist through any other medium and be lost. The world will not have it.

"It is not your business to determine how good it is nor how valuable nor how it compares with other expressions. It is your business to keep it yours clearly and directly, to keep the channel open. You do not even have to believe in yourself or your work. You have to keep open and aware directly to the urges that motivate you. Keep the channel open.

—Martha Graham

This rule probably has the most far-reaching implications of the three.

Other ways of stating *Say the first thing that comes into your head* are

- Dare to be obvious.
- Dare to be average.
- Do not try to be clever.

Huh? Isn't most improvisation about just the *opposite* . . . wildly clever people coming up with punch line after punch line?

I make a distinction between two kinds of improv: *gag improv* and *narrative improv*. Most people are intimidated by improv because most of the improvisation they are familiar with is gag improv: two stand-up comedians trying to top each other. This can be an exciting art form in the hands of skilled performers. However, it is highly competitive and dangerous in the hands of unskilled performers.

Gag Improv

- Gag improv is based on you and your own *personal* success or failure with the audience, not the success or failure of the character you're creating in conflict with the character your partner is creating.
- The criteria for this success or failure are cleverness and jokes. These *have* to come quickly and regularly.
- Your primary relationship is with your audience. In fact, gag improvisers will often abandon their partners, block their offers, even put them down, etc., if it gets them a laugh from this primary audience relationship.
- It can become highly competitive. As a result, you can lose your partner's trust and he will begin to shut down; you lose his support *and* eventually—as the scene begins to bog down—you can lose your audience's interest.
- The skills developed in gag improv, which is *competitive* and *audience focused*, do not translate readily to scripted theater, which is *cooperative* and *partner focused*.

Narrative Improv

- Narrative improv is based on a character's success or failure with another character, not on your personal success or failure with the audience. The irony is that character can fail and theatrically you will *still* succeed with the audience.
- The humor is a result of that character's passionate pursuit of his objective, not your own ability to say clever things.
- Your primary relationship is with your partner, not the audience.

- It is cooperative.
- Because it is cooperative, you instill trust in your partner, and consequently begin to have fun with each other, releasing yourselves into bigger and better spontaneous choices.
- Because it's not based on cleverness, it's a lot easier. And because it instills trust in your partner—who again, if he's responding in kind, is instilling trust in you—it can be a *lot* more fun.

So, while in gag improv you sacrifice dramatic action for a laugh, often at your partner's expense, in narrative improv, as in scripted theater, you advance dramatic action by working *with* your partner.

By the way, narrative improv is just as funny as gag improv; but for different reasons. Again, gag improv is funny because of the jokes. It is witty and highly cerebral. The humor in narrative improv, on the other hand, is character based: people with strong passions and commitments throwing themselves into an unknown future, giving up control in the process, and staying where they suddenly find themselves to work it out. What could be funnier than a scene where a bag lady turns to a businessman on a subway and says, "Let's dance like the wind!" and the actor says, "Yes! And. . . ." Immediately the audience leans forward.

This, I feel, *is* the "moment of theater:" when the audience is leaning forward, convinced that the character they're watching doesn't know what's going to happen next and yet he continues to step forward into the unknown future. In scripted theater, your ability to create the illusion of these moments is essential. However, in improvisation these moments can't be helped. Just say "Yes! And . . ." to every offer and you'll be in trouble . . . guaranteed . . . the kind of trouble audiences will pay a lot to watch. What improvisers come to realize is that if they say "Yes! And . . . ," create the danger, and then just keep moving forward, as *performers* they will *always* succeed, even if the *characters* they're playing fail. The drama you create by stepping into the unknown future is always satisfying to the audience, whatever the outcome.

This is one of the great lessons in improvisation that translates so readily into scripted theater. The actors who delight us the most are the ones who know the lines, execute the blocking they've rehearsed, and yet can *still* convince themselves on some level that they don't know what their scene partner is going to do next—don't know if the objective they're pursuing with all their might will be achieved. Improv helps you do this: helps you get comfortable with being uncomfortable, that feeling of "treading air" as you lunge forward into the unknown. And it's this danger the characters find themselves in and their passionate commitment to work it out that makes the audience laugh if the situation is farcical and broad, or gasp if the scene is realistic.

Fear #1—Revealing Yourself

In the previous chapter I said that, as you try to follow these three rules, you probably will find that they are antithetical to everything life has taught you. In the case of this first rule, one of the reasons people are afraid to say the first thing that comes into their heads is because life has taught them that if they do, they will reveal themselves.

You will.

Why would anyone want to do that?

Because if you say the first thing that comes into your head, if you dare to be obvious, dare to be average, you will end up parading before us a story that no one else could tell because no one else has lived your life. And this is the first step to becoming the unique voice in the arts *that you already are.*

For example, I encourage my students when they write papers for my class to illustrate quotes from the text we use by telling stories from their own lives. And I'm sure at times many of them feel nothing could be more mundane than a story about their dorm life. *I* haven't lived in a dorm in over thirty years, however, and *anything* they tell me is fascinating. A student came into the class the other day, plopped into a seat and said, "I went to a Bulgarian bar last night with my friend Rinka . . ." This was an ordinary event in her life, an obvious statement. I was fascinated!

However, we've all been through high school. The *last* thing that that experience encouraged was saying the first thing that comes into your head. And high school tends to mark us for life with lessons that become knee-jerk for many of us. From the most popular kid to the least popular, everyone labored under the belief that we weren't good enough as we were. And so much of America is geared to confirming that.

We live in a society of templates. There is the "God" template: *I am perfect; you are a sinner. You must spend your life trying to be*

as good as me, but of course you never will be. So keep asking for forgiveness. There is the "Teacher" template: *I'm smart. You're not. Try to imitate me and I'll give you a good grade.* Because we can't be *like* anyone else, both of these struggles are doomed to failure. And we internalize this sense of failure. Saying the first thing that comes into our heads, daring to be obviously ourselves, is out of the question.

In addition, there is the stranger in your living room who not only has more money than anybody in the world, but more money than anybody in *history* to accomplish his purpose. And his *sole purpose* is to make you dissatisfied with yourself. I'm talking about commercial television. TV *must* succeed in making you dissatisfied with yourself, or you won't buy things. And commercial TV's extraordinary power is this: No one questions it. If I came to you and said I wanted to teach your child, you'd investigate me. But no one questions TV.

This TV/media template, which includes magazines, movies, etc., is bad enough for men. It's worse for women. I think every guy should read a women's magazine at least once a year to see what they're up against. The first fifteen to thirty pages are advertising. This is even before you get to the table of contents. And what are these advertising pictures of? Women who,

a) Are genetically eccentric. Look at a billboard and then look at the people surrounding you on the street. How many people in your immediate vicinity look like the models on the billboard?
b) Have spent most of their days following a very strict regimen to maintain their "perfection." Most of the people I know don't have time for this. I don't.
c) Have spent as much as two hours getting made up for the shoot.
d) Are then lit to perfection in a way that seldom if ever occurs in nature.
e) And then . . . the photos are air brushed!

And what do you see when you look at the picture? A smiling, relaxed woman who looks, "just great."

How can you argue with that? How can you argue with someone who looks "just great?" So you look at your naked body in the mirror and find it's not good enough (for whom? You're the only person in the room). And decide that maybe if you spent $50 on .014 oz. of mascara, you could be just like her. A female minister in my church gave up wearing makeup for Lent. She thought it was a token gesture, only to discover the truth: that there was a template for women's beauty called "perfection," and as a woman, she was constantly being judged on her ability to fake it.

Now don't get me wrong. If you're going to be a performer, the way you look is extremely important. You have to take care of yourself and go to auditions looking like yourself at your very best. I'm not saying "Don't wear makeup." I am saying be aware of these templates, these standards that tell you that this is the way you *should* be and that you're a failure if you're not. You, as you are, are sufficient and a unique presence in the arts. Makeup is a costume you put on to achieve an effect for a particular occasion, not a standard you fall short of when you're without it.

In brief, the God/teacher/media templates invade our lives. And so, saying the first thing that comes into our heads, and thus revealing the unique voice in the arts, we already are suppressed at every turn. The message is repeated over and over: You're not good enough as you are. And the first thing that comes into *your* head isn't good enough either. So we reject it, try to be "clever," usually choose to *imitate* something "clever" we saw that was considered acceptable, and end up being just like everybody else. More about this later.

Imagination

Children are often admired for their imaginations. Adults feel they lose touch with this, and look back in admiration, making it something magical and unattainable. However, what children are is the epitome of daring to be obvious, of saying the first thing that comes into their heads. What we call "imagination" in children *is just being obvious.*

For example, I went to visit a friend. Her son Jeremy was on the floor in the living room with his small plastic dinosaurs and a pocket camera. He said he was giving them a screen test before he would cast them in his next movie.

I was delighted, and initially thought, "Wow! What an imagination." Now, when people say that, what they usually mean is, "How clever!" In fact, what Jeremy was doing was perfectly *obvious* to him. He had a limited number of toys, which included some dinosaurs, and his folks had thrown away a disposable camera. He'd seen movies. And if I'd said, "How clever, Jeremy!" he probably would have looked at me like I was from Mars. Or else, got bitten by the "clever" bug and tried to impress me, at which time he probably would have done a lot of ordinary things he thought I'd think were clever.

I now believe what Keith Johnstone suggests: that self-expression and imagination should be as *effortless* as perceiving. In his book *Impro: Improvisation and the Theatre* he points out that it takes enormous mental gymnastics to recognize a face in a crowd, considering how little information our eyes actually receive and how many thousands of variations there are in the human face. And yet when you recognize your father, are you aware of *any* mental effort *at all*? (It's only when you make a *mistake* in your perceptions and try to clarify it that you are aware of making any *effort*.)

A good improviser knows that his imagination should be just as effortless; that his best choices are his first, obvious, "average" ones. A bad improviser often monitors his first choice, labels it "not clever enough," and then struggles to find a clever one. And it's been my experience time and time again that he ends up simply conforming to some standardized "cleverness." Ask an audience for a room in a house to start a scene in and inevitably some clever person will say "bathroom." Always. Ask for an occupation, and you'll get "proctologist" or "gynecologist." Every night. We once asked for a location to start a scene, and a child said "Under the dining room table." "How clever," someone said. How obvious. The kid was three feet tall and, I suspect, not out to impress anyone.

The hardest thing to convince improvisers is to trust their first obvious instinct. To dare to be average. If I ask for a loaf of bread, hand me a loaf of bread, not a flaming gerbil. "Flaming gerbil" will get a laugh, your partner will feel abandoned, and the scene will die. If I say, "Dad," say "Yes, son," not "I'm your mother." This, too, will get a laugh; again your partner will feel abandoned and will either try to top you or will haul out another offer, which you, giddy because of the last laugh, will probably again take as a "set-up" and deliver another punch line. In either case, the dramatic action of the scene will hiccup to death.

By starting with basic, obvious responses, students begin to trust their first impulses. And I believe this is the first step toward healthy self-expression. Again, the great life lesson improv has taught me is that if you say what's obvious to you, you will begin to parade before us a life that is unique and fascinating and not necessarily obvious to anyone else. How could it be? No one has had the same life experiences you have had.

Fear #2—Obscenity

People are also afraid to say the first thing that comes into their heads because they're afraid they're going to say something obscene. Besides, they argue to themselves, they're secretly convinced that they're a little crazier than everybody else.

You will. And you're not.

When people are finally given permission to say the first thing that comes into their heads, one of the phases most people go through is an obscenity phase. Everything is "fuck" and "shit" and "piss."

I'm smiling as I realize that I'm now going to introduce this topic in a section titled "Obscenity." But we're addressing taboos and shame, powerful elements that society uses to keep us "in our place." And prevent us from becoming all that we are. And it's this very freedom of gleeful self-discovery, of which the obscenity phase is only symptomatic, that makes improvisation such a powerful tool.

So much of my work as a teacher and performer is based on a fundamental belief that my role in life is two-fold: My first purpose is to uncover more and more of the best of myself. And by that best, I don't mean the "goody-goody." I mean everything that makes Dan the unique voice in life, let alone the arts, that he is. This is an on-going process, and that "best" changes continually as I synthesize more and more of the world around me. My second purpose is to help others do the same.

Two Moralities

Now, as an artist, I feel I have two separate moralities: One morality is the basis for actions I permit myself to take in daily life. The other is for actions I permit myself to take as a performer. Each of these must be both honored and examined continually. But the standards for one should not be confused with the other.

For example, in life, I probably would not betray Jesus. But if I'm asked to play Judas, *and I believe in what the play has to say*, it would be inappropriate for me to say, "Oh no! I could never betray Jesus!" I wouldn't appear nude in downtown New York. But if I'm asked to do so in a movie, *and I believe in what the movie has to say*, I would. If a bag lady turned to me on the subway and said "Let's dance like the wind!" I'd probably move to another car. In my class, however, I insist that the student say, "Yes! And . . ."

As a performer, your voice and your body are your instrument. And everything the human race is capable of, you can be capable of reflecting on stage. Your mission as a performer is two-fold: to delight the audience and to give them insight. Some of the things you'll do will be more delightful than insightful: musical comedies, Neil Simon plays. Others will be more insightful than delightful: *Oedipus Rex, Death of a Salesman*. As an artist, this is the service you provide the community, what people come to you for. Therefore, to refrain from certain activity on stage *if you believe in what the play has to say* simply because it's something you personally wouldn't do is to cloud this mission with personal issues.

Breaking through the obscenity issue is a marvelous way to clarify and confirm the distinction between these two moralities. I tell my students that simply because an actor has given himself permission to spout obscenity on stage doesn't mean that's who he is in all his life. Just because you say "Yes! And . . ." to someone in a subway improv who asks you to dance like the wind doesn't mean that it's advisable to do so in New York. Morality in life must be honored and examined because it protects us.

It also represses us. And audiences flock to watch us break through this repression. This is what farce is all about. One of the best, most practical books on acting styles is *Acting with Style* by John Harrop and Sabin R. Epstein. In their chapter on farce, they say:

> *Farce goes for the belly and the backside. It makes us laugh at the fact that we look funny, or at a disadvantage, with our pants down. Yet three of the five basic human physical functions—shitting, pissing, and fucking—can only be performed with the*

pants off. We have deliberately used the Anglo-Saxon terms, which our dictionary tells us are "usually considered vulgar," because that is part of what farce does—it removes polite masks to show the primitive realities beneath, and asks us to laugh at the discrepancy between what we show and what we are.

Handling Obscenity in Class

Again, one of the reasons actors are afraid to say the first thing that comes into their heads is a fear of being obscene. As an instructor I've found that, though obscenity in the classroom may seem like a risky issue, it can be handled well in two phases.

At the beginning of a course, students don't know each other and they probably already have a preconception of improv as something dangerous and competitive. The instructor's first task is to create an atmosphere of safety. So at the beginning of the "Gift-Giving" game (see Class 2) I tell the students that later on in the semester they'll be given permission to say anything or do anything in this class, except take their clothes off (which they can mime and create exactly the same effect on the audience), manhandle another performer (which is a control issue and breaks that performer's trust in you), and abuse the furniture (which the institution gets upset about) (see Class 5: Permission).

However, at this point in the course, since they're not used to working with each other, for the Gift-Giving exercise, I ask them not to make any deliberately funny offers—which starts competitive "gag" improvising—or to make any sexual offers. A sexual offer will get a laugh, and the partner will probably accept it because she thinks that's the adult thing to do, but she may feel very uncomfortable doing so in a room of strangers and she will begin to shut down. Also, the person making the sexual offer has put the partner on the spot and then sits back safely, abandoning the partner to struggle through the issue. This isn't fair and, more importantly, doesn't make your partner look good.

By the way, if the partner's *response* to an offer in the game is sexual or obscene, let it ride. Good for her for taking the risk! *Don't* stop it or imply that it's bad. But if you say too much in response, it may start competitive obscenity, which, again, puts students who aren't ready for this just yet on the spot.

Fear #3—I'm Crazier Than Everybody

Another reason people are afraid to say the first thing that comes into their heads is their fear of revealing that they're crazier than everybody else.

I ask my students early in the semester to raise their hands if they think that if anybody *really* found out the truth about them, he would realize how crazy they were. Usually all the hands go up, including mine. Then I tell them that they don't have to raise their hands this time, but how many right now are thinking, "Well, everyone else may *think* they're crazier than everyone else, but I *know* I am!"

A friend of mine told me that one of the things that pulled her through a very difficult time in her life was a statement her therapist had made: Crazy people are just like everyone else. Only more so.

I think contact with and acceptance of my craziness and my humanity is one of the redeeming things my life in the arts has given me. Most people don't bother to examine their lives: then when things go up in crap, they're bereft of the skills required to deal. Actors, on the other hand, are frequently called on to play parts that they often, at first glance, don't like . . . e.g., a businessman so repressed and lonely that he suddenly springs to his feet on the subway at the invitation of a bag lady and joins her as they dance like the wind. No character dislikes himself, so the actor is forced to figure out what about this character makes him like himself. And in fact it broadens our understanding of human experience in a way others don't ever reach. We begin to see "weirdness" or "life going up in crap" as simply another aspect of the human condition—no crazier than any other. And, ultimately, people turn to us for this understanding.

Making Fun

In the previous chapter, I talked about the value of play, how one of the great gifts of improvisation is its ability to take the difficult journey through revelation and self-discovery and make it fun. One of the great tricks I've learned is to take issues an actor or improviser may be having, aspects of themselves they may be afraid to manifest for fear of appearing "crazier than everybody else," and deliberately "make fun" of them. This is a far more powerful tool than you'd imagine.

I'd always been a pretty bad singer. I was an OK boy soprano in our church choir, but between my voice changing at puberty and my own determination to do everything "right," my voice just closed up. Whenever I tried to sing solo, I clenched and squeaked. All my life. I had a couple of leads in musicals. If the song was within my speaking range, I was OK. But the worst was the lead in *Plain and Fancy*, a musical about the Amish, where I had the only memorable song: "Young and Foolish." Well, the audience learned by my second act reprise that it was time to look at the program, talk with their spouses, and unwrap candies.

Years passed. And one day our improvisation company was driving in a van to a retreat. On the way, we started making fun of country-western songs. We made up titles that we thought were pretty funny, ("Drop-Kick Me, Jesus, Through the Goal Posts of Life"–which may be an actual title) and then improvised the song. About twenty minutes into this it dawned on me . . . I was singing awfully well. I was in tune, had vibrato, was making up rhyming lyrics, and was *harmonizing*, for Pete's sake.

What had happened?

I was "making fun" of singing. As soon as I stopped taking it seriously, I was free. During the shooting of *Presenting Lily Mars*, Judy Garland had been having a very difficult time with the final dance number, a glamorous ballroom production. During a break, she admitted to the choreographer, Chuck Walters, that she was afraid of it. He asked her who her favorite dancer was. She told him (Tony DeMarco) and he suggested she forget that she was Judy Garland dancing and to do an imitation of Tony DeMarco. According to Judy, it was a breakthrough.

I had a student once, a huge lummox of a guy who worked as a bouncer. He was extremely gentle, however, and never got angry in any scene he did. We were working on one of the neutral scenes at the end of this book and I was encouraging him to lose his temper with his partner. He couldn't, and explained that he was afraid of his own anger. And the problem was compounded by the fact that since he didn't get angry, he didn't even know how to use his body and voice to do a bad imitation of it.

I asked him who he knew who got angry easily. "My mother!" he said, grinning. Evidently she was this petite spitfire. I told him to show me, to make fun of her. He hedged; he felt uncomfortable about "making fun" of his mom. I told him it was merely an exercise and that she would never know. Bingo! Suddenly his voice and body were inhabited with all the trappings of anger. The transformation was amazing. And as long as he was making fun he could keep it up.

Making fun of something lowers the status of the finished product and makes it less intimidating. "You mean, make it funny?" a student asked me. No. *Making it funny* raises the status of the finished product: you have to make the audience laugh or you fail. *Making fun* of something on the other hand doesn't need audience feedback. You don't think it's worth much to start with. And the fear of failure is eliminated.

I have found this to be such a freeing approach and such a powerful teaching tool with anyone who is intimidated. Now with my current voice coach—who is very sympathetic to my learning techniques—after vocalizing and working on breath control, etc., I'll make fun of opera singers, and we're astonished how everything galvanizes.

So, should you make fun of your performance issues for the rest of your life? No. After a while, when you're feeling more secure, make fun *with* your issues. This is more than just clever semantics. It's an attitude. As long as you are being playful, you will take the risks and continue to grow and develop. Take things *seriously*, and your fear can tend to cramp your style.

So how do you deal with your fear that you'll expose yourself in improv as crazier than everyone else? First, remember that your artistic morality and your private morality are separate: you're under no obligation to hold yourself accountable in life for what you do in class, rehearsal or performance, anymore than you should mistake Blanche DuBois' wantonness or Hamlet's murderous revenge for your own. And then make fun of the things you're afraid to express. Make fun with your partner. And here's the important, freeing step: make him look good as he makes fun of his own issues. This is all part of the education, the "leading out" process. Revealing oneself, even while making fun, is infinitely easier in an environment that is safe and supportive. The more trust you instill in your partner, the safer you'll feel when it's your turn.

We performers are here to reflect the human condition—all aspects of it. The seven deadly sins are Anger, Lust, Gluttony, Greed, Sloth, Envy, and Pride. You now have the titles for seven movies that audiences will flock to watch. You can star in all of them. Just as everyone else can. Annette Benning stood in front of the camera and slapped herself over and over in shame and humiliation in the movie

An American Beauty. You can too. And "crazy" as that seems, we will be as grateful to you as we are to Ms. Benning for delighting us and giving us insight into ourselves.

All seven of these "sins" are part of the best of you. Just as your love and compassion are. One thing acting has taught me is that I'm not responsible for the way I feel, because I can't *control* my feelings. I feel anger, lust, greed, etc., *just like everyone else.* Morality in life isn't based on how you feel. It's based on the actions you choose in the face of those feelings. Hooray for anger, compassion, lust, and friendship! They give you color and texture and it's your job as an artist to uncover and celebrate them all. It's by accepting only the "wholesome" and "acceptable" aspects of self that lead to insanity, and it's society's insistence that we do dwell on these alone that leads us all to suspect that we're crazier than everyone else.

On the other hand, I repeat: *Say the first thing that comes into your head*, dare to be obvious, and you will tell us a story, warts and all, that no one else can tell because no one has lived your life. And trusting the value of this is the first step toward revealing the unique voice in the arts that you already are.

Chapter

[3] Make Your Partner Look Good

The improviser has to understand that his first skill lies in releasing his partner's imagination. What happens in my classes, if the actors stay with me long enough, is that they learn how their 'normal' procedures destroy other people's talent. Then, one day they have a flash of satori [a moment of illumination]—they suddenly understand that all the weapons they were using against other people they also use inwardly, against themselves.
—Impro: Improvisation and the Theatre, *Keith Johnstone*

As I mention in the introduction, when students ask me, "Am I a good improviser?" my immediate response is, "Do people want to play with you?" People seek out people with whom they enjoy playing. They grow in their presence. They feel freer and safer and are released to be more creative. And equally importantly, people *hire* people with whom they enjoy playing.

Plato once said that you can learn more about someone in an hour of play than you can in an hour of conversation. Think about it. You probably know people with whom you get along well, only to find when you're playing a game that there are aspects of their personalities that take you completely by surprise. I remember going to a paint ball fight and being amazed to watch a meek friend transform into a screaming suicide warrior.

I remember how shocked I was when I realized that at my parents' cocktail parties, no one was there to have fun. This was a *party*, I thought. I now realize that if you have fun and engender fun in someone else, you are exposing yourself, giving yourself away, and inviting your partner to do the same. This is the last thing people in suits and, at the time, sheath dresses wanted. Have you ever seen footage of "sophisticated" partygoers from the late fifties doing the twist? Men in suits like armor and women who've encased themselves in girdles, immobilized their hair with hairspray, hobbled on high, thin heels, and everyone thoroughly deodorized . . . trying to dance with "wild abandon." Their parent's Depression was over, the war was over, everyone had cars and homes and appliances, and America was struggling against the Eisenhower years and Eisenhower clothing and trying hard to play. Fortunately the sense of play won out in ways they never could have anticipated, and their children moved into the liberated sixties with an abandon and sense of play that revolutionized America.

When you play, you and your partner give yourselves away. As I said in the chapter on *Say the first thing that comes into your head*, people are afraid to do this for fear of exposing themselves. They will. And your job as your partner's "educator" is to respond to everything that pops out of him spontaneously and unexpectedly with celebration. You e-duco him: you lead him out. You make him look good.

The Expert's Game

To illustrate this attitude, I'll describe "The Expert's Game," which you'll be introduced to in the third class of this course. This exercise directly addresses this rule.

The premise of the game is that the two of you are on a talk show; one is the host, the other an expert. The person playing the expert, however, doesn't know his area of expertise until the host springs it on him during his introduction. You may be introduced to the audience and suddenly find out that you're an expert in teaching penguins how to knit; or soothing troubled cans of tomato soup; or using dead bodies to ski. (These areas of expertise, by the way, are random combinations of suggestions given by the audience before the exercise begins; not clever inventions the host is pressured to come up with.)

I love this game because it draws equally on all three rules. And what participants discover is that the two positions—host and expert—are very different skills. I'll describe the expert's role first. Then I'll describe the role of host, which is what this chapter is about: making your partner look good.

The role of the expert is to know that he's fabulous. He knows everything about the subject and answers all questions confidently with, "Yes!" (*Say "Yes! And . . ."* *to all of your partner's offers*). It's a wonderful exercise in saying the first thing that comes into your head because you have no time to think ahead. "Do penguins knit other things besides mittens?" asks the host. "Yes!" replies the expert, having no idea what he's about to say. So he glances around the room as he's answering and taking obvious offers from the environment he's sitting in (*Say the first thing that comes into your head*). "They knit window blinds, black boxes, and students." he says. "Students!" says the host. "Like yourself?" *"Yes!"* replies the expert confidently, "I'm knit from top to bottom!"

Grabbing this stuff out of the air and proclaiming it with confidence is scary. I repeat: we've all been to high school. Open your mouth, say the first thing that comes into your head, and you could say something stupid—or worse, personal and revealing. You're on display, giving yourself away. I read somewhere that according to some studies, there are very few things in life more stressful than standing in front of a group and performing or lecturing. (In fact the *only* thing I can remember as being more stressful for some people, according to this study, is landing on an aircraft carrier; appearing before a group can be *that* stressful.) It's your host's role to address this fear of yours, to make his partner look good, which I'll explain in a moment.

I pause here for a moment in this explanation to point out once again one of the big differences between gag improv and narrative improv. The humor in gag improv is based on cleverness and jokes. Your success with the audience is based on your ability to deliver funny one-liners as regularly as possible. This is the main reason why so many students dread an improv class. I'm teaching a class as I write this book, and as I was interviewing one of the students in the Expert's Game, she completely froze up. Putting the game on hold for a moment, I asked her to place herself in her mother's kitchen and name three things as she looked around it (*Say the first thing that comes into your head*). After struggling, she collapsed her head on her knees and said, "I'm blank!!" Now, before any of you reading this book go, "Oh god! I don't want to play!," let me tell you that after twenty years of teaching, this is highly unusual.

But it is a classic example of someone who's seen a lot of gag improv and who has crippled herself with the belief that there's a "right" way to do it and she's going to get it wrong.

As the semester progressed, this student has found what most of my students find—much to their amazement: that they are hysterically funny, that it's very easy, and that it's *not* because they're thinking up clever jokes. Although Neil Simon's *The Odd Couple* is filled with funny one-liners, the real humor in the play is the passion with which the two characters pursue their objectives. You know you're doing Neil Simon correctly when you have your first audience, and their laughter *angers you!* "Why are you laughing!? This isn't funny!" (Unfortunately, what happens in too many productions is that you get familiar with the laugh lines and then start playing for laughs. And the show is a lot less funny.)

This is the first, and one of the most difficult things that improv students have to learn: In the Expert's Game, and in narrative improv in general, it's this passion, the conviction, the confidence with which you announce your spontaneous choices that makes the audience laugh, not the funny things you say.

Why is this funny? This is improvisation: the audience *knows* you have no idea what you're about to say, that you have no control over the future. And you'll find that simply by saying the most ordinary things with conviction will make them laugh.

I was interviewing an expert once who said he cleaned his ears with a toothbrush, "What brand?" I asked. "Oral B." he said without missing a beat, and the class erupted with laughter. What? I think you'll agree there's nothing intrinsically funny about "Oral B." But the audience knew he was on the spot, invited by my saying "What brand?" to step into an unknown future . . . and that "moment of theater" was in the air, where the audience knows the actor is in trouble. But instead of blocking the offer to save himself, he announces the first brand name that comes into his head with confidence. This kind of rapid problem solving by simply announcing the first thing that comes into your head, creating a character who moves into the unknown future rapidly and with conviction, makes an audience giddy. What is hard to convince students in the beginning is that *it really makes no difference what you say* . . . as long as you say it with conviction.

But many of you may be thinking, I'm *still* scared.

Again, this is where the host comes in. As I said before, the two positions in this game—host and expert—are very different skills. The expert's job is to know that he's fabulous.

The host's job is to make his partner look good.

Two Skills in Acting

As I mention in the introduction, I went into theater probably for the same reason many of you did: I enjoyed showing off. I found I could get attention and validation, and that people liked me. High school athletes were getting this kind of attention all the time and had letter sweaters to prove it. I couldn't compete in that arena. High school theater, however, gave me the opportunity to show off, to rise into this kind of recognition and at the same time become more of who *I* was.

In the Expert's Game, the role of the *expert*, as described above, capitalizes on this "showing off" skill. Most actors don't have to learn it. That's why we went into the business in the first place. We know how to walk on stage, show off, and become the center of the audience's focus and attention. It's a wonderful experience. And when we are alone on stage, we are responsible for 100 percent of the audience's experience.

However, when there are two of you on stage, you're only responsible for 50 percent of the audience's experience. Ten of you, and you're only responsible for 10 percent. Therefore, there is another skill that actors have to learn. And that's how to *throw* focus. Actors must develop a sense of what the stage picture is at any given time; they must discover in rehearsal and through the director what effect this stage picture is supposed to be having on the audience at that moment, and then what part they play in that effect. As the focus of audience attention shifts from place to place on stage, you must play your part in either taking that focus and projecting your choices clearly and efficiently (showing off), or throwing the focus where it's appropriate, and in many cases "disappearing" on stage. You must learn how to make yourself un-interesting. And make your partner look good.

For example, in a play if your scene partner has an important monologue, it's up to you to make sure the audience pays attention to that monologue. Now, if you're downstage of your partner, facing the audience, fidgeting with your nails, pushing your hair out of your face, shifting your body weight from foot to foot, etc., you're stealing focus.

On the other hand, there are any number of things you can do to throw the focus at your partner.

- Freeze.
- Find an excuse, before your partner's monologue begins, to stand in profile, or even better facing 3/4 upstage, both of which are less interesting for the audience than standing full front. For example, before the monologue begins, turn upstage to pick something up then stop suddenly as you turn your head to listen, body in 3/4 position.
- Look at your partner. This is more powerful than people imagine. When you stare steadily at your partner, if the audience glances at you, they'll immediately wonder what's so interesting and go to where your eyes are directed.

Dancers develop this sense of stage picture and the part they play in it very early in their careers. If they've ever danced in an ensemble, they develop a keen sense of what the picture is that the ensemble is creating at any given moment and what part they play in that picture. They can even sense what's going on behind them, moving on cue like a school of fish. Actors must develop this sense of ensemble.

You may be wondering why I'm including what seems like basic acting technique in a book about improvisation. The importance of "throwing focus" may be obvious to you. It's certainly essential in scripted theater, though even when performers are stealing focus in scripted theater, the scene can still limp along. In improvisation, however, the scene dies.

Theater and improvisation are communal art forms and one of the great things about a class in narrative improvisation is that it emphasizes how essential cooperation is. The Expert's Game is a scene about a fabulous expert. The host's role is to convince himself, the expert, and the audience just how fabulous this expert is. The focus should always be on the expert as the host makes him look good.

Remember, the person playing the expert is afraid. Scripted theater is scary enough where you at least know your lines and blocking. But this is improvisation and, without a script, he has absolutely no control over the future. As the host, your job is to make him feel wonderful; to throw awe and affection in his direction. Make him look good. You've been *dying* to get this expert on your talk show and you are *thrilled* to have him there. And everything he says amazes you. This kind of validation encourages your partner to open up.

The host should sit in profile, which again is less interesting to an audience than the expert, who should be sitting turned out toward them. Lean in to him and stare with admiration, directing the audience's focus: if they look at you, they'll look immediately at him to see what's so interesting.

Nod a lot! This is another very simple thing, the power of which is seldom appreciated. It does two things. On a theatrical level, you look like you're participating in your guest's responses and it makes the scene more real, and consequently funnier. Here's an expert talking about using dead bodies for skis and you're nodding gently and sincerely.

Secondly, and equally importantly, you are subtly but continually releasing your partner: Again, he's frightened and usually ahead of himself. But seeing someone else on stage nodding at him with encouragement, making him look good whatever is tumbling out of his mouth, is extraordinarily validating. Try it in conversation. When you're conversing with a friend, freeze your head as he talks. This is very intimidating (when people are yelling or giving orders, they don't move their heads). After a while, start nodding . . . and watch the difference. You will actually see your partner relax, and he'll probably begin to use his hands as his body animates in relief.

The Subconscious

If your expert partner is on a roll, he has probably launched into answering your question with a "Yes! And . . ." *before* he has any idea what's going to come out of his mouth. And he is making up his answer completely on the fly. I call this "motormouth."

It's a marvelous place to be. In fact, getting comfortable with this motormouth state is the reason for this game. Because the expert has had no time to prepare, he is in direct connection with his subconscious, saying the first thing that comes into his head, grabbing "obvious" answers out of the air as fast as he can, answers that, in their obviousness, reveal him in a way all artists hope to achieve.

I remember waking up in the middle of the night at the end of an amazing dream. It was an extremely vivid murder mystery and I still remember the grounds of the estate on which the mystery took place, and the faces in the dream; faces I'd never seen in my waking life. And it even had a surprise ending. I suspected on awakening that the surprise really wasn't as clever as it felt in the dream. However . . . it was an astonishingly clever mystery. I remember thinking at the time, "I could never write something like that."

But I just had. No one wrote that dream but me. There is this wealth of random, creative material in our subconscious that most of us are out of touch with. I suspect it's because one of the jobs of our conscious brain is to quell the subconscious while we're awake so we don't go crazy. In any event, your subconscious is rich and unique and more *you* than anything clever you can imitate.

There are all kinds of acting exercises designed to help you release it. What I love about the Expert's Game is that if you are not informed of your expertise before the game and therefore have no time to plan, if you say "Yes! And . . ." to all the host's questions and you launch into motormouth, you are in direct connection with your subconscious. There is no other way to be. You're treading air up there and your mind reaches frantically for vocabulary hand-holds to spew out. And the most amazing things come out.

As the host, ask simple questions: "How did you get started?" "Tell us what happened last Tuesday." "What kind of yarn do you use?" Your job is simply to keep your expert's motormouth ball in the air, gently sending him off again as his last answer wends to a conclusion.

Can't think of what to ask next?

The Improvisational Cylinder of Panic

One of the things that most beginning improvisers are afraid of, as "hosts" in this case, is not knowing what to say next. *Say the first thing that comes into your head* sounds good on paper, but at the moment, they are convinced that their minds are blanks. And as an audience member, you can see "blankness" happening. The way it manifests itself is so common, I gave it a name: "The Improvisational Cylinder of Panic." Your face goes flat, your eyes glaze, your body freezes, and you disconnect from everything around you as you turn your attention inward.

Like the three rules of improv, the solution is very simple. And like the three rules, at the time this simple solution is the farthest thing from your mind:

Look at your partner.

He is making a million offers a minute, even if he is unaware of it. As the expert is coming to the end of his answer, if you can't think of another question, look at him. "You're wearing a green sweatshirt. Is that significant to the penguins?" The answer will always be "Yes! And . . .". Remember, your task as a host isn't to show the audience how clever your questions are. Your task is to make your partner look good. To spur him on to another session of motormouth. His answer to *any* question you ask will always be "Yes! And . . ." "You're wearing a single earring. How does that tie in?" "I notice you're wearing Reeboks. Is that significant?" "You're nodding a lot. Do penguins like that?"

Conclusion

The world is competitive enough as it is. One solution to artistic expression in this competitive world is solo art forms: writing, sculpting, painting, etc. In these you are in complete control from beginning to end. You can even name your own hours, getting up when you choose, working when you choose, and quitting when you want.

But if you choose a communal art form like theater—or improvisation—your ability to release your partner is a part of this bargain. Theater is not about you. It's about you and your fellow cast members, and the director, and the lighting designer, and the costumer, etc., all creating something that is bigger than all of you. And if you've ever done a scene where afterward you were amazed by what had just happened, you know what I mean.

By bouncing off your partner, taking and receiving, making every offer of his look good, something enormous happens. It is an expression of the vitality of all involved, not just you. And it is that enormity that makes theater so breathtaking to be a part of. Something equally wonderful can be created later by another combination of talent, but nothing identical. Communal artists must commit themselves to losing themselves in the process. To contributing in cycles of moving forward to become the "figure" of audience focus when the creation demands, then receding into "ground" that supports the moment, the other actor, making him look good. And when you can do this on the fly, as you are required to do in improvisation, this recruiting of individual egos in creation of a greater stage picture is breathtaking to watch. And I think you'll agree, it is one of the most exhilarating things we are capable of doing.

Chapter

[4] Say "Yes! And . . ." to All of Your Partner's Offers

Whatever your partner says, say "Yes!" to it . . . and add one more thing to make the offer even better. This is what makes narrative improv "narrative." It's this response, back and forth from each partner, that generates the narrative story one step at a time.

For example, I may walk on stage with a great idea for a psychiatrist/patient scene. But just as I'm about to start, my scene partner says:

"Dad!"

What I don't say is:

"I'm not your father. I'm your shrink."

This is blocking an offer; it stops the scene. And in addition, it makes your partner look bad. Instead, I have to immediately give up my psychiatrist scenario, however brilliant I may think it is, say "Yes." to my partner's offer *and* add one more thing to make it better.

For example, in response to his "Dad!" offer, I might "Yes! And . . ." it by saying:

"Hello, son." (*"Yes."*) "I brought your lunch." (*"And . . ."*).

I have no idea where this lunch offer is going. Neither does my partner. It was the first thing that came into my head. We have both given up control of the future. And now it's up to my partner to "Yes! And . . ." my offer.

"Thanks." he might say, opening the bag. (*"Yes."*) "Baloney sand-wiches." (*"And . . ."*)

Again, neither one of us has any idea where the scene is going.

"I brought your lunch to school because your mother couldn't."

With this offer, I continue to "Yes!" the father/son offer and the lunch offer, *and* I've added a location, my wife, and, without really thinking about it or planning it, a plot element: Mom couldn't pack lunch.

"Yes, I know." my partner might say. "She left you."

And I would say, "Yes."

Or he might say, "Yes, I know. You killed her last night."

And I would say, "Yes."

Or, "Yes I know. She's not my mom."

And I would say, "Yes."

To the audience, this looks like mind reading. How did we both know she'd left? How did we both know she was dead or not his mother? We don't. All that's happened is that one of us made an offer and the other accepted it. And offer-by-offer, the plot advances.

An improviser is like a man walking backwards. He doesn't know where he's going, but he knows where he's been. As you begin an improvisation, you're going to have a "treading air" sensation, not knowing where you're going. But as you "walk backwards" into the future, offer-by-offer, you will gradually leave behind you a ground-work of history, relationship, location, plot elements, etc., as the framework of the scene begins to structure itself.

Now, if, in a panic, you decide you have to make the scene "inter-esting" and introduce something sensational—"God! Your hair's on fire!"—you will get a laugh. However, the narrative tension and the believability of the scene will be destroyed. Audiences *want* to be seduced into thinking that they are looking at a private moment on stage, at characters unaware that they are being observed, at a father and son dealing with the murder of the wife. It's hard to convince yourself of this when you're up there with no script or sense of direction. Trusting that an audience's silence is actually rapt atten-tion is difficult. Their laughter, on the other hand, is audible valida-tion. And it's also a drug. Once you've thrown in a gag—"Your hair's on fire!"—and gotten a laugh, your partner will feel required to do the same. You will have lost the sense of drama, and although you may have won the audience, they've given up interest in the story just as you have, and now want as many jokes as you can possibly make as fast as you can possibly make them. We're now into "gag" improv, and the pressure on you to be funny is enormous.

Give Up the Future

As I said in the introduction, as simple as the three rules of improv sound, they are antithetical to everything our culture has taught us. Saying "Yes! And . . ." is difficult because it means giving up control of the future. Whatever brilliant "psychiatrist" scenario you may have projected before you go on stage, whatever future you may intend by saying that mom couldn't pack lunch . . . those futures can and will be instantly redirected by your partner's next offer.

Now, if you gauge your personal success by your relationship with the *audience*, as in gag improv, obviously this way lies failure. You may be building to a "punch line" that you're convinced the audience will think is a riot, and your partner thwarts it. And you're going to end up annoyed at him for not "playing along" and perceiving the brilliance of your scenario. (If you keep insisting that your scenario is best and deflect all contrary offers in order to achieve that scenario, you're doing what is called "driving": taking the wheel and making the scene go where *you* want it to go.)

If instead you gauge your personal success by your relationship with your *partner*, trusting that he will make you look good as you will make him look good, you will *always* succeed by "Yes! And . . ."-ing his offer, because by doing so, you consistently create "the moment of theater"—that moment where the audience is aware that you have no idea where you are going, or whether you are going to succeed or not, and you step forward anyway.

And my firm belief is that audiences go to the theater primarily to be present at moments like this.

I remember watching the movie *River Wild* with Meryl Streep and Kevin Bacon. It's about a woman and her family on a white-water rafting trip. Kevin Bacon is a criminal on the run who forces her at gunpoint to take them down rapids that few people have survived, because it's his only route away from the police.

Now I *knew* that Meryl Streep wasn't going to die. I'd seen her interviewed recently. She's just an actress in a movie. But I didn't sit in the theater thinking, *Oh look. There's Meryl Streep. She's such a good actress. Interesting choices.* No, I remember screaming at least twice. How did she effect this reaction in me? I mean face it, it isn't *really* happening.

She achieved this, I believe, because she, like all fine actors, had convinced herself somehow that despite the lines she had memorized, all the rehearsals they had been through, all the blocking she had to execute, and despite the twenty or so technicians that were surrounding her with cameras, lights, and boom mikes that we couldn't see . . . despite all that, she had somehow convinced herself, face to face with Kevin Bacon, that she really didn't know what was going to happen next and that every choice of hers was a step into an unknown future.

It's this skill of getting comfortable with being uncomfortable that a class in improv can teach you in a way nothing else can.

But, you may be thinking, she's not really *improvising*.

Acting Techniques

There are two skills common to all acting techniques, whether it's Meisner, Stanislavski, or Uta Hagen, to name a few:

- The ability to *analyze* a script, i.e., break it down into beats and objectives appropriate to the playwright's intentions.
- The ability to *improvise tactics* at each performance to *achieve* those objectives based on your partner's behavior *at that moment*.

The ability to improvise tactics at each performance is what keeps a performance fresh. Unfortunately, too many performances are simply repetitions of both the objectives and tactics that were discovered once in rehearsal. However, the willingness to *maintain* the analyzed objectives, the lines, and the blocking), but *improvise* the tactics each night gives a performance continuity, freshness, and the illusion of the first time.

As I've said before, everything in life tells you not to follow the three rules of improv. Not only is improvising risky, it also isn't encouraged. Acting is a business where other participants—directors, playwrights, designers, producers, etc.—demand control. For many of these, the only good actor is a predictable one. Yet, ironically, they keep hiring those very "stars" who surprise us with every performance.

I'd had two days of improvisation when I was in graduate school. That was all. I remembered liking it, but hadn't given it much thought afterwards. However, years later I was playing Horace in a production of Moliere's *The School for Wives* at the McCarter Theater. It was the fifth performance in a five-show weekend late in the run. I was a little tired and was aware that my performance was too. I was waiting backstage about to go on to do a scene with the actor playing Arnolphe, when those two days of improv came back to me. And as I looked at him from the wings I thought, *What if I really didn't know what he was going to say to me next?* I walked on stage with this attitude, a little scared at the risk I felt I was taking, and it galvanized my performance. I couldn't remember having felt so giddy and alive on stage. In fact it was this event that convinced me of the value of improv.

"Do you mean you actually improvised in a professional production?" Yes. I *was* able to convince myself, line by line, that I had no idea how Arnolphe was going to respond. And I spontaneously altered my tone of voice, based on whether I could see in his eyes if I was getting what I wanted, if I was achieving my objective. I whined, I yelled, I got intimate, I high-statused him, I low-statused him. (More about status in the next chapter.) But because the play is so well written, because we'd rehearsed so well and because the blocking was so organic, the lines and the blocking seemed like the natural extension of my improvised tactics.

But isn't improvising in a scripted play dangerous?

Not with practice. When you are performing, you are working on so many levels. Improvising tactics are only one part of a complex series of checks and balances that is informing your performance. The command center in your brain is constantly shifting awareness:

- Pursue my objective: Get this woman to fall in love with me.
- Project my voice to the back of the house.
- Face downstage.
- Someone's moved the sofa; walk around it.
- Where's my light?
- Coughing fit in the audience. Talk louder.
- Pace is too slow; pick it up.

I'm sure you've also experienced that moment at the movies or theater that I did watching *River Wild* . . . when you've literally gasped with delight at an unexpected turn of events that seemed to throw the characters into immediate danger. It's what audiences pay for. And this moment happens in improvisation *all the time*. The way to become the kind of vital, exciting performer that creates these moments for the audience is this: Develop the courage to abandon control of the future, to throw yourself forward into the unknown by saying "Yes! And . . ." to all of your partner's offers. The resulting moment-to-moment risks may feel like you're treading air without a sense of direction. But by continuing to "Yes! And . . . ," and, like a man walking backwards, remembering and re-incorporating things you've established along the way, the cumulative effect is breathtaking in it's cooperative spontaneity.

Planning is Death

No one ever follows the three rules flawlessly. And if that's your goal as it was mine for a while, you'll spend much of your time frustrated and thinking you're a bad actor/improviser. And you'll stop having fun. Remember, you are released when you are having fun, being playful. The best of you comes to the surface. Your job is to create that playfulness in yourself and in your partner. Picking on yourself isn't just a bad idea; it stunts you.

I've been improvising for years and still don't follow the rules perfectly. I do three things, however:

- I follow them more consistently than before, simply through practice.
- I don't pick on myself when I fail, but simply notice when it happens, decide to do it differently next time . . . and then let it go.

This is a meditation technique. In meditation, if a thought interrupts and you let it distract you, it has you. If you fight to ignore it, it has you. If, however, you acknowledge its presence, *I'm thinking about my folks again*, and then choose to let it go each time the "folks" thought reoccurs, your meditation grows with success. If as an improviser I berate myself when I "break" the rules, I stop growing. If I ignore the mistake, I also stop growing. If I admit its existence, however, and don't engage with it emotionally but simply choose to do otherwise in the future each time it happens (and it will happen again and again) and then turn my attention back to my partner, I develop *and* the scene continues.

And finally,

- I try to set up situations where breaking the rules is difficult, if not impossible.

I've chosen exercises in this course that put you in those situations, where all you *can* do is follow the rules. For example, earlier I described the Expert's Game. In that game, the host waits until he has introduced both the show and his guest before he reveals the guest's expertise. He does this for a reason: to prevent his guest from planning ahead.

Because planning is death, and the end of saying "Yes! And . . .". As soon as you have time to plan, you arrive with a "brilliant" scenario and a whole set of jokes . . . and the last thing you want to do is "Yes! And . . ." your partner's offer. In fact you disconnect from his offers. Either that, or try to bend them toward your material, shoehorning the funny bits into your responses. And without the give-and-take that saying "Yes! And . . ." involves, the scene quickly becomes a series of gags, your partner disconnects because you have, and again, the audience begins to demand jokes and more jokes.

I'd been an actor for many years before I started performing as an improviser. And acting had always involved a lot of off-stage preparation and planning: scene analysis; choosing objectives; memorizing lines; researching periods in history, etc. One of the hardest things I had to adjust to as an improviser was spending a day before a show knowing that not only could I *not* prepare for the performance, I'd be in trouble if I did. And I'd betray the cast. This was crazy-making at first and every performance felt like jumping out of a window face first. No handholds. And what made it worse was that I felt I had to rely on the good will of other equally nervous improvisers.

What I ended up realizing was that in scripted plays, I'd never really relied on my partners in the first place. I'd known my lines and blocking and assumed they'd know theirs, and then I'd simply shown the audience what I'd discovered in rehearsal, expecting my partner to be where he was supposed to be. The decision to actually *rely* on my partner in improvisation, trust that we'd be safe if we jumped out that window hand-in-hand, treading air indeed, but "Yes! And . . ."–ing each other's offers . . . well, at first it was embarrassing. I was scared, where I'd always been so self-reliant. My fear was naked and I had to trust that someone else would go out of his or her way to make me look good.

But when it worked, when we accepted each other's offers and sent our next obvious offer back with delight, the sense of camaraderie was exhilarating. And the resulting scene felt out of our control, as if it were creating itself. It's an exceptional high that still leaves me amazed each time it happens. Each time is unique, and each time I'm convinced it will never happen like that again. And with each subsequent improv, I have to give up trying to duplicate the last scene or plan the course of this one, "Yes! And . . ." my current partner's offers, and step into another unknown future.

Avoid Conflict

Arguments can kill an improvisation.
  "Let's jump off this cliff!"
  "No, that's a stupid idea."
  "It's not stupid, it's an adventure."
  "No it isn't."
Meanwhile, the audience is all dying for you to jump off the cliff. Jump! Don't argue. Don't set yourself in conflict with your partner. It brings scenes to a standstill. Instead, say "Yes."
  "But isn't conflict what theater is about?"
  Yes. But there are all kinds of conflict.

When You Can Say "No"

When you're a beginning improviser, saying "No" is usually a choice to stop the action in order to remain safe. However, once you've drilled this skill of "Yes! And . . ." and you begin to feel more confident with continually stepping into an unknown future, you can begin to say "No" in ways that advance the action as well. In a scene at a singles bar where a guy is trying to pick up a girl, for example, she can say "No" in a way that makes it clear she wants him to actually continue, thus advancing the action.

Waffling

It's amazing how inventive we can be in avoiding the three rules. There's nothing "wrong" with this, it's normal: Life has conditioned us to do this. In fact we are so good at this that we can seem to be following the rules, still do dull scenes, and not know why. One way we do this is by saying, "Yes! But . . . ," or "waffling."

"Let's jump off the cliff."

"Yes! But I want to tell you something first . . ."

And the scene becomes talky and goes nowhere.

But, you may argue, I said "Yes!"

Yes, you appear to accept the offer, and then you immediately deflect it by saying "but." The word "but" is a flag. Be alert to it as a response to an offer, and try to avoid it.

Say "Yes! But . . ." and the momentum of the scene always pauses as it turns a corner. This may be appropriate occasionally. But for most beginning improvisers, it's a way to avoid conflict and regain control. On the other hand, when you "Yes! And . . ." your partner's offer, the scene progresses in a linear fashion. Say it faster and faster and you both begin to lose control as the scene seems to take off on its own, exploding into a unique expression of your two creative minds solving problems in rapid cooperation.

Conclusion

The choreographer Agnes DeMille once said:

> *Living is a form of not being sure, not knowing what next or how. The moment you know how, you begin to die a little. The artist never entirely knows. We guess. We may be wrong, but we take leap after leap in the dark.*

In other words, get used to saying "Yes! And . . ." and it becomes more than a device that guarantees exciting improv. It guarantees adventure on every plane.

Chapter

[5] Status

- A female lawyer in a suit walks into a singles bar. She has just won a big case for her firm. She is approached at the bar by a taller male co-worker. The bar is crowded so he is very close, looking steadily down on her, as he congratulates her. Startled, she giggles, avoiding his eyes, and thanks him as her head tilts to the side and her hand goes to her hair. He raises his palm between them to stop conversation as he signals the bartender and orders a Scotch and a Daiquiri. She glances at him, smiling, but looks immediately back at the bar, her head moving slightly right to left. When his hand comes down, she says, "So, uh, you were, uh, there in court today?" He says, "Yeah. I didn't think women could handle criminal litigation." Her head immediately straightens and freezes. Turning toward him, she brings her face closer to his. "I didn't think men drank Daiquiris."
- Two students have failed to turn in a paper that was due. One approaches the teacher rapidly and slaps him on the shoulder. Looking directly into his eyes he says in a loud voice, "I didn't get my paper done, Bill. Big game last night. Hold on." he says, turning away and talking to another student, his hand resting on the teacher's shoulder. He finally turns back. "So next week's OK,

right?" As he leaves, the second student walks slowly toward the teacher, catching his eye and looking away immediately. Standing about two feet away, head lowered, rocking from side to side, he says in a quiet voice that he's been taking care of his sick father and had to spend the night at the hospital. The teacher asks him to speak up. He looks at the teacher, but looks away immediately as he stutters, admitting how important this class is to him, eyes to the ground, and asks if he can turn his paper in next week.

- Oedipus Rex is king of Thebes. The city is ridden with plague. In the course of a day, he finds that he has killed his father, married his mother, and that the plague on his beloved city is the gods' punishment for his crimes. He puts out his eyes and is driven from the city like a pariah by his own people.
- A huge policeman with a billy club threatens Charlie Chaplin. As Chaplin turns away, head lowered, the policeman slips on a banana peel.

All of the above are examples of status and status transactions. My experience has been that an understanding of status, and the ability to apply status and status transactions to scenes gives them a vitality and sense of reality that are theatrical, immediate, and based in truth. And that there is nothing more interesting on stage than a status transfer. I'll explain how status plays out in the above examples in a moment.

Definition of Status

The concept of status, as I use the term in this chapter, is probably different than what most people understand. We tend to associate high status with money, fancy homes, and big cars and we feel that high status is good and desirable. We associate low status with blue-collar workers, heavy regional accents, bad use of language, etc., and feel low status is bad and undesirable.

Status, as I use it in this chapter, however, is not about ranking in the community, but about behavior. There is high-status behavior and low-status behavior.

And this is the message of this chapter:

High status isn't good. High status isn't bad. Low status isn't good. Low status isn't bad. Status is a tactic you use to achieve an objective.

Sometimes high-status behavior works in a given situation. Sometimes low works. What's important to realize is that whenever we are face-to-face with anybody, we are continually altering our status from moment-to-moment to achieve our objective. And the more alert an actor is to these transactions in real life, the more facile he is at creating scenes on stage that feel like real life to the audience.

Why We Go to the Theater

Audiences don't go to the theater just to hear the script. They can buy the script. And it's a lot cheaper. Audiences go to the theater for a catharsis: What happens on stage, happens in the audience.

If you doubt this, go on stage sometime and hold your breath for as long as you can. When you finally release it, you will hear some members of the audience release theirs as well, many of whom will be unaware that they were holding their breath.

Something communicates across the footlights or from the screen: a dynamic, a vitality that works on a level that's hard to understand. But we are programmed this way. When someone panics around us, our own panic begins to rise. When a baby is crying, we are alarmed. This is why a crying baby is so much more annoying to passengers on an airline than it is to the mother. When she sees that the baby is all right, she's heard crying often enough to be able to turn down her alarm reaction. We passengers, on the other hand, aren't used to it and we remain alarmed, struggling to ignore this programmed reaction. We are continually alert to all human behavior around us. And to a greater or lesser extent, we reflect that behavior in our own bodies. In short, people are frequently amazed how a school of fish can all turn at the same time. But we do the same.

How does a performer create this effect in the audience?

In two ways: by what your body does and how your voice sounds.

Your feelings aren't enough to create this effect in the audience. I gave an example in the Introduction where I sat myself with my back to the class, felt truly angry, and then asked the class if they felt it as well. Of course not. Without the skills required to physically and vocally project your intentions efficiently to an audience, it can make no difference *how* you feel.

Why Work on Status

One technique that I'm a great believer in for creating a character is using externals: creating or imitating behavior that is like the characters before I've justified it internally. For example, I get my character shoes as soon as I can because I walk differently and *feel* different in different kinds of shoes. You can't rehearse Moliere or Restoration in running shoes. If you do, when the character shoes arrive, you're going to be jolted into a new way of carrying yourself through space that will radically alter everything you've done in rehearsal up to then.

I was in a production of *Otherwise Engaged* by Simon Gray, playing a character who was pretty defeated by life. He had very little energy and dragged himself, exhausted and annoyed, through the play. Well, this wasn't me. I'm a pretty perky guy and I was having a terrible time finding this character. So I bought a pair of ankle weights, those padded things filled with lead shot that Velcro around your ankles. By the end of rehearsal that day, I had not only found the character, I was exhausted.

Or so I thought. As I was taking off the weights, a cast member asked if we could go for a drink. I wanted to go to bed, but agreed. And half an hour later in the bar . . . perky Dan was back. I had been so convinced that I was truly exhausted. What had happened?

True exhaustion can cause a person to drag his feet. And it seems that the opposite is also true: dragging your feet over a period of time can *create* a feeling of exhaustion. Start thinking about something sad, place two drops of glycerin just below your eyes and let them run down your cheeks. You will be amazed at how amplified the feeling becomes just by adding the sensation of "tears."

We're addressing status in this chapter, and there are classic high-status and low-status postures. Drilling these postures can have the same effect as ankle weights or glycerin tears. On the one hand, they can be used subtly or in extremes to amplify and reinforce the feelings your character is experiencing on stage, helping you communicate that reality subtly and with greater vitality. On the other, they can also help you create the same effect in the audience on those performance nights when you *don't* experience those feelings when the play begins. And that is your job: to give the audience the experience they've paid for whether you feel it or not.

Classic Status Behavior

So what is status? I'll give examples of classic status behavior, both low and high.

High Status
- Keep your eyes locked on your partner's eyes whenever you are speaking or listening. Direct eye contact, which is high status, or lack of it, which is low status, is the strongest indicator of status.
- Take up space, physically and vocally.
- Invade your partner's space: extend your hand first to shake hands; touch your partner; put your arm around him; sit or stand close to him.
- Stand tall with your head up.
- Arrange things so that your head is higher than your partner's: stand while he sits; sit straight when he slumps; sit on a throne.
- Don't move your head while you're talking.
- Start sentences with a long, "Uhhhhh," essentially keeping your partner on "hold" until you gather your thoughts.
- Make your body a study in contrasting body lines: e.g., hands on hips; leg up with ankle on knee when seated; arms held away from the body; one foot on the chair when standing.

Ballet is an extremely high-status form of dance. The bodies are erect, and the arms are held away from the body, taking up space and expanding into it. Ballet teachers tell their pupils to imagine that every gesture stretches into infinity, filling and commanding space.

Low Status
- When you make eye contact with someone, instantly look away, then look back, look away again, etc.
- Shrink from space by pulling into yourself. Contract your body, slump.
- Sit and stand in parallel lines: e.g., arms close to the body, legs together when standing or seated.
- Never invade someone else's space. And when you do, apologize instantly.

- Move your head while you're talking, tilting frequently from side to side.
- Touch your face and hair.
- Fidget.
- Insert short "uhs" throughout your sentences.
- Giggle.

Geishas are low-status experts. They not only speak in a very high, soft voice, but they actually enter a room on their knees. Both of these actions take up very little space. You'd never hear a geisha bellow.

In addition to the above behavior patterns, there are some standard status assumptions we learn as members of our society. In our culture, for example, men tend to be assigned higher status than women. Raise a curtain on stage with a man and a woman standing side by side dressed similarly, and the audience will automatically assign higher status to the man until the play proves otherwise. "That's not fair!" some of you may say. Again, don't let the morality you hold and honor in your real life hamper what you permit yourself on stage. If you observe status honestly in real life and are aware of audience expectations, you can use these expectations skillfully—however you may feel about them personally—to deliver the playwright's message.

Other cultural status markers: people in suits tend to be assigned higher status than people in jeans. My students have done the following exercise to amazing effect: Go into a very high-end clothing store dressed in jeans, T-shirt, and sneakers, and observe how the staff treats you. Then a week later dress upscale: guys wear suits and women put your hair up and wear heels. Go back to the same store and notice the difference in your treatment. And while you're choosing clothes and asking for help, talk to the staff *without making eye contact.* Your status will skyrocket.

Doesn't this contradict the statement that direct eye contact raises your status? Looking and then holding eye contact raises your status. Looking, then looking away and *never* looking back also raises your status, implying that your partner isn't interesting enough to engage your attention. It's the looking *back* that lowers your status. Then darting your eyes away immediately again, looking back again, away, etc., lowers it even more. This low-status behavior implies that your partner's presence is so high status that you're hesitant to invade his space even with your eyes.

Status Analysis

In the first of the scenarios at the beginning of this chapter, a female lawyer walks into a bar wearing a suit. She's a female, which is low, and wearing a suit, which is high. There are several things to bear in mind as I work through these scenes. First, we seldom send high- or low-status signals exclusively. We are masters, whether we are aware of it or not, of subtly blending combinations of high- and low-status tactics to achieve our objectives, balancing one with the other with amazing sophistication. Second, when I say "female" is low and "suit" is high, these aren't polar extremes, but subtle gradations relative to the character's surroundings. And finally, remember, sometimes our status tactics work, sometimes they don't. Choosing a status tactic doesn't guarantee its success.

The woman is approached at the bar by a *taller* (high status) *male* (high status) co-worker. These are cultural status assignments and not tactical choices on his part, though like all privileged people (and in our society, men are privileged) he probably works from that higher-status posture, taking it for granted without even realizing the mechanisms that have placed him there.

But now we'll move on to his conscious status choices. I'm going to project what seems to be an obvious objective on him. He wants this woman to like him. It could be because she's powerful and she can advance his career. Or because he wants to sleep with her. In either case, the bar is crowded so he is very close to her, invading her space (*high*) looking steadily (*high*) down (*high*) on her. (High-status people maintain eye contact.)

He congratulates her (*low*).

She is startled (*low*), and now begins a series of low-status tactics: she giggles, avoids his eyes, thanks him, tilts her head, and plays with her hair. Projecting an objective on her, I'd assume she finds him attractive, is slightly intimidated, and rapidly sends low-status messages to appear non-threatening. This, by the way, is the classic male/female dating relationship. He is strong and bold (*high*) because many men tend to think that will work and she is giggly and weak (*low*) because many women tend to think *that* will work.

He raises his palm between them to stop conversation. This is *very* high status, actually putting someone on "hold." He orders himself a Scotch and her a Daiquiri, which is a low-status drink in our culture compared to the Scotch. And he is in fact lowering her status by doing so without asking her.

Meanwhile, she's still sending low-status signals: glances but looks away immediately; sways her head. She says, "So, uh, you were, uh, in court today?" Hesitant speech and using "uh" lowers her status even more.

We're now headed for what I consider the most interesting thing that ever happens on stage: a status transfer. There is *nothing* more interesting than a status transfer: someone starts high, someone low . . . and they switch. He presses her status down even further by saying, "I didn't think women could handle criminal litigation." At this point the audience is probably *screaming* for him to get his. And she does it. She straightens her head and holds it steady (*high*) turns toward him (*high*) and leans into him, invading his space (*high*). "I didn't think men drank Daiquiris." With this, she lowers him rapidly by associating Daiquiris with him and by being clever enough to turn the tables with a very witty remark.

Again, I feel that there is nothing more interesting on stage than a status transfer. It can happen rapidly as in farce: the big policeman with a billy club who is threatening Charlie Chaplin slips on a banana peel. His status goes down; Charlie's goes up. Or it can take an entire play to happen: Oedipus, King of Thebes, is chased from town, blind and ragged, by his own people.

Look at the two examples of students asking forgiveness for not getting their papers done. Who has chosen high status, who has chosen low status, and what are their tactics? If their objective is to be forgiven, which tactics do you think have a better chance of succeeding?

Be Specific in Your Observations

When students are asked to describe a status transaction, they often say things like, "He was intimidating her!" or "He's acting like a wimp!" The question to ask yourself immediately is, how do you *know* these things? How do you *know* he's intimidating, or a wimp? Again, the effect is being created on you because of what that person's body is doing and what his voice sounds like. Name the specific activities. "He's standing very close to her and yelling." "He's giggling and avoiding eye contact." These are things that you can imitate on stage, and probably have the very same effect on the audience—intimidating; acting like a wimp—that that person is having on you.

Address this issue by observing status transactions in life and then bringing them into the classroom and imitating them. As I describe in chapter 2, make fun of the people you're imitating. If your mom was raging in a high status manner, make fun of her as you imitate for the classroom. "Making fun of" frees you of inhibitions and consequently gets more and more of the physical and vocal feeling into your body vocabulary.

Comedy

I said earlier that you'd never hear a geisha bellow. Except in comedy. A tiny geisha with a voice like a cannon and smoking a cigar is funny. Why? Because it's contrary to the expected status. Take the expected status and play the opposite, and you have instant comedy. Play God as a stutterer who can't make eye contact and keeps pulling at his pants, and people will laugh. Stick a cigar in a baby's mouth and people will laugh.

Status and Space

We not only adjust our status tactics at every given moment with everyone we meet, we do the same with the spaces that we enter. If you want to show an audience that the bedroom you've just walked into is yours, abuse the furniture. Plop onto the bed, or put your feet on the chair. In short, treat the surroundings as low status.

If, on the other hand, you walk onto an empty stage with someone, look around, and start to whisper, the audience will suspect that the space has very high status: a church, a library, a funeral parlor.

Status Postures in Our Own Lives

While most of us mix status signals to achieve our objectives in life, the exercises in this class starting with Class 7 are extreme, single status choices. I chose these extremes because they are designed to help you get this status vocabulary into your body.

And I invite you to go as far with them as you can, even if you don't "feel" them at first. Some status choices will feel natural to you; others may not, and you may feel you're just doing them mechanically.

In many cases, the ones that don't feel organic to you are exercises in a status you don't feel comfortable with in real life. All of us have chosen a status posture that we feel comfortable with relative to most of the world. Some of us choose higher, and some lower. There is no value judgment connected with this statement. We choose the status posture we do because experience has taught us that *it works for us.*

For example, I realize now that, up until high school, I was a pretty accomplished low-status player. Whenever tension built in our family I found that I could disappear and avoid the crossfire. Low status was a choice that worked for me. As a young teacher, however, I learned quickly that low status didn't work. Good students *need* a high-status figure that they willingly play lower status to. Also, as a performer walking into an audition, I learned to present myself in a high-status pose that hopefully exuded confidence. On the other hand, as I got used to this new high-status posture, I found I wasn't dating very successfully. High status was turning people off. So other adjustments were necessary as I learned to balance high-status signals that hopefully exuded confidence and strength with low-status signals that kept these from being intimidating, raised the status of my partner, and that made me seem inviting and engaging.

So if a particular status exercise is difficult, there's a good chance it's because you're working in a status that you're not comfortable with in life. First, tell yourself that there's nothing wrong with the status you're comfortable playing. You can get cast playing that status all your life. Then pursue the uncomfortable exercises to stretch your range. This will only make you *more* castable.

Body Vocabulary

Again, as you're doing these exercises, even the ones that don't feel organic, do them to the extreme. The purpose is to get these extremes into your body vocabulary. You may be asked at an audition to play a street beggar who truly thanks people when they kick him. This is as low status as you can get. If you've done it in class, you'll find it easy to drop that low at the audition.

There's nothing pretty about a ballet dancer doing 100 pliés at a ballet barre, or 100 stag leaps in a row. She doesn't do it in class to be pretty. She does it so that when she's dancing or choreographing and a feeling comes to her, she can naturally extend that feeling into a stag leap because those 100 leaps have ingrained it into her body vocabulary. Similarly, you do these exaggerated status exercises in class so that you can recall high- and low-status postures and adjust them on the fly when you're performing or auditioning.

The extremes of some of these exercises are very clearly in the style of acting that we call Farce. Farce is probably the most demanding of all acting styles. As John Harrop and Sabin Epstein say in *Acting with Style*, "Acting in farce requires the energy and fortitude of a laborer combined with the physical agility of a tap dancer." My feeling is that if you can do the kind of status work required in farce, you can adjust this work to any of the other acting styles.

"I Don't Play Status Games with My Friends!"

A lot of students bridle when they first encounter status work. Some consider it calculating and manipulative. Then as the concept becomes clearer, they may grudgingly admit that in fact they *are* "guilty" of status work, but don't like that part of themselves.

Status work *can* be calculating and manipulative. It can also be helpful and compassionate, just as all the other skills you develop as an actor can be used to lift the hearts and minds of your audience as well as to spread propaganda. These skills in themselves, including status work, are morally neutral. They are tactics. It's the objective you're trying to achieve when using these skills that is value laden.

And here's the truth: Whenever you are to face-to-face with any individual, group, and often spaces (churches, libraries, your dorm room) you are constantly adjusting your status to achieve your objective.

Here's an example:

Imagine you're a student in my class. A camera is turned on in our classroom and someone is viewing the class from the next room on a monitor. They see you and the rest of my students sitting in a circle on the floor as I stand, lecturing. Without knowing anything about the class or what is going on, simply from the visuals and body language they're observing, to whom would they assign high status?

Me, right? And what is it about this picture they see on the screen that gives me high status? I'm standing; you're sitting, which makes me taller than all of you. I'm talking in a loud, clear voice, invading the space with it, using pauses and speaking articulately in a manner I probably would not use with you in a restaurant, where I'd speak quietly, mumble occasionally, leave sentences unfinished, etc. You are listening silently. I'm gesturing, filling the space with my physical and vocal presence. I'm older than all of you. I'm a guy. I'm tall.

On the other hand, you have agreed to sit on the floor, by your own choice making yourselves lower than me. You're all facing in my direction, again by choice. None of you are interrupting me, and if you decide to, you raise your hand first, essentially asking for permission to invade the space that I've taken charge of and made mine. And you're probably younger than I am.

Some of these status indicators are social: our age, my being a guy. Most, however, are tactics both of us have chosen in order to achieve an objective: in this case, an education. If the teacher/student relationship is to succeed and information is to be conveyed, students in every culture that I'm familiar with take a lower-status posture to their teachers. If any one of you in my classroom were to suddenly start singing, or stand up and go to the window, thereby raising your status by invading "my" space in this case, I would probably stop teaching for the moment. And if all of you did this, I'd cancel class—and the objective, an education, wouldn't be achieved.

Now I didn't enter the classroom with my dialogue planned and my status choices mapped out. I'm *improvising* tactics to achieve my objective, making them up as I'm going along. Because of my objective and cultural conditioning, these high-status choices come to me spontaneously.

So here you are in a voluntary low-status position. My question is, do you feel *diminished* by taking this posture? I never did as a student. It was simply a tactic I used to achieve what I wanted—an *agreed-upon* tactic with my teacher that was ultimately to the benefit of both of us. In fact, teachers *must* exhibit behavior that is generally high status because students demand these signals and willingly lower their status in turn. Imagine me walking into the classroom and falling down, leaving, re-entering, mumbling "Is this my, uh, class?" in a high squeaky voice, avoiding eye contact, apologizing for interrupting you, and then standing in the corner facing the wall until class begins. It wouldn't make much difference what kind of credentials I had as a teacher; my credibility in your eyes as a dependable source of wisdom would be seriously jeopardized.

Another example:

When a child injures himself, a good, compassionate parent will exhibit an incredibly sophisticated combination of both low- and high-status signals to achieve his objective: to console the child and reassure him. For example, he may rush forward into the child's space and hold him (high-status people invade other people's space), using direct eye contact. This is a high-status, "It's OK, honey, I'm in charge," signal. But in order not to frighten the child who's scared enough as it is, he may lower his status and the hugeness and suddenness of his presence by speaking in a soft low voice and tilting his head, both low-status signals.

Now imagine the same situation, only this time the parent runs, falls six feet short of the child and screams, "Are you all right!!!" while nervously avoiding eye contact. Again, this is a combination of low status—falling and avoiding eye contact—and high status—screaming. But if the objective is to console the child, the combination of tactics probably isn't going to work.

Status on Stage

Ideally when you're given a part in a play, it will be so close to who you are that all you have to do is be yourself and say the lines and the character will be authentic, along the lines of the playwright's intentions, and fully fleshed out.

However, unless the part is written for you, you'll be lucky if this happens even once in your entire career. Most parts are *not* like you.

Looking for status transfers in a script and altering your status arbitrarily during rehearsals is a great way to investigate a part and shuffle those varying aspects of your own voice and body until they fit the character's from moment to moment.

Once you're familiar with status work, take it into all of your scene work. In rehearsal, enter high at one point: commanding the space and taking charge, holding eye contact. Next rehearsal, enter low: cringing or weary, avoiding eye contact, giggling, weeping, or sighing. Look for moments, triggered by your partner's lines and actions, that begin a status transfer. See the scene as one long status transfer; then try it as several transfers. Make the transfers gross; then make them very, very subtle: your partner says a line and you stare him straight in the face without moving your head; next line and you look away and slump slightly, fidgeting with a button.

Most importantly, however high or low your status, however gross or subtle, feel the change throughout your *entire* body. Feel the collapsing sensation of low status even if you're just looking away; feel the growing, expanding sensation of high status, even if you're just making eye contact for the first time across the room. This is why the exercises in this course are so exaggerated, to get you familiar with this internal sense of expansion and contraction even if the externals you choose are small and subtle.

You're Not Listening

One of the great difficulties in communal art forms like theater is the necessity for actors and directors to communicate subtleties, feelings, and impressions to one another during rehearsals in an attempt to analyze what is right and wrong with the work. Much as I honor spoken language as a miracle, vocabulary can in fact be clumsy. A director or actor who feels he is being perfectly clear can be completely enigmatic to another director or actor.

The bottom line is, words are handles we put on life experiences. And since we don't have common life experiences those handles don't connect to the same freight when heard by someone else. For example, I know what I mean when I use the word "depressed." However, I suspect that when a survivor of a concentration camp uses the word "depressed," my understanding falls far short.

So, part of our task as artists when we hear advice or criticism of our performance is to figure out what we were doing that created a particular effect that the director perceives as "wild," or "too slow," or "unconnected," and then decide what we can do differently to create a different effect. Yes, this elaborate translation process can be difficult, particularly if a director doesn't work the way you do—"speak your language," so to speak. But it's part of your job.

An example that's appropriate for this chapter on status is when a director says, "You're not listening." This direction always threw me. I'd always *thought* I was listening. Heck, there were just two of us on a dark stage, I was facing my partner and I wasn't thinking about Chinese food. If I wasn't listening, what was I doing? So the next time through the scene I'd be thinking, "I have to listen, I have to listen," and then I *wouldn't* be listening.

So what was I doing that was creating a particular effect that the director was perceiving as "not listening"?

I wasn't being *changed* by what I was hearing, changed in a way that was manifesting itself in my voice and body. In fact, I eventually realized that it's these physical changes after every line that reinforce the "illusion of the first time," no matter how many performances you've given. It looks like everything is happening on the spot.

And one of the easiest and most powerful ways to manifest those changes is status adjustment and status transfers.

Some of the finest "status experts," for example, are the really fine soap opera actors. Sometimes they're called upon to do scenes that are largely fillers between commercials where in fact nothing happens. Or they simply talk about what happened last week while they drink coffee. (These are usually the Monday scripts. Everything tends to happen on Fridays to make sure you come back next week. Monday, they often just chat.)

How do they make this interesting? One way is to flirt, raising and lowering your status as you lock eyes with your partner, then look down and fidget, then suddenly look back and freeze again with a smile, subtly straightening your posture, then suddenly slumping just as slowly. You can be talking about pineapple upside-down cake, but as the audience watches these changes manifest themselves in your body, they are fascinated.

But, you may be thinking, this is just a technical trick. Exactly. Status work is one of many technical skills that you acquire to make sure the audience gets what they've come for, as you amplify scripts already full of richness and texture on the one hand, and create drama and excitement where there is none on the other.

Part II
A Flexible Class Plan for a Course in Improvisation

Introduction to the Class Plan

The following chapters are a class plan for teaching a course in improvisation. Each chapter begins with a discussion of the concepts in the chapter. This is followed by a warm-up, which involves some deliberate silliness and ends with a short, energetic game. Then there are one or two exercises, and finally an occasional assignment, where you're asked to use the principles learned in class outside of class.

Depending on the number of students and the time allotted for the class, you may or may not be able to complete a chapter per class as I've laid it out. That's not important. What is important is that you take as much time as you need to make sure that every student has an opportunity to do everything.

When I began teaching improvisation, I think I did what many beginning improv teachers do: I tried to give the class a lot of variety by introducing as many new games as possible. However, each game required a new skill or a new combination of old skills. And what ended up happening was that none of the students worked at any game long enough to feel confident with those skills, to get good at the exercise, and to feel a sense of accomplishment. And many ended up feeling that I was terribly clever and they weren't good enough.

In response to that, I've introduced a limited number of exercises in this course and have chosen specific exercises/games that incorporate the skills you have just learned in previous ones, building one on the other.

For those who may be interested in taking what they learn from this class and forming an improvisation group, there are a lot of books and source materials for games that you can use to extend your skills and to develop and expand a repertory. I've given some examples in Appendix 6: Source Materials. If that's your intention, I encourage you to do what our improvisation company did: find a game that interests you, and then spend an entire rehearsal period playing it over and over. If you're firmly grounded in the three rules as they are addressed in this course and then take the time to drill the skills required for a particular game, I can pretty much guarantee that whatever games you choose, your group will flourish.

I can say this pretty confidently. Our improvisation company, for example, began as a "TheaterSports" company, an improvisational format developed by Keith Johnstone. TheaterSports is improvisation done as a competitive sport with two teams of improvisers competing for points. But the secret for a successful evening of TheaterSports—as all TheaterSports companies around the world discovered—was that the event wasn't really a competition. It was a show *about* a competition, where in fact everyone on both teams was cooperating to make it the best show possible. For example, if one team was doing a scene and needed a crowd, the other team jumped on stage eagerly. And when I've analyzed why a particular TheaterSports game was a success, I realized that whatever happened that evening, the three rules were always in play.

Another reason I've chosen the specific games I have is that they emphasize skills that are important not only in improvisation, but in scripted theater as well. As a result, I've found that whether students of this course branch off into performance improv or scripted theater, the skills learned here will hold them in good stead.

So, again, however much class time it takes, make certain that each student participates in each exercise. Take your time. What I've described as one class may in fact take you two or three classes.

It's very important, however, that each of your classes begins with a warm-up that incorporates something deliberately silly, and then a fast, energetic game. Don't begin a class by moving right into an exercise.

In addition, since these warm-up games are intended to make everyone lose face at the same time, change them frequently. This may sound like I'm contradicting what I've just said above about working an exercise until you have it. But the warm-up game has a different purpose than the exercises within the class themselves. They should be designed to engender a sense of mutual ridiculousness and camaraderie by making everyone feel slightly off-kilter. Their purpose is to help everyone to drop attitude, meld with the group, and begin exercises from a base of mutual humanity.

Class

[1] Getting Acquainted

Most participants beginning a new improvisation class are nervous and apprehensive. Their experience has probably been either watching or participating in gag improv. And they feel that:

- They know nothing about improvisation and assume that everyone around them is already much better than they are.
- They've tried improvisation and feel they've failed miserably and that everyone around them is much better than they are.
- They've tried it, been successful with it, and bring all the dangerous habits and skills of gag improv: cleverness, punch lines, and a sense of competition.

The purpose of this opening class is to defuse the participants' apprehensions, create a sense of safety, and to get them comfortable with the leader and with each other. The "getting to know you" exercises are simple, low key, and very important. Next, the three rules are described in the class, and exercises are introduced that give students an opportunity to familiarize themselves and succeed with each of them.

A note: In one of the exercises below, the "Introduction Circle," you greet each member of the group and tell him something obvious about yourself that he probably doesn't know, which he repeats. For example, "My name is Dan and I had a dachshund when I was younger." This should be something simple and not something soul-baring, like "My name is Dan, and my father was mean to me." You should also say something different to each person. And if you can't think of anything, the instruction is to place yourself, for example, in your living room or your kitchen, look around, see something, and report. "My name is Dan, and I have an electric can opener." "My name is Dan and my walls are a cream-yellow." This is an exercise in *Saying the first thing that comes into your head . . .* in daring to be obvious, daring to be average. And in doing so, revealing a story no one else could tell.

In an improv performance once I was asked to describe a character's bedroom. "Oh, it was a desolate place." I said. "The bed had an orange-and-green-striped bedspread he'd bought in Poland and a headboard he'd made himself out of floor boarding. And above the bed hung a picture of 'The Incense Pot' by John Singer Sargent, a woman in pur-dah holding her veils over her head to capture the fumes." Afterward I was congratulated on such a vivid, imaginative description.

I'd simply described my bedroom. Everyone assumed it was a desolate description because I told them it was. I could have said, "It was a beautiful place," and given the same description and everyone would have thought it was beautiful. This isn't a description I prob-ably would have made up. It is unique and vivid simply because I spontaneously described what was obvious to me in detail. And at the time I remember feeling I was probably doing it wrong because I wasn't working hard enough. It's this very "effortlessness" that I had to get comfortable with as an improviser. And that's the purpose of this particular opening exercise.

Breaking the Ice

Sit in a circle. It's helpful at the beginning of class for the leader to talk about himself for a while. It raises his status and establishes a sense of control in the room with this group of people who are con-cerned about their safety and need to feel that someone's in charge.

This also gives them time to check each other out. The leader's comments should all be friendly and reassuring.

Then ask all participants to:

- Introduce themselves.
- Say what their experience with improv has been.
- Say what they hope to get from taking a class in improv.

Let them know that improv experience or lack of it has no bearing on this class at all. And that they are probably going to find the approach very different than what they expected.

This round of introductions gives everyone an easy chance to speak up in a room of strangers for the first time and, again, to get an impression of each other.

Exercise: Introduction Circle

Have everyone stand in a circle.

Then have every other person step inside the circle, turn around and face the person to his right. This will form an inside circle and an outside circle. If there are an odd number of participants, the leader joins one of the circles to even out the number. If there is an even number, the leader also participates but does so by traveling with another participant side by side as a couple.

Have the outside circle join hands temporarily and then step backwards as far as they can. This will space the circle evenly. Then drop hands.

You now have a circle of couples facing each other. Have each couple decide who will go first. Then, the following happens with each facing couple participating at the same time.

- Introduce yourself by first name, "My name is Dan . . ."
- Say something about yourself that the other person probably doesn't know, ". . . and I had a dachshund named Fritz."

When participant A finishes, participant B should repeat what A just told him, "Your name is Dan and you had a dachshund named Fritz." Then B should take his turn, again shaking hands and saying his name and something about himself. A then repeats what B told him.

This exchange should be brief. When the leader is done with his own partner, announce that the inside circle should move one person to the right. After each shift, the leader should swap places with the new person he's facing, going from the inside circle to the outside circle or vice versa each time. Everyone now repeats the exercise with the new partner. After this exchange, again the leader announces that the inside circle should move one person to the right, and he moves with the inside circle if he's inside, or remains stationery if he's outside. And again, he swaps positions with whomever his new partner is. With the leader acting as a "shuttle" this way, it guarantees that by the time the game is over, every participant will have met every other participant.

The participants should tell each person they meet something different about themselves. This is important. The temptation may be to repeat oneself, which is simply a way of dealing with fear. This exercise is a simple but important one about self-revelation and risk-taking.

When everyone has met everyone else, form one big circle. The leader should arbitrarily point to someone and ask the class to say what they learned about that person. When they've run out of things to say, point to someone else at random and have the class report. The leader should include himself. By the way, as you get to the final few, most people will have forgotten what they've heard. Make clear that it's simply because everyone's had a lot of time to forget and that it has nothing to do with the individual, personally.

Again, choose people at random until everyone's been chosen. Don't do it in a sequential circle, starting with the person on your left, then the next, etc. In fact, try to avoid doing any exercise in a sequential circle. Participants know when they're next and are either apprehensive or start planning, depending on the exercise. Catch them by surprise. It's kinder.

Again, there is nothing sensational about this exercise. It's an icebreaker. The purpose is:

- To create a sense of trust;
- To give the class a chance to hear each other talk and get familiar with each other's dynamics (how they move, hold themselves, what they're particular energy is); and
- To feel comfortable being observed this way as they reveal themselves.

This exercise, simple as it sounds, and these feelings of trust it's designed to engender, are essential for successful narrative improvisation.

Exercise: Slap Pass

Form a circle. The leader starts the game by clapping his hands then lunging forward onto one leg, pointing his arm straight at another player and making clear eye contact. That player then claps his hands and lunges at another, again making clear eye contact. As the game continues, side-coach to make it go faster and faster as they pass the slap around the circle. (For more information on side-coaching, see Appendix 4: Side-Coaching.)

This is equivalent in improvisation to "making an offer." And the person sending the pass should make each offer crystal clear with full body movement and direct eye contact to whomever he's passing.

The second time you play the game, the leader sends out two slap passes to two separate people so that two slap passes are flying around the room and, after a while, maybe a third. This is where it's important to make your passes clear both physically and with direct eye contact. Generally people are looking everywhere to see where the passes are coming from and may miss your offer/slap. If someone misses your offer, don't say anything; just keep clapping, lunging and making eye contact with the same person until the receiver sees you. (If you receive two slap passes, send out two to two different people.)

This game is another great icebreaker and at this point people are usually pretty giddy. The reason for these opening games and others like them is to get everyone to "lose face" all together, to lower his or her guard, i.e., the high-status defensive posture we tend to greet any new, risky experience. If you have time, add a third round where, if you receive a pass, you have to spin 360 degrees in place *quickly* before sending it to someone else.

When this game is flying, individual differences begin to drop and it feels like a machine that is running away with everybody. This feeling of being lost in the energy of a communal endeavor by simply "Yes! And . . ." –ing each offer is the playful giddiness that should invade every good improvisation.

Play this game one more time, and this time, when you pass the slap, you have to call the receiver by their first name. Gasp. I'm terrible with names and I say as much. And here's where we introduce the first rule: *Make your partner look good.*

If you see someone lunging at you and trying to remember your name, your job is to make him look good *as quickly as possible* by saying your name. No standing back or making him wait. It will get a laugh but your partner will feel abandoned and begin to shut down. Help him quickly. And the leader should reward the helper by saying "Good, Jill." or whatever the name is. In this course, I can't emphasize enough the importance of simple, continual positive reinforcement on the part of the leader. I make a habit of muttering the word "good" for everything I approve of. In a risky class like improvisation where participants are encouraged to get way ahead of themselves, this kind of reinforcement buoys them up and carries them forward.

Discussion, and Introduction of the Three Rules

Now is a good time to sit down and discuss the class plan if there is one, or explain school policies, attendance, grades, etc.

As I mention above, continual, positive reinforcement from the leader is essential to the success of this class. Calling participants by their first names is part of this—I know I was always delighted when a teacher called me by name and disappointed when they got it wrong. Still, I'm terrible with names. So I take a picture of the whole class at this point and, at the end when it's developed, write everyone's name beneath it; then, before each class I check the names.

Introduce the three rules of improv and have the class discuss how the exercises have so far illustrated them. If there's still time, move on to exercises from the next class.

Assignment

Read chapters 1–4 by next class.

[2] Warm-up and the Three Rules

Martha Graham, the dancer/choreographer who revolutionized modern dance, once said that wherever a dancer stands, poised and ready, that ground is sacred. I believe this is true wherever you are as a performing artist. Whether you're on stage, in a rehearsal hall, in a classroom, or in your own room rehearsing a scene, that ground is sacred. And I believe that if you're going to find happiness and contentment in this art form called theater, you have to believe this is true. You're probably not going to make much money for a long time. Without the enthusiasm that comes from this sense of respect for what you do, a career in the arts can feel pointless.

As an artist, you perform two services for the community: to delight them and to give them insight. Unfortunately, this community may not treat the event you create with the same respect: they'll talk and answer cell phones and unwrap candies. You may think, "Stupid audience!" But in fact, they're usually doing the best they can, which can fall far short of your expectations. You, on the other hand, owe them everything; that is what you're there for.

So it's important that you come to any space that you're going to be working in ready to work. The sacred space is about the work, what's happening now, and not your outside life. You will have to struggle with this focus throughout your career. Ideally, whenever you step into that sacred space, you must take all the distractions you're dealing with—the papers you haven't written, the boyfriend who left you, the fellow classmates who annoy you—and hang them on the rack outside saying, "I'll get back to you at the end of class." And as they annoy you during class, in particular with the "You're just avoiding!" message, say, "No. I'm not. I'll get back to you at the end of class." You have to be here for these people in this room for the class period.

That's your job.

Now you will *never* fully succeed in eliminating the voices and distractions that will clamor to invade your rehearsal time, classroom time, etc. And if your goal is perfection, you're going to spend a lot of time feeling like a failure. Your task instead is to minimize these distractions in a way that works for you, a way that is caring and loving. In part I, chapter 4, I discussed a meditation technique, acknowledging distractions as they enter your mind without engaging with them emotionally, and then gently releasing them and turning your attention back to the task at hand. They may, and probably will, return within a matter of seconds. Acknowledge them again, and turn your attention back. The more you do this, the easier it becomes.

And it's also important to begin each session—a rehearsal, a class, a performance—with some routine that acknowledges this passage from your daily life to this focused communal event. One that gets you ready to work. I've found that if you jump directly into class, it takes a while for everyone to finally focus. So I've developed the following warm-up to ease the participants into a unified group in the sacred space.

By the way, if the term "sacred" bothers you, choose whatever term you like. Class, however, is not a social event, and whatever you call the space, there should be a feeling that you're participating in something special and "other" that requires professional focus and commitment as a group. I've found that the term "sacred" and the opening warm-up help turn my mind to the task at hand.

The purpose of the following warm-up is to get you out of your head and into your body, balanced on your two feet; and equally important, to be silly and have fun in the process. A class in improvisation is high risk for a lot of people. Again, the purpose of being silly and having fun is to make sure that everyone "loses face" and lowers his or her status so that no individual is perceived by the others as "cooler" than they, detached—in short, threatening. The basic warm-up is described below followed by variations that you can introduce throughout the course to keep everyone on their toes and slightly but deliberately off guard.

Physical Warm-up

- Stand in a circle.
- Shake out your hands.
- Shake out your feet.
- As you continue shaking out your hands and feet, move your face around, squinching your face muscles and expanding them while you make vocal noises.
- Make a "motorboat" noise with your lips: force air through them as you hum, making them flap up and down.
- Jump up and down. (By the way, the sillier you do all of the above, the better.)
- Take a deep breath and reach for the ceiling going up on your toes and hold, as you stretch higher and higher for about five seconds. Release.
- Resume shaking out your hands and feet. Turn to your partners on your left and right and introduce yourself by your first name and as you do so, make faces at them. "Hi. My name's Dan." "My name's Mark." "It's a pleasure to meet you," etc. Turn around and repeat with the partner behind you. (See Appendix 1: Warm-up Games" for alternate games.)
- Take another deep breath and reach for the ceiling once again, stretching with all your might.
- Now collapse from the waist and hang, going from the high-energy movement above to complete release and relaxation.

At this point, imagine you're a string marionette and all of your strings have been cut except the one holding you up at your tail-bone. This should now be in complete silence. Another image: you're a big sandbag supported at the waist with holes in your fingers and at the top of your head through which sand is gradually pouring out. The leader (still standing) should side-coach with instructions in a low, calm voice. "Let everything go. All the irritations and confusion of the day . . . worrying about a sick parent, the teachers you don't like, the folks at work you can't stand . . . let them all go. And make a commitment to be here for these people for the next hour. That's your job." At this point, the leader may want to go around and very gently and carefully take a participant's head in his hands and move it easily left to right to help them release. Most of us hold a lot of tension in our neck and the head is the last thing to give up. The leader should give each participant positive, verbal encouragement: "Good." "Let it go. Excellent." (Remember: There can never be too much of this positive, verbal feedback throughout the course. See Appendix 4: Side-Coaching.)

NOTE: If this hanging position hurts at all, try adjusting. Bending your legs slightly might help. If it still hurts, feel free to squat and let your head hang between your knees. But *don't do it if it hurts*. The purpose here is to release into deep relaxation, not to endure because the leader told you to. If standing erect and just breathing quietly is most comfortable, then do that. You know what is best for you.

- Then the leader gives a slow count of twenty.

During this count, the participants should inhale on four as the leader counts "one, two, three, four" and exhale on four "five, six, seven, eight" up to the count of twenty as they raise their torsos, arms dangling, stacking their vertebrae one on top of the other "like greased poker chips." In other words, don't raise your torso like solid plank. But uncurl from the base of the spine gradually: first the stomach, then stack the lower chest on top, then the upper chest, then begin to stack your neck and your head on top around the count of sixteen. Keep your eyes closed when you reach the top and don't adjust your hair or your clothes. Let them lay where they are and just keep breathing slowly and deeply.

- Place one hand on your stomach, eyes still closed and take a deep breath.

Together on the leader's cue, make this a slow, deep breath, pushing your hand away with your stomach muscles, leaving your chest where it is, breathing as deeply and as low as you can. Imagine you're filling a big spare tire that surrounds your waist, expanding in front, as well as on the sides and in back. Hold. Then let the breath just drop out through your nose without forcing it and sink deeply into the exhale. Pause.

- Take another breath on cue, pushing out your hand as described above. Hold. Then, as you exhale, "touch sound." That is, gently engage your vocal chords in a quiet, vocalized sigh. Pause.
- Take a final breath, as described above. Hold. Then pull in more air. Hold. Pull in more air, expanding your stomach as much as possible. Then let it all out together with a loud groan.
- Open your eyes and shake your hands out.

Notes on Breathing

All babies breathe correctly, which is why they can cry for hours and never damage their voices. If you watch them sleep, you'll notice that their stomach is the only thing rising and falling. We unlearn this correct breathing technique in a society that insists we keep our stomachs flat and held in. We also tend to hold a great deal of tension in our stomachs, our viscera; hence the term "visceral emotions." The kind of breathing described above helps us to get back in touch with correct breathing, and to release and relax.

Above I've suggested introducing yourselves to each other while you're making faces. I've included alternate exercises in Appendix 1: Warm-up Games.

Opening Games

The purpose of an opening game, once again, is to "lose face" universally and cooperate collectively.

For an opening game in this class, start with a round of Slap Pass. Then Slap Pass with names, bearing in mind that it's a game about making your partner look good. Help your partner out *immediately* if he's forgotten your name. This game at this point in the course also helps everyone learn everyone else's name.

Whoosh!

Stand in a circle. The leader should demonstrate each of the following moves, and then add them to the game one at a time. There are additional rules to this game, which can be introduced in subsequent classes as well as alternate games described in Appendix 1: Warm-up Games.

- **"Whoosh!":** Whoever starts swings his arms up and to the right toward the next person and says, "Whoosh!," that person continues the direction of energy, saying "Whoosh" and swinging his arms toward the next person in the circle. You can't change the direction of the "Whoosh!" but must pass it on to the next person. Do this as rapidly as you can. In the demo, after it gets back to the leader, demonstrate it going in the opposite direction.
- Now demonstrate **"Whoa!":** If someone whooshes you, you can either continue the "Whoosh!" in the same direction as I've described above, or throw both arms up in the air and scream, "Whoa!" This reverses the energy back to the person who just whooshed you and that person must then continue the "Whoosh!" in the new direction, or "Whoa!" your offer, reversing it back to you again.
- **"Zap!":** If someone whooshes you, you can continue the "Whoosh!", "Whoa!" it back as described above, or clap your hands and lunge forward pointing directly at someone else in the circle with your arm fully extended and say "Zap!" That person can then "Whoosh!" it on to someone on either side of him, or "Zap!" someone else in the circle. (You can't "Whoa!" a "Zap!")

Moment of Theater in "Whoosh!"

Remember, one of the aims of this class is to get comfortable with being uncomfortable, to willingly throw yourself into an unknown future and risk "failure." Check in after each game: When was it funniest? Most interesting? When did you laugh hardest? It's usually when someone screws up and fumbles to correct himself. As I explain in part I, chapter 4, that is the "moment of theater," when the audience perceives that you don't know where you're going, and yet you move forward anyway, risking failure. Congratulate those who did; they have delighted those around them by taking the risk. That is their job.

Discussion

Briefly discuss the introductory chapters and the three rules. What is the purpose of each? Why are they difficult to follow? Every exercise in this course focuses on one or all of these rules. Review the rules at the start of every class. When an exercise isn't working, analyze it in terms of these rules. And as an artist, be honest with yourself and the other participants as you discover how you're breaking the rules.

In the process, congratulate each other on your honesty. This isn't just nice. It's essential to support this kind analysis in a caring fashion in the name of communal creativity. If you see your partner breaking a rule in a way he doesn't perceive himself, *suggest* what you perceive; never accuse.

There are two messages in every act of communication: a content message and a relationship message. One message, the content message, is the information you wish to convey. The other message, the relationship message, is how you feel about and relate to your partner. Artists are particularly sensitive to the latter, and many of our most creative potential artists have been shut down by harsh relationship messages, needling, being made fun of; in short, feeling as if they've failed a standard and are being diminished for it. Foster a feeling of support, particularly in your critical observations of one another. Make your partner look good.

Gift Giving: Make Your Partner Look Good

Sit on the floor in a tight circle, knees touching those on your left and right. The leader randomly chooses a participant to give a gift to the person on his left. The participant turns to that person, gives a reason for the gift, then offers the gift. For example, this initial offer could be: "It's your birthday. I got you this puppy." Or, "I understand you're afraid of school. I got you this eraser." Or, "I hear your dog died. I bought you this sweater."

The reason for the gift should be simple. And the gift itself is also simple and incidental, and doesn't have to be related to the reason. The attitude must be one of sincerity and affection.

At this point, as I'm explaining the game, I tell everyone that although later in the semester they will have permission to say and do anything in this class, for this beginning exercise they are to avoid trying to be funny, and they should avoid sexual offers. At this stage in the course, your partner doesn't know you well. And although he may play along with a sexual offer because he thinks he should, he may very well be uncomfortable, begin to shut down, and cease to trust you. Again, make the offers bland and simple. Make your partner look good.

The receiver should now "over-accept" the offer. By his wild enthusiasm he should make it clear that this is the best gift he has ever received, making his partner's offer look good. And he should give a reason for his enthusiasm. He then touches his partner and says, "Thank you!"

"A puppy!! I'm the loneliest man in the world and now I have a friend! I'll walk him every day! (*touch*) Thank you!"

"An eraser! Oh my god! How did I ever get along without one! I've just been throwing things away and now I can save paper! (*touch*) Thank you!"

"A sweater! Wow! I can wear it like a hat! (*touch*) Thank you!"

Just as the reason for giving the gift can have nothing to do with the gift, the reason for the recipient's enthusiasm is also completely incidental. It's the enthusiasm that's important and equally importantly, his eagerness to make his partner's offer look so good that he's willing to accept it with a "Yes! And . . . ," flinging himself into an unknown future, go into motormouth, and make a "moment of theater" as we watch with delight.

Watch what happens. What you're going to find is that the audience's delight has very little to do with what he actually says. It's the tension that is created by his over-the-top acceptance, and then released by *whatever* he grabs out of the air that causes us delight. Again, in narrative improv it's not the funny things you say that make audiences laugh; it's the passion with which we throw ourselves into unknown futures and then quickly grab "obvious" solutions, saying the first thing that comes into our heads, that make audiences laugh. They love your bravery and laugh with your victory.

The touch at the end of the response is extremely important. It could also be a hug, but there should be some kind of body contact. If the receiver forgets to touch his partner, remind him.

I feel very strongly about this. It's been proven over and over that infants who are touched actually grow larger than those that aren't. Touch is literally nourishing. It educates us, leads us out. And we are deprived of it in our culture—to a criminal degree, I feel. There is very little that is more reassuring and growth-producing than touch.

We do have touch issues in our culture, and a person's privacy and sense of physical safety must be honored. But I think we all know what we intend when we touch one another, when our touch is appropriate and when it's not. Our partners need it, and appropriate, reassuring touch helps release them.

The leader should then choose someone else at random, and continue until everyone, including himself, has had a turn.

Gift Giving: Part Two

This time, partner A (again, chosen at random) turns to his right (opposite direction), gives a reason for a gift and then passes the gift to partner B but this time without identifying it.

"I know you're moving to New York. So I got you this."

"Your sister's coming for a visit, so I got you this."

Partner B then opens the gift and immediately identifies what it is and adds why it's so wonderful. And partner A nods, "Yes! And . . ."-ing his partner's response.

"Oh my gosh! It's a Cuisinart! Now I can have friends over for dinner! (*touch*) Thank you!"

"Wow! It's a gun! Now I can shoot her. Oh, (*touch*) thank you so much!"

This version is slightly riskier because the recipient not only has to explain his enthusiasm on the fly as he did in the first version, but name the gift as well.

Again, this is not about being clever, but about enthusiasm and immediate response. You can't get this wrong.

Commenting

I spoke earlier about two improvisation no-no's: blocking and driving. Commenting is a third. Watch for it in particular during this exercise.

Commenting is when the receiver of the gift gets this concerned look on his face and looks to the leader or the rest of the class as he's responding. The message is "This is weird. What am I doing?" Commenting is another way to deal with fear, an attempt to get the audience on your side. "I'm with you, audience. I don't know what this game is or who this bizarre guy is." And with that, you abandon your partner, making him look bad.

We already know that you don't know what you're doing. Commenting simply reduces performing to a social event, getting the audience to like you. Responding with enthusiasm, on the other hand, no matter how lost you feel, creates a theatrical event as the audience watches you moving forward into a future that they know you have no control over. People who say "no" . . . or "comment" in this case are rewarded by the safety they maintain. People who say "yes" are rewarded with the adventures they have—and in improvisation, that they share—with their audience.

"Yes! Let's!": "Yes! And . . ." to Your Partner's Offers

Everyone stands. Anyone at any moment can yell, "Let's do . . ." something or "Let's be . . ." something. Everyone else must respond by yelling, "Yes! Let's!" as loudly as they can, and immediately begin doing it until someone else makes a new offer.

"Let's all be jet airplanes!"
"Yes! Let's!" And you do, until . . .
"Let's all do classical ballet!"
"Yes! Let's!" And you do, until . . .
"Let's do transcendental meditation!"
"Yes! Let's!"
"Let's pick lice off each other and eat them!"
"Yes! Let's!"

Two things: Keep in mind that you can't do anything wrong. If someone says, "Let's all dance the Farandola!" you know exactly what the Farandola is and you do it with complete confidence.

The second is that if anyone suggests something you don't like, you can't say, "No!" You still must yell, "Yes! Let's!" But you can change the activity quickly by yelling another suggestion:

"Let's all do 500 jumping jacks!"
"Yes! Let's!" (*do five*) "Let's all take a nap!"

The purpose of this exercise is to introduce saying, "Yes! And," to cooperate as a group, to lose yourself in the group energy. Do it for about three minutes.

If there is time left in the class, introduce the Expert's Game (next class).

Ending Class

If you can, keep your eye on the clock and leave about five minutes at the end of each class to review the three rules, and then check in. By that I mean, ask how everyone is doing, if there are any comments, positive or negative. For example, at the end of this first class, you might ask how it compared to their expectations of an improv class, their fears at the beginning of class, etc. Make it clear that there are no wrong answers. If you're a student and you're having trouble, or don't like what's going on, say so. You can only address the issues and work through them by first saying them out loud. These issues don't have to be resolved at the end of each class. If you're the leader, ask students with issues to keep monitoring them as the classes progress and report on how they're doing, if they're getting better or worse and, if worse, what they might suggest to improve them.

Class

[3] Experts

The Expert's Game is one of my favorite games for a number of reasons. It's always been a good performance game. And it's an excellent, supportive, and safe way to drill all three rules. Have the students read the section in part II, chapter 3, describing the Expert's Game before class.

Warm-up

- Physical Warm-up
- Slap pass
- Slap pass with names
- "Whoosh!" Add "Groovalicious!" (See Appendix 1: Warm-up Games)

Expert's Game

A note to the players: With this game as with all the games and exercises in this course, give yourself all the room in the world to "fail" and get it "wrong." If you were already good at them, you wouldn't be taking this course. This is a class, not a performance; a place you've come to develop skills that you don't already have through trial and error. It is about process, not about product. Be kind, accepting, and forgiving to yourself and encouraging to your classmates. And I think that ultimately what you'll find is that this attitude will begin to permeate not only your work in class, but in all your creative endeavors including rehearsals, games you play with friends, etc.

The Set-Up

The Expert's Game is a live talk show before a studio audience. Place two chairs, one for the Expert, one for the Interviewer side by side. The Expert's chair should be facing more toward the audience, the Interviewer's more toward the Expert.

In addition to the Expert and the Interviewer, choose an Observer who will remain in the audience. At the end of the exercise, he will be asked to give three examples that he observed during the interview, one for each of the three rules. Each interview should last no longer than three to four minutes. But use as many classes as needed to do at least two rounds of this game.

I'll explain the role of the Interviewer first:

The Interviewer's Job

Before the game begins, ask the audience for two suggestions: an object and an activity. You can phrase it that way; for example, "Can I have an object and an activity?" Or you can be more specific such as "Can I have something you'd find in a garage [an object]?" "A lawn mower." "And can I have something you do in the summer [an activity]?" "Go to the zoo." As a general rule of thumb, when people are asked to think of *anything*, they can go blank. If you narrow down the choices as in the above example, however, it's easier.

Then combine these two suggestions into an expertise: For example, taking lawn mowers to the zoo, or creating a zoo of lawn mowers. Try to make up something that wouldn't ordinarily happen (unlike "mowing lawns at the zoo" which is a normal activity). Instead you could anthropomorphize the object, that is, turn it into something intelligent that you're teaching a skill to, for example, teaching lawn mowers to run a zoo. At the same time, don't worry about how clever your idea is. Often an expertise that is extremely funny on its own defeats the game. Just make the expertise odd. The humor will come from the expert's passionate commitment to this expertise, not the cleverness of the expertise itself.

- *Do not tell the Expert his expertise in advance!*

If you do, he will begin to plan and, as I've explained, planning is death.

Now begin the show: "Hi! And welcome to the Jill Sanders show!" Applause. "Today I have a very special guest, someone I've wanted to have here forever. . ." (*touch the expert*) Thanks so much for coming. This is Bill Frayne and Bill is an expert in mowing animals at the zoo. Bill, how did you get started?"

As the Expert launches into his answer, stare at him with full attention and continue to nod your head. As soon as the Expert begins to flag, ask another simple question to keep the Expert's ball in the air.

Remember that the show is about the Expert, not about you. Your job is to throw awe and affection in his direction and to make him look good, and, as much as possible, to disappear from the audience's awareness.

If the Expert is on a roll, don't interrupt. I've seen Expert's Game where the Interviewer asked an opening question and the Expert talked for five minutes. There was no need for the Interviewer to do anything but nod, and occasionally make appropriate side comments: "Really!" "Wow." "That's fascinating . . ." enough to encourage the Expert but not enough to interrupt him. Remember, the focus of the show is the Expert. Your job is to reinforce and validate his expertise, then disappear as he expands.

If the Expert says anything contradictory, make him look good by helping resolve the issue. If the Expert has said that this is his first time in America, then later says he was in Cleveland last year, the audience will know a "mistake" has been made. Clear the mistake: "Oh yes. You flew in for your one and only visit before your current one." This frees the Expert to continue taking risks without worrying about the consequences. He *must* feel that he can't say anything wrong. *You* will make it right.

After a while, the Interviewer should "open the floor" to questions. If an audience member has a question, it is his job also to make his partner look good. As the audience member asks the Expert questions, he must never confront him, never get angry with him. Everyone must show him the same awe and admiration the Interviewer is showing. The class should be making a unified effort to support and release the student/Expert, urging him with delight to take greater risks, and applauding him on his way. Confrontation can shut him down.

As Interviewer, ask at least one question based on what your partner is wearing or doing. "I notice you're all in black. Is that significant?" "You're laughing. You must enjoy your work." If the Interviewer fails to ask such a question, the leader should side-coach him to remind him. The purpose is for you, the Interviewer, to have the experience of not knowing what to say next and then, rather than going into your head and "The Improvisational Cylinder of Panic," *look at your partner* for an offer. He is making thousands. Pick one.

Try to avoid elaborate questions that contain their own answers and so require a one-word response. For example, "When you're taking your penguins for a day out, do you go to the park or do they prefer art museums?" "Art museums." End of reply. This is usually a sign of an Interviewer who feels he has to come up with something clever in order to shine, which is perfectly normal. Instead, ask very simple, open-ended questions."When you're taking your penguins for a day out, what do you do?" "How do they entertain themselves?" "Tell the audience what happened last Tuesday." "And now you're in love with? . . ." The answer will *always* be "Yes! And . . ." in some form. Remember, the Interviewer's focus shouldn't be on pleasing the audience or the group leader, but on how much he loves and admires his partner.

The Expert's Job

As soon as you hear your first question, open your mouth and go! Remember: You're the Expert; you can't say anything wrong. Among other things, for example, you speak every language in the world with absolute fluency. If the Interviewer asks you how you ask animals to get out of the way in French, you say it. No matter what comes out of your mouth, everyone in the room is going to be in awe. That's their job: to make you look good. If you are asked to whistle and you can't, you can. If they ask why there's no sound coming out of your mouth, be patient with them. Clearly the sound is so high they can't hear it. They will thank you for your patience.

Use specifics in your answers. "What kind of lawn mowers do you use?" "Lawn Pro 3000." Make it up. "When did you last mow the animals at the Bronx zoo?" "Tuesday, March the 22nd." The answers in themselves aren't particularly funny; respond rapidly, however, and everyone will laugh. Again, with every question the Interviewer offers, there is a "moment of theater" where the audience knows the Expert has no idea of the future. When you plunge ahead with a quick, specific answer, they laugh with delight as the tension is immediately and confidently resolved.

Don't just accept each new question/offer from the Interviewer: *over*-accept it. "Do you enjoy surfing on refrigerators?" Instead of simply saying "Yes, I do," try "It's my life!" Or, "Dear god, it's redeemed my soul!"

And in this over-accepting mode, occasionally try making a big emotional choice in response to a question before you know why. Start crying suddenly. Start laughing. Emit a deep, satisfied sigh. Explode. As you launch into motormouth, you'll be amazed how quickly you find an explanation for this emotion.

A final note: When you've finished being an Expert, you will become the Interviewer in the next round. And there's a tendency to take this wonderful "show-off" Expert energy with you. The Interviewer's skills, however, are very different than the Expert's. As Interviewer, pull back and focus entirely on your partner. Get him started with a question, then instead of filling the space with your presence like you did as the Expert, "disappear," lost in the admiration of this new Expert. This is making your partner look good.

The Instructor's Job

As the class does more and more interviews, it's easy for them to get side-tracked by the humor, to reach for it by trying to say/do clever things, and to forget how the humor's happening in the first place. So before every interview begins, the leader should remind the two participants of their jobs. Tell the Expert he's hot stuff. And instruct each Interviewer to throw awe and affection in the Expert's direction; and to take at least one question off what the Expert is wearing or doing.

If the Expert ever answers "No," even if it seems to be logical, side-coach "Yes!" immediately. Prompt him to get used to saying "Yes! And . . ." to all of his partner's offers.

In addition, side-coach by quietly saying, "good," frequently, validating the Interviewer whenever a question is asked; validating the Expert whenever he "Yes! And . . ."s a question or goes into motormouth.

And when the expert takes a particularly risky choice, such as "Actually, this penguin is my wife," side-coach with "Go! Go! Go!" to help push him over the edge into even more creative motormouth as he tries to solve the issue. Again, I can't over-emphasize the value of this kind of positive reinforcement throughout this course. With continuous, enthusiastic support, people are willing to take greater and greater creative risks. (See Appendix 4: Side-coaching.)

At the end of the exercise, ask for feedback from the two participants. Some students are going to find the Expert position more challenging; some the Interviewer. All that means is that is the particular arena they should focus on to stretch their own range as a performer. Also, some students will have no comments to make. That's fine. For many, the experience is so unusual they don't yet have vocabulary for it. Always asking for comments at the end of an exercise simply gives students an opportunity to say something if they wish.

The Observer's Job

Finally, have the Observer report his examples of the three rules. And congratulate him as well. Again, there can't be enough positive feedback in this class. In addition, praising the Observer—someone in the "audience"—emphasizes that this theatrical event is a communal one that is contributed to by everyone, not simply one created by the performers.

If you are the Observer, when the interview is over report on your observations of the three rules. "An example of *Say the first thing that comes into your head* was when she . . ." "An example of *Make your partner look good* was . . ." Phrase it this way, naming the rule you're about to illustrate, to emphasize the three rules for both yourself and the class.

Often these reports will be repetitious: "He made his partner look good by nodding a lot." Excellent. The reports should be as obvious as "Saying the first thing that comes into your head." Repetition is fine; just tell us what you saw.

As you report, be aware of statements like, "She made her partner look good by being so supportive." As I discuss in the Introduction and the chapter on status, you feel she's being "supportive" because she's *doing* something with her voice and body that's creating this effect on you. *What* specifically is she doing that comes across as supportive and that you could imitate on stage and possibly create the same effect on another audience? "She's nodding her head." "She's leaning into him." "She's saying 'Wow.' all the time."

Conclusion

For the next round, move the Observer into the Expert position and the Expert into the Interviewer position. Choose a new Observer and continue in this rotating fashion until everyone has had a chance to do all three positions, ending with the original Interviewer becoming an Observer, then the final Expert.

Class

[4] "I Love You" Scenes with Expertise

As I've mentioned in the Introduction, this course has been planned so that each new exercise incorporates skills learned in previous exercises. You are now going to improvise two-person scenes using skills learned in the Expert's Game.

There are rules for the *"I Love You" Scenes with Expertise* as there are rules for all the exercises that follow. And I think you'll find that these rules, rather than making the exercise more difficult, actually make it easier. As you're improvising, if you don't know what to do next, simply move on to the next step.

Warm-up

- Physical Warm-up
- Slap pass
- Slap pass with names
- "Whoosh!" Add "Freak out!" (See Appendix 1 for "Whoosh!" rules.)

"I Love You" Scenes with Expertise

We're now going to begin improvising scenes. As I mention in part I, chapter 4, in order to help you internalize the three rules—rules that everything in your conditioning has taught you *not* to follow—I've tried to devise exercises where breaking the rules is difficult. This exercise is an extension of the Expert's Game, with which you're already familiar.

Setting Up a Scene

At the beginning of most of the improvised scenes in this class, you'll start by asking for either a location or a relationship. Because of the nature of this particular exercise described below, just ask for a location this time. And for those of you in the audience suggesting locations, make it something that fits on a stage. For example, *Paris, France*, doesn't fit on a stage. On the other hand, a *bistro* or a *street* or a *hotel room in Paris* does. *Bill's house* doesn't fit on a stage. *Bill's kitchen* does. This gives the actors and audience something definite they can see around them.

Choose two actors to do the scene and two observers in the audience, one observer for each of the actors. When the scene is over, each observer will report back on the actor he was observing with examples where he fulfilled each of the three rules. And then the two observers will become actors in the next scene. Having students observe and report back on others before doing a scene themselves is another way to help them integrate the three rules into their work.

As soon as the scene partners get the suggestion for a location, they start pushing furniture around to make a set *without* discussing it with their partner and *without* necessarily knowing what they're building. Just make the space different than the scene that took place before. You'll discover what these furnishings are as the scene progresses. Some will be obvious: a chair, a table; some may turn out to be a soda machine or a gas pump depending on how the scene goes.

As the performers are setting the stage, the instructor should get two of the fields of expertise from the list in Appendix 2: Lists for Jump-Starting Games, Expertise; for example, "Sticking his tongue in electrical outlets" and "Sucking Nerf balls." He whispers one into the ear of participant A, and the other to participant B. The expertise he has given A is B's expertise, which B isn't aware of at the beginning of the scene. And B knows A's expertise.

If you choose to invent your own fields of expertise, keep them nonsensical. Once the student has accepted the offer and made the quantum leap into believing himself an expert on something completely nonsensical, it's easier and feels safer to lunge ahead into spontaneous motormouth since there is *no* precedent to worry him.

For example, if he's an expert on something real, like Scottish Dancing, he can either do it or he can't and there's less inclination to take it to extremes for fear of being "wrong". Teach pencils to Scottish Dance, on the other hand, and the Expert knows his audience has no expectations. In short, the purpose of this game is to get over that initial fear of getting it "wrong". Once that hurdle is crossed, a nonsensical expertise leaves you unbounded.

One of the performers begins on stage; when the scene begins, the other will make an entrance. I usually announce the beginning of each scene by saying from the audience, "The curtain is going up . . . and LIGHTS!" Do this to help make the transition clear between the social feeling that is class, and the new relationship you now have with the actors. This transition should include complete silence in the audience before "raising the curtain."

The Characters

The premise of the game is this: The two characters haven't seen each other for many, many years. When your characters did know each other years ago, neither one had the courage to tell the other how deeply, deeply in love they were with each other, how much they admired one another. As a result, when the scene begins and they see each other (and one can see the other before the other is aware), lightning strikes! They might even embrace each other. Each one can't believe how fortunate she or he is to be back in the presence of the other person.

One needs to establish this tone, this kind of relationship, for a reason. Too often, new improvisers in their nervousness and fear begin scenes with arguments, or with "make-wrongs." "Make-wrongs" are statements like "What's wrong with your hair?" "Don't sit there!" "I'm sorry, I was first in line," each statement implying that there's something wrong with your partner. An example of an argument:

"Can you get me a drink?"

"No I can't get you a drink. Get it yourself!"

Arguments and make-wrongs keep you safe: you can deflect all your partner's offers and stay exactly where you want to be—whatever unexpected offer he makes, he's wrong after all—and at the same time you can bully the scene where you want it to go. What you've done, however, is immediately made your partner look bad. And instead of tuning into a cooperative give-and-take that's required for narrative improv, every argument counters the previous offer and brings the scene to a full stop.

At the top of the scene, carry on a conversation; discuss what you've been up to for however long it's been, or why you're here in the bistro, etc. You may never tell your partner how strongly you feel about him, or you may. That's not important. What is important is the energy this feeling provides that draws the two of you together in mutual support and admiration.

And finally, one of you says to the other that one of the things you'd always admired so much about him in the past was how he used to stick his tongue in electrical outlets.

Although this is the first time you have heard your expertise, like the expert in the Expert's Game, you are wild about it and should immediately "Yes! And . . ." and over-accept this offer. Go into motormouth, saying the first thing that comes into your head. "I had no idea anyone knew how important that was to me!" as you leap to your feet and put your hands to your head, or start weeping quietly, or kiss your partner's hand. Go on to explain in detail *why* this was so important to you. And illustrate it with a story about your childhood and what led up to that first electrical outlet incident, or the best electrical outlet you've ever encountered.

This should go on for at least a minute. Meanwhile, the other actor should take the Interviewer position. Nod, add little rejoinders such as "I know," "Oh, wow," "I see how much it meant to you." In short, support. He shouldn't interrupt; he should make you, his partner, look good.

Then you begin to wind down and eventually turn to your partner and say, "But you know what I really admired about you was the amount of time you spent sucking those Nerf balls." Again, an explosion of over-acceptance, immediate motormouth explaining this enthusiasm and telling a story about it.

Finally, at the end, the two characters should find a reason to leave. It could be anything and the reason isn't important. "Let's go get a soda." Or, you can incorporate either expertise: "I've got a Nerf ball in my room!" It's just a device to bring the scene to an end in a way that's dramatically satisfying.

When the exercise is over, the instructor should check in with both participants, then ask the observers to give examples of when they were following the three rules.

Things to Keep in Mind

- Again, if you don't know what to say next, look at your partner, or look at your environment, or make an emotional choice and go with it.

Trust that what your subconscious will supply spontaneously will be more than sufficient; all you need to do is trigger it by grabbing something obvious from around you.

- Remember, your internal "mantra" throughout the scene should be, *I love you, I love you, I love you.*

This is extremely important. Musical comedies for the most part have such stupid plots. But we love them. To have someone look you in the eyes and sing "If I Loved You" . . . well, most of the audience sits there wishing someone would do that to them. The lyrics may sometimes be really sappy, but we all long for that, for someone to take that big risk and say that to us. And in this exercise, it draws your partner to you. In addition, it has the audience wishing for your success. On the other hand, start any scene with a fight and you alienate your partner *and* the audience, who see fights every day.

- As in all the exercises in this class, some of you will find this game easy, some difficult. Give yourself permission to feel whatever you feel.

This is the first time you've done it so of course you haven't developed that particular balance of skills that this game seems to demand. You're going to do variations on this game as the course progresses, and you're only going to get better at it as you do it again and again.

- In this game and throughout the course, the instructor should be alert to "gags" and point them out afterward.

By "gags" I mean anything funny, jokes, etc., that seems to have less to do with the relationship between the two characters and the development of the scene, and more with the performer's relationship to the audience, getting them to laugh, to "like" him. The purpose of this course is to develop skills that can be readily used in scripted theater. The audience *wants* to believe what's happening on stage. In this case they *want* to believe that this is a reunion of two people desperately in love with each other. And they'll alternately hold their breath creating moments of silence, wishing the best for this yearning couple; and then they'll laugh at your struggle for mutual understanding, your passion for your absurd expertise.

On the other hand, start telling jokes, and you've turned the exercise into stand-up comedy. The drama disappears, the audience is only going to want jokes, and your partner will lose trust. Instead, stay focused on your partner and risk the scary, unknown future together.

Establishing Sets and Costumes in Improvised Scenes

In scripted theater, unlike improvisation, you have a set designer and a costume designer. The curtain goes up on a dentist's office and the audience thinks, *dentist office*. You walk on in a dentist smock and the audience thinks *dentist*. This is all clear to them before you even open your mouth.

However, in improv, as the scene begins, the audience has no clue as to who you are or what they're looking at. You have to supply them with this information. And you can't be too verbose.

Let's say the location is an orchestra pit. As your partner enters, you might open the scene with:

"My God! Jim Larssen. You're the new cellist! (*identifying his name and profession*) Put your cello over here against this chair (*establishing the cello and a chair*). I'm the first violinist (*hold up the violin, establishing its presence and your profession*). Here let me move these music stands (*establishing music stands and a sense of clutter*). The conductor hates a mess (*gesture towards the conductor's podium, establishing its presence and where you are relative to the rest of the orchestra pit*)."

An audience is greedy for detail. And as you give them clues like these they will immediately populate the set. Notice this when you're in the audience: The actors give you a number of clues about their hospital waiting room, and immediately you fill in the blanks with space, detail, color, furniture, windows, etc. Again, as a performer you can't be overly descriptive. It may feel weird because you never have to do this in life. But it's one sign of a good improviser: one who spontaneously imagines his environment and then immediately shares it with his audience in as much detail as possible.

I remember doing a scene where I was a G.I. meeting a Japanese geisha in a dark alley. I told her I was surprised to find anyone so beautiful leaning against a wet brick wall. Years later someone came to me and said how much they'd enjoyed the scene in the brick alley with the wet walls. The simple, one-sentence description had clearly made so much of an impression on him that that was how he defined the scene. (By the way, Shakespeare does this all the time.)

And *use* the set. Go to the water cooler. Get a beer from the fridge to give to your partner. Wave to people in the distance or say something to someone offstage as you enter. Check yourself out in a mirror. And try to do this in such a way so that your partner sees what you're doing and what it is you're establishing so that he can use the refrigerator himself if he chooses, and doesn't walk through it later on in the scene.

Be Specific
In all of your descriptions, be specific. If you mention a high school, give its name: *P.S. 35,* or *Brother Rice High School.* And don't "make them up." Get these specifics from your own life; it's so much easier. (I went to Brother Rice High School.)

Reincorporation

Later on in the course, we're going to work on the elements of a good story. "Reincorporation" is one element that you can begin working with here. If you use something or mention something in the beginning of a scene, use it or mention it again somewhere else. Audiences find this deeply, deeply satisfying. I can't overemphasize what an amazingly simple yet powerful story-telling device this is.

And you don't have to be clever about it; just remember what you did. If you enter carrying a suitcase, pick it up as you leave. If you enter drinking a soda, pick it up later and throw it away when you get angry. If your partner mentions your time together in Dayton, Ohio, at the beginning of the scene, later say something like, "Boy, a lot's changed since Dayton, hasn't it?" Notice how many plays and movies end up at the same location they began? There's a reason for this—reincorporation of anything toward the end of a story sort of closes the arc, book-ending it. And audiences think you're brilliant. I'm not exaggerating.

The Observer

When you're working as an observer and reporting back on the use of the three rules, report back on the use of environment and reincorporation as well if you notice them. Again, one of the reasons for being an observer is to then become a performer in the next scene with these elements fresh in mind.

Class

[5]   Permission

As I mention in part I, chapter 2, Say the First Thing That Comes into Your Head, at the beginning of a course, students don't know each other and they probably already have a preconception of improv as something dangerous and competitive. The instructor's first task is to create an atmosphere of safety.

At this point in the course, the class is probably feeling a lot more comfortable with each other now. Before this class, have the students review the sections in part I, chapter 2 under the subheads Fear #2: Obscenity and Two Moralities. Begin this class with the "Whoosh!" game. Then do a second round of "I Love You" scenes. And add the permission that follows below.

Warm-up

- Physical Warm-up
- "Whoosh!"

Permission to Say or Do Anything

The class now has permission to say anything or do anything . . . except take their clothes off (which they can mime and create exactly the same effect on the audience), manhandle another performer (which is a control issue and breaks that performer's trust in you), and abuse the furniture (which the institution gets upset about).

Manhandling includes grabbing one's partner in a "dance" and hauling him around the room. It also includes physically fighting with one's partner. Fighting with him three feet away and swinging wild punches while he reacts as if he's being hit can achieve the same effect. And by doing it this way, partners can still maintain each other's trust.

When I give this permission speech in class, I tell the class that I'm gay, and they have permission to use the word "faggot." Using myself as an example, I find, helps level all taboos suddenly. I tell the girls that I hope they don't mind the guys saying "bitch," and the guys that I hope they don't mind the girls saying "dickhead."

I go on to make it clear, however, that just because I've given them permission to be obscene doesn't mean they *have* to go there. That they're not to think that if they're not obscene, Mr. Instructor will think they're a bad improviser. This clears the air for those who in fact don't go through the obscenity phase. But if they choose obscenity, go for it!

At the same time, however, I still retain the power to veto an obscene *suggestion* from the audience for a place to start a scene if I choose; for example, a whorehouse or a sex party. It's not fair for someone from the audience to put fellow performers on the spot like that and then sit back, uninvolved in the consequences. This is essentially making one's partner look bad.

Educating Your Partner

The next part of this speech is extremely important: I explain that part of their job as "educators" for each other, leading out the best of each other, is to maintain an atmosphere of safety so that everyone feels comfortable going into arenas that are risky for them.

This means that whatever goes on in the classroom should stay in the classroom. On the one hand, it's OK to talk with a non-class member outside the classroom about a scene where someone picked up a hooker in a convent. On the other hand, it's *not* OK to name the student who participated in the scene. The last thing a student struggling with a breakthrough needs is to hear her name bandied about in the lunchroom.

Having made this speech, I then ask them if they agree to this, look each student in the eye, name his or her name and get a nod from him or her.

This doesn't guarantee they won't talk about it. And if it gets back to you later in the semester that someone has spoken inappropriately about someone else outside of class, address it. Without identifying who it is, say that you've heard about it. That it's probably a case of someone simply forgetting their promise, but for the sake of safety in the class it behooves them to strengthen their promise by taking the difficult step of apologizing outside the class to the person they've offended. My experience has been that they will.

Reminders

Periodically throughout the course remind students of this promise, particularly after a class where wonderfully outrageous things have happened or a where student has made a significant breakthrough. They *can* talk about what happened outside of class, just don't name names.

Class

[6] Introduction to Status

We're now going to put the exercises we've done so far on hold for a while, and introduce status work. Later we'll go back to scene work, adding status to these exercises. Review part I, chapter 5: Status, before class.

Most of the work in this section consists of exercises in extreme status postures. Exaggerate these postures when indicated, taking them to the extreme even if you feel you're just doing it mechanically.

Be alert to the exercises that you have the most difficulty with—you are probably working with a type of status that you don't normally use in your daily life. Make fun of it. If unpleasant low status is uncomfortable for you, make fun of bag ladies: put your hair in your face, pick your nose, and spit. If high is difficult, become Queen of the Monkey People and order your monkeys to bring you stuff.

Don't take yourself seriously. Making fun of someone else helps you achieve this by releasing the pressure you may be feeling to do "quality" work. I've chosen exercises that will make it easier for you to do so. If the class honors its agreement to mention no names outside the workroom, no one's going to find out you're making fun of them. It's a tool. You've seen other actors make fun of people in the movies and on stage. So can you. "Make fun," and I think you'll be amazed how the status suddenly fills your body.

Warm-up

- Physical Warm-up
- "Whoosh!"

Exercise #1: Status Wander

This is a simple but powerful exercise that introduces you not only to the concept of status, but to the sensation of status as well. The instructor divides the class in half; one half is A and the other B. When the exercise begins, everyone—students and instructor—will be wandering through the space, moving the entire length of it and making eye contact with whomever you pass.

If you are an A and you make eye contact with anyone (whether they are an A or a B), continue staring that person in the eyes as you walk until he has passed. Don't crane your neck to accomplish this; simply break eye contact comfortably as your partner passes.

If you are a B, on the other hand, whenever you make eye contact with anyone, look, then look away *instantly*, then look back at him, then look away instantly again, etc., and keep this up until you have passed. Make sure you are looking away immediately. Don't hold eye contact for a while, then look away. It should be as if eye contact were painful—but you must look back to see if your partner is still looking at you. Also, when you look away from your partner, make sure you look to the side and not down. Looking down can look like you're raking your partner's body with your eyes, which has a totally different message.

Do this for about a minute as you wander up and down the whole length of the room in silence. Change directions occasionally so that you encounter new people. You may notice as you do this exercise that it actually invades your body, your posture, the way you walk.

Then stop and take turns reporting back how this made you feel. There will probably be a lot of laughter because on some level the exercise is disturbing for many people.

Keep in mind when you report back that there is no right or wrong way to feel. Everyone will have individual responses to this exercise. Consequently, make "I" statements as you report back. In fact make "I" statements whenever you report back on all of the exercises. When I say "I" statements I mean, "I felt powerful." or "I felt afraid." Not, "When you're an A you feel powerful." "You feel like such a Valley Girl!" These are general conclusions about everyone, but other people are not going to have the same experience as you. We tend to make all-inclusive statements like this because it feels safer to be part of a group. Own the fact that your feelings are unique and valid and well worth expressing, whether anyone else is in agreement or not. This may begin to feel isolating, but your reactions to this and all other exercises are part of what makes you the unique voice in the arts that you already are.

I think you're going to be surprised at the depth of feeling this simple exercise brings up. Comments I've heard are:

- "I was an A and when I made eye contact with another A I felt like we owned the room."
- "I was an A, and I felt very powerful, but very challenged whenever I met another A".
- "I was a B and it reminded me of a nightmare I had where I was walking down the streets of New York and everyone was staring at me. It made me feel very uncomfortable."
- "I was an A and when I looked at Rebecca she looked away instantly and it really freaked me out. I felt frustrated."
- "I was a B and I wanted to be an A the whole time. I normally make eye contact with everyone and I hated it."

Maintaining eye contact is high status. Looking, looking away, then looking back is low status. As I mention in the chapter on status, eye contact is the strongest status signal we send. And, again: high status isn't good or bad; low status isn't good or bad. Status is a tactic we use to achieve an objective. Sometimes high status works; sometimes low.

After reporting back, switch parts . . . As become Bs, etc. . . and do it again.

Reporting Your Impressions of Others

This time report back not only on how this particular eye contact made you feel, but how other individuals came across to you. Were they intimidating? Stupid? Cute? Again, there are no right or wrong observations, and don't worry about hurting their feelings. Name names. "Bill, you really scared me." "Jane, I didn't know what was wrong but I wanted to hug you." "Steve, you looked like such a jerk and I wanted to smack you." Notice, for example, how college-age students tend to look like freshmen when they're doing low status, and like seniors when they're doing high status.

I spoke earlier of the catharsis the audience comes to the theater for: what happens on stage happens in the audience. And I talked about how that catharsis is achieved by what your body is doing and what your voice sounds like. These are the instruments you use to communicate. In this exercise and all subsequent exercises, as people report back on how you come across, listen closely *and* take nothing personally. If someone says, "As an A, you were such a bitch!" or "As a B you looked like someone I wanted to pick up and take home," congratulations! Now, if you ever have to play a bitch or someone cute on stage all you have to do to begin is this particular kind of eye contact. While others come across their own way, when *you* did it in this class, it had this particular effect on this student and will probably have a similar effect on an audience.

Listen closely to these reports; in fact, *any* time someone comments on how you're coming across—in class or out. For example, if during the day someone says, "Are you OK?" and you feel perfectly fine, clearly something about your appearance and behavior has triggered this feeling in someone else. Perhaps you'd just come in from jogging and felt great, but with your head in your hand feeling your pulse and your disheveled clothes, you may have looked sick. You can reproduce this "sick look" on stage. These observations by others are a goldmine of information about how you personally affect the people and space around you. Every actor creates these effects in his own unique way, just as all your friends with their varying personalities affect you in unique ways. The more alert you are to how your body and voice are coming across to other people, the more versatile you are as an actor.

You've now created two unique effects, two very different character types just by changing the way you were making eye contact. As you listen to what your fellow students say, you may find that although doing B you may have felt scared, in fact, other people found you threatening. Now if you ever have to play "threatening" you know where you can start. Also bear in mind that part of what contributes to these effects is the unique look and shape of your particular body in addition to this eye contact. Someone six feet one inches tall with a day's growth of beard and no smile doing *look, look away, look back* may look like a criminal. Someone small, boy or girl, with a round face and a sweet smile, on the other hand, may look adorable. These are both low status, unique to these two individuals.

Exercise #2: Status Conversations

Now find a partner, face him and decide who is A and who is B. If there are an odd number of people, assemble a trio where an A is facing two Bs.

You're going to carry on a conversation; you can talk about anything. During this conversation, if you're an A:

- Keep your eyes locked on your partner's eyes the whole time.
- Talk without moving your head. This is going to be very hard for some people, many of whom will not realize they're moving their heads. If you want to move your head, you can *only* do so in the silence between your sentences . . . tilt it to the side, say, or lean it in, and then begin talking again.
- Whenever possible, begin your sentences with a long "Uhhhhhhhhh". The intent here is to put your partner on hold, sending a *Don't interrupt me* signal until you get your next thought together. "Uhhhhhhhhh, Dan. How was your day?" Be careful with the tone of this sound. Don't make it sound like "Duhhhhhhh . . ." Make it a normal, voiced vowel.

All of these are high-status behavior.
If you're a B:

- *Look, look away, look back* over and over again, making the actual eye contact as brief as possible. Don't hold eyes at any moment with the A.
- Fidget.
- Touch your face and your hair a lot.
- Giggle.
- Pepper your sentences with lots of short "Uhs." "I . . . uh . . . went to the . . . uh . . . (*giggle*) movies with (*giggle*) . . . uh . . . my sister."
- Move your head a lot.

All of these are low-status behavior. And, again, even if the instructions above don't feel organic, do them mechanically.

During these conversations, the instructor should wander from couple to couple, repeating the instructions as they talk, prompting the Bs to giggle, touch their faces, etc., and the As to not move their heads, etc. For the As who *do* move their heads, I find it's helpful for the instructor to place fingertips on the back of the student's head to hold it still. Locking your head while talking is an extremely high-status tactic. When we move our head, our status goes down and we seem friendlier, less threatening. On the other hand, when you yell angrily in order to threaten someone else, you automatically lock your head. Try it: yell with your head locked; then yell while you wiggle your head. People around you will probably laugh at the latter, which is exactly what an angry person *doesn't* want. This still-head signal is so powerful and you'll notice there are some people who are such dedicated low-status players that they seem almost unable to do it. I want to underscore again that there is nothing *wrong* with this. They have chosen relatively low-status signals as a life norm because they work for them. Practicing high status in their case, however, will make them even more versatile as a performer.

When the exercise is over, report back on how you felt . . . and again on how your partner came across to you. If you found your partner annoying, etc., say as much. You're giving him a gift: now he knows one way to play "annoying" on stage. Hearing this kind of feedback can be a breakthrough for some people. For example, often when actors are asked to play an annoying character, they actively try to annoy their partner. In fact, the last thing most annoying people are trying to be is annoying. Often they want you to like them, but they just don't let up. Frequently the high-status people in this game *want* to like their low-status partner who also *wants* to be liked, but he is acting like such a low-status idiot that it's annoying.

After reporting, switch roles. (If there's a trio, the two Bs should now be high status to the A.)

You're going to be amazed at the total transformation that happens during the two conversations. You'll see tall guys who are playing low status actually struggling to get physically smaller than the short women they're opposite, often without being aware of it. Toward the end, the instructor can single out a couple to continue conversation as the others watch. Anyone can describe the scenario they seem to be observing: "He looks like a college freshman and she's a senior sorority girl."

"She's a teacher and he's a student in trouble."

"I thought she had a crush on him."

"It looked like he was talking to the autistic guy in *Rainman*."

"You said you felt intimidated by these two low-status guys but it looked like you had them on skewers."

For those of you who have trouble maintaining one status or the other in this exercise, it may be because these are extreme status postures I've given you (and they're going to get even more extreme in the next few exercises.) In life, however, we seldom send an exclusively high- or exclusively low-status message at any given moment. As I've mentioned, we are masters at balancing status signals depending on what we want to achieve. But for the purposes of this class, no matter how *you* feel while you're doing these tactics, they *will* have an effect on your *partner*, just as they will have an effect on an audience. In addition, if you do these things mechanically, they are going to start invading the way you feel, ultimately begin to feel organic, and become a part of your vocabulary. These are all classic human behavior patterns, patterns you and all humans are capable of.

Exercise #3: Status Bench

Use two chairs side-by-side to create a park bench facing the audience. Two volunteers, A and B, sit on the bench.

The premise of this exercise is that an imaginary curtain will rise, revealing these two characters at the beginning of a play, and the class's job as director is to pose them so that A's status is as high as it can go, and B's is low. There is no dialogue, we're simply positioning two actors.

You might begin posing them before the curtain goes up by telling A to sit well back in the bench with his arm along the length of it, essentially invading B's space. And tell B to pull his arms and legs close to his body and slouch forward.

The class should now take turns giving instructions to A and B, adjusting their body positions in an attempt to raise A and lower B. After each adjustment, the class should take vote on how effective the adjustment was. There will be disagreement, which is fine. And some adjustments will simply leave the status where it was. Go back and forth occasionally from the new pose to the pose before it so everyone can see the difference.

Some suggestions for A:

- Stare at B.
- Lean into B.
- Cross your leg, ankle on knee. Raise and lower the toe of that foot slowly as if you're thinking.
- Stand up.
- Stand with one foot on the bench.
- Put your hand on B.
- Laugh loudly.
- Expose your crotch.
- If B is lying on the ground, put your foot on his head.

Some suggestions for B:

- Fidget.
- Look at A, look away, look back.
- Cross your leg, ankle on knee. Raise and lower the toe of that foot *rapidly*.
- Giggle.
- Touch your face and hair.
- Turn your toes in. (This is an exceptionally strong low-status signal. In fact, there's been a study that showed that if two people are on a date and at any moment one of them turns in his or her toes under the table, the success of the other is guaranteed. Just as dogs roll over on their backs and expose their throats to the pack leader to show submission, "toes in" seems to signal willing surrender.)
- Sit on the ground.
- Lean your head against A's leg.
- Cry.
- Crawl under the bench.

After doing it one way, switch status roles and re-direct it to raise B and lower A. Notice the amazing difference achieved with the same two individuals.

I want to point out that the stage picture you end up creating will often be so powerful that students, particularly younger students, may resent being a B while the audience yells at him "Get him back!" Rather than resenting this low-status posture, congratulate yourself for creating this effect in the audience. If you feel personally affronted by this or by any exercise where status is required, then you're reducing the class and possibly other opportunities to work in a communal art form into social events, which is inappropriate. The feelings may be strong and that is exactly where you should be. Because, once again, if you can cause feelings like that here, you can have the same effect on stage.

Some Status Observations

The Stereotypical Dating Relationship

In the stereotypical dating relationship, the guy plays high status and the girl plays low status. He invades her space by putting his arm around her. He looks her straight in the eye. He talks in a low-pitched voice—in our culture, bass voices are given higher status than treble voices. A bass voice in a man, a result of testosterone, implies strength and muscles, which are also a result of testosterone. He calls the woman "baby," which diminishes the woman physically and implies softness and dependence. She, on the other hand, fidgets, giggles, speaks in a high voice, and, most importantly, looks, looks away, looks back, reinforcing in a very flattering way the strength and power of his stare.

Again this model I've just described is stereotypical. The two are using status tactics to achieve a mutual objective. But all the guy has to do is insult the woman, and it can result in an immediate status transfer. Her objective (connecting with him) may change to protecting herself. And she may choose to defend herself by raising her status and taking the offensive. She turns on him full in the face, locking eye contact and pointing, and without moving her head she lowers the pitch of her voice and raises the volume as she sits upright and announces to the whole bar that if he doesn't want her drink on his nice new shirt, he might consider moving on—essentially imposing her space on him by altering her voice, by threatening him with a liquid mortar shell, and then by insisting he *leave* that space.

I took a self-defense course once and they taught us that one of the most powerful weapons we have is our voice. If someone attacks, scream in his face. This sudden, powerful high-status invasion of his space can throw him back physically for a moment, which can be all you need to dart around him and run away. I'm not saying that this will always work. No status tactic, high or low, is guaranteed. I am saying that if your *objective* is safety, this is a wise, high status *tactical* choice that may, like all status tactics, increase your chances of achieving that objective.

Love Scenes in Comedies

The secret to a lot of successful musical and comedy love scenes is that they are low-status struggles.

"You're wonderful!"

"What!? No! I'm not wonderful! You're wonderful. I mean you're smart and good looking and . . ."

"Me!? I'm not smart. You get As and always know what to say in class. Would you like to go out sometime?"

"Wow! You want to go out with me!" and so on. This can be extremely endearing to watch.

Sex and Status

Almost anytime someone introduces sex into a situation or scene, his or her status goes up. This is cultural. Despite the fact that in America we are bombarded with sexual imagery, we still feel it's inappropriate to talk about it. Bring sex up, and your partner is almost immediately on the alert. For example, if you sit on a subway or bus pulled into yourself as most people do, everyone will probably ignore you. However sit across from someone, slouch and spread your knees open, exposing your crotch . . . and you'll see a flurry of *look, look away, look back*, etc. Even at a distance, you are invading their space with sexuality.

I remember the first time I saw female window mannequins sitting "like guys" with their legs spread and their elbows at their knees. Everyone in the street slowed down to rubberneck at this unexpected display of high status.

Posture

A straight spine is high status because it makes you taller and it takes up more space. In addition, a straight spine exposes the most vulnerable part of your body, your heart and soft stomach area. When we are being attacked, we tend to curl up in a ball, exposing the more protected back and spine, protecting our organs, and in doing so sending a low-status "I'm not a threat" signal to the attacker. Exposing those organs with a straight spine on the other hand implies confidence. Kings sit with straight spines on thrones above the crowd: "Try to attack me. I dare you!", whereas servants bow and contract: "Don't hit me. I'm not worth it."

Assignment #1: Observing Status in Life

Watch conversations in restaurants, particularly conversations among several people at a distance that you can't hear, and decide who is an A or a number one and who is a B or a number two. How do you *know* this? What is the one *doing* that makes you know that he's a one, actions that you can imitate on stage to create the same effect on an audience. Who is a two; a three?

I once was standing in Penn Station looking across the room at a group of four teenage girls and a guy. I couldn't hear the conversation, but it was clear that one of the girls was the guy's girlfriend because she was standing next to him facing the other three. Two of the other girls weren't saying anything. And a larger, overweight girl was carrying on a conversation in a fairly animated way with the guy. The girlfriend wasn't saying anything.

My feeling was that the guy was number one for two reasons: he was "the guy" which is high in our culture, and he had a girlfriend, which guaranteed—whether he intends it or not—that the remaining girls, all facing the couple, look unattached and lower status. He was also taller than everyone. The girlfriend was number two. She had a guy and the others didn't, was facing the same direction as number one and standing close to him, invading his space with his permission.

But the heavyset girl who was in conversation with the guy wasn't addressing the girlfriend; in fact, she was essentially ignoring her. This girl carrying on the conversation was a three: she had the full attention of number one, though not the attachment that two had; she was ignoring the remaining two girls as well, and she was bigger than all the other girls—in short, taking up space both physically and vocally. The remaining girls were fours; not four and five because they were so identical in their silence, posture, and positioning.

Now, as you observe interactions like these at restaurants, etc., watch what happens when someone leaves. In this Penn Station example, the boyfriend left, and suddenly the status, or "pecking order," changed. Immediately the heavyset girl became number one as she continued to monopolize the conversation. And as the girlfriend now joined the others and faced her as well, they all became twos.

I'm using the term "pecking order" deliberately. The term actually comes from the status behavior of chickens on the farm. All flocks of chickens decide who is number one, who is number two, etc., all the way down to the last chicken. Number one can peck on everyone. Number two can peck on everyone but number one; number three on everyone but one and two, etc. As a result, there's always a chicken whose feathers are ragged and who may be missing an eye because everyone can peck on her, while she can't peck on anyone.

Now I want to make it clear that despite my pecking order analogy, there was nothing mean-spirited in any of the interaction I observed at Penn Station, at least not that I was aware of at that distance. Again, status transactions are morally neutral: they are a tactic you use to achieve an objective. Status *can* be used maliciously; it can also be used compassionately and to foster friendship, just as language can be used for both.

But it is used *constantly*. And the power of status work on stage is similar in its effect to the power of stage lighting: most audience members are completely *unaware* of its effect on them. Just as stage lighting can totally transform the mood of scene for an audience who is ignorant of how it's happening, so status work, gross and subtle, sends powerful signals to an audience, giving them that catharsis that they've come for in ways they aren't alert to. The more observant you are of status transactions in life and how voice and body signals affect you, the better your ability to affect the audience in a similar manner with greater and greater sophistication.

Assignment #2: Reporting Status Transactions

From this point on and for the rest of course, as you observe status transactions in life, bring them into the classroom. When someone is standing opposite you outside of class and you feel afraid or intimidated or in awe, or annoyed at, or more powerful than, or tickled by . . . make a habit of observing what that person is *doing* that makes you feel that way, activity that you can reproduce on stage and possibly have the same effect on an audience that this person is having on you.

And bring it to the class. Don't just describe it. *Do* it. Imitate the person: A boss who drives you crazy. A snotty lady on the street. A puppy you just want to pick up and take home. Physically and vocally imitate what you've observed; make fun of it. The instructor should then ask the class to analyze what the status signals are: Is he taking up space (high)? Using loud vulgarity (high)? Is the puppy fidgeting (low)? The more you break it down into parts, the more the individual elements of status become part of your vocabulary, a vocabulary you can begin to regulate consciously and with greater effectiveness on stage.

As we were working on status in class one day, one of my female students started laughing. She's a tall, confident woman who always maintains steady eye contact in conversation and is very articulate. She said that whenever she is with her friends, guys or girls, she is always number one, always in charge. But she was on a date the other day and she felt like "a girl" as she put it, insecure and little. And she thought "What the *hell* am I doing!?" I asked her if she remembered how it was she was behaving. She said she couldn't keep eye contact, she giggled, she played with her hair, etc.

It's this kind of awareness that is so useful for an actor. Her first description of acting like a girl may be a true report of her feelings. But it's too general, and if later she's asked by a director to "act like a girl," she may or may not recall her actions. But by separating and identifying her actions, giggling, playing with her hair, etc., she's aware of them. They comprise a vocabulary, in this case a low-status vocabulary, which she can now apply to any character because she knows the "steps."

Or course, your first obligation in situations like hers is to deal with them as best you can in the moment to achieve what you want. What I'm inviting you to do in addition to this is to observe your and your partner's actions, to become more and more aware of how status signals are used so that you can transfer them to the stage.

I was in a production of *When You Comin' Back, Red Ryder?*, playing a kind of glad-handing, backslapping, junior-executive type. I was having a terrible time finding the character until my parents came to visit. At dinner a penny dropped as I began to watch my dad, a very successful salesman who is always number one in any room. The next day I started incorporating his high status actions into rehearsal—talking louder than everyone, invading everyone's space, keeping people on hold as he gathered his thoughts, etc. Since I'd lived with him all my life, it was easy to remember these things. And it transformed my performance.

Class

[7] The Four Status States

Again, status work is ethically neutral. It's merely a tactic you use to achieve an objective; it's the objective itself that has ethical value. On the one hand, you can use status tactics to soothe a child; on the other, you can use them to con an investor. As an actor you can be cast to do both, and you can do them more effectively with a greater understanding of your own status tactics.

However, when many students begin to understand how status work permeates every human encounter, they tend to label it manipulative and consequently find it suspect. As a result, when they are invited in class to exaggerate high and low status, they tend to exaggerate only the unpleasant aspects. High-status people can become arrogant and dismissive and low-status people idiotic and gross.

To help redeem status tactics, I've broken status down into four status states: unpleasant high, unpleasant low, pleasant high, and pleasant low. There's an exercise for each of these four states to help emphasize the characteristic tactics of each.

Warm-up

- Physical Warm-up
- Blind Offers (See Appendix 1: Warm-up Games.)

Exercise #1: Review Status Conversations

Repeat the Status Conversations exercise from the previous class. Report back both on how it made you feel and on how your partner came across to you, bearing in mind that there is no right or wrong way to feel. And pay close attention to what your partner says about you.

And again, *strong* reactions from your partner, like "Oh, yuk. You were such a creep!" while offensive in life are in fact the *best* kind of response. It's times like these that the instructor should jump in to congratulate both partners and reinforce the purpose of this work. You've created a strong emotional reaction in someone else, the kind of thing you want to create on stage: a reaction so strong that in this case the emotion of it invades your partner's report. This is the kind of work that brings scenes to life and that audiences love to watch.

The Four Status States

Again, for instructional purposes, I have arbitrarily divided status into four states: unpleasant high, unpleasant low, pleasant high, and pleasant low. Exercises follow that emphasize the attributes of each state.

Status State #1: Unpleasant High

Everyone stands in a circle. Take a moment to imagine yourself the king or queen of something. You can be the king or queen of anything. In fact, I recommend you look around the room and take the first thing you see: "King of the Light Switch People," "Queen of the Water Bottle People," "King of the Teacher People," and think up one thing that makes this position so wonderful.

If you're the instructor, demonstrate this and all other exercises to start, going over-the-top each time. It makes it a lot easier for others to follow when they see the leader taking the risks first. Then pick someone to go next.

Throw your arms into the air from your shoulders (not just from the elbows) in a grand manner, taking up as much space as possible. And in a booming, arrogant voice, announce to the world at large who you are and what makes your position so wonderful. Fill the space with your presence! Then finish by turning to the person on your right, and in your snottiest and most condescending manner, ask him who *he* is. And so on, all the way around the circle. Your objective is to intimidate the entire world until they tremble with understanding at your feet, giving you the worship you deserve. Meanwhile, the instructor should stand in the center and coach with a smile, side-coaching, encouraging louder voices, bigger gestures, more condescension toward that pathetic idiot to your right. It's the *exaggeration* of these states that helps give you the status body vocabulary.

Here's a transcription from one of my recent classes, to give you an idea of where this should go and the kind of side-coaching I'm encouraging. The parenthetical remarks are the coach's:

"I AM THE KING OF STARBUCKS! *(Yes! Go! Keep your arms up!)* AND IT'S GREAT TO BE ME BECAUSE I MAKE YOU PAY SO MUCH! *(Yes! Yes!)* And WHO are YOU!?"

"*(Go!)* I *(Yes!)* AM THE QUEEN *(Yes!)* OF VICTORIA'S SECRET! *(Yes!)* AND MY LIFE IS SO WONDERFUL BECAUSE I GET FREE BRAS! *(Find out who this jerk is!)* AND WHOOOO ARE YOU!?"

"*(Go!)* I AM THE KING OF UNDERWEAR! *(Snottier! Get snotty!)* I HAVE MORE PAIRS THAN YOU AND EVERY ONE OF THEM IS NOT CLEAN! *(Yes! And who's this?)* AND WHO THE HELL ARE YOU?"

"I AM THE KING OF FRUITS AND VEGETABLES! *(You are!!! Keep it up! Arms up!)* I PROVIDE NINE ESSENTIAL VITAMINS AND MINERALS. AND WHO ARE YOU?!"

"I AM THE QUEEN OF THE OCEANS! *(Go! No laughing! Nail these sons of bitches! Go!)* AND I AM FABULOUS BECAUSE I RULE 70 PERCENT OF THE KNOWN WORLD! AND WHO ARE YOU!"

Take yourselves very seriously! And when I say that, I mean make *fun* by doing exaggerated imitations of people who take themselves so seriously. One of my instructions above was *"No laughing!"* Laughter is a way to avoid the over-the-top absurdity of this exercise, to show everyone that you're really just like them and short circuit it into a social event. However, the more serious you are, the funnier it becomes.

Remember, the humor in narrative improv doesn't come from jokes but from people passionately pursuing *anything* that the reasonably prudent man wouldn't. It is character humor, not joke humor. And I think you'll begin to find that character humor is much easier. Even when an audience isn't laughing, they are grinning in expectation, dazzled by the absurdity of your character. There's this feeling the audience has of looking over a fence at ridiculous people who don't know they're being watched. And this feeling can hold a voyeuristic audience to narrative improv far longer than gag improv, where you're more like a friend saying funny things—and the moment you stop saying funny things, they're bored and impatient.

By the way, when I say, "*No laughing.*" . . . it's the person performing who shouldn't laugh. It's fine if the rest of the class—the "audience"—laughs.

When everyone has had a turn, review the elements that have made these characters high status.

- Throwing your arms up and taking up space.
- Projecting your voice and, again, taking up space with it.
- Direct eye contact, etc.
- Obscenity.
- Lowering the pitch of your voice.
- Invading the space of the person next to you when you ask them who they are.

By the way, instructors, this is a good time to remind the class that they now have permission to say anything and to do anything in this class—except take their clothes off, manhandle another partner, or abuse the furniture. If obscenity comes out, go for it. Keeping in mind that if students choose *not* to be obscene, that's OK too. And remind everyone again to keep their promise: what goes on in the class stays, in the class.

Status State #2: Unpleasant Low

Now imagine yourself the most disgusting thing that you could possibly be. You loathe yourself, so much that if anyone were to kick you, you'd thank him. A different person in the circle begins. That person announces who he is and why he is so disgusting in a pathetic voice like gravel as he crumples to the floor, ending up on his stomach and vomiting. Collapse in on yourself as you take up as little space as possible trying to bury your presence into invisibility on the floor:

"I am the booger on the end of a two-year-old's finger (*You are! You're disgusting!*) that's green and slimy (*God, you are so gross!*)

and he eats in church while saliva drools down his face (*YES! Puke! Puke!*) BLEAAAAAAAGH!"

At this point the instructor can stomp his foot on the floor as if he's kicking this booger person, who responds . . . "Oohhh, thank you!" then on to the next person.

"I . . . (*Oh God! You're disgusting! Tell us who you are!*) am . . . (*You're so stupid you can't even* say *it!*) the pus-filled pimple on the nose of a dead dog (*Oh my GOD that's disgusting!!*) that flies eat BLEAAAAAAGH!!"

Your objective is to warn the world away, making sure they loathe you on their way out as much as you already loathe yourself.

When you're done, review the low-status behaviors.

Exercise to Review the Two "Unpleasant" Status States
Now you'll review the two unpleasant personas you just created. This time around the instructor chooses someone in the circle and gives him a thumbs up or a thumbs down. If you get a thumbs up, do your unpleasant high-status character. If you get a thumbs down, your unpleasant low. The instructor then moves to the next person giving a thumbs up or thumbs down and so on.

Your willingness to go all the way down and your willingness to go all the way up is so important as an actor. This is farce work, and, again, my feeling is that if you can do farce, you can do anything.

Status State #3: Pleasant High
Now choose a very pleasant high-status persona: a Mother Superior, a principal of a high school, a guidance counselor, the President, the Pope. Turn to the person on your right and in a very pleasant, confident manner, shake hands as you introduce yourself, making it clear that you're in charge and will take care of him. Then ask him who he is. He then turns to his partner on the right and does his pleasant high persona in turn.

"Hello. (*shaking hands*) I'm nurse Wilson. I'm here to take your temperature and blood pressure and I know you're going to do just fine. And who are you?"

That person turns to the person on *her* right and continues:

"Hello. I'm Mrs. Turner, head of the Junior League. We're so pleased to have you on board and know that you're going to make a wonderful contribution to our group. And who are you?"

And so on. As I've mentioned before, most of our status transactions in life are neither strictly high nor strictly low but sophisticated combinations of both as we adjust our tactics on the fly. Keep your eye contact direct and steady in this pleasant high persona and I think many of you will find that you'll automatically tilt your head as you speak. This is a low-status signal that softens the high-status impact of the steady stare.

Status State #4: Pleasant Low

Finally, pleasant low status. There's a scenario to this exercise:

When it's your turn, imagine that the person on your left is someone famous that you've worshipped all your life. You are unaware that he's there, so when you turn and find him, you scream in recognition as you back away slightly so as not to invade his space. This could be a TV personality, your favorite singer, your favorite actor, etc.

Run on about how much you adore this person, how you've seen all his movies, know all his songs, etc. Until suddenly . . . uh oh! You notice something wrong with his grooming: some mustard on his shirt or a hair out of place or dog poop on his shoes.

Gently and carefully draw this person's attention to the problem. Be careful, he may find it insulting: he's famous and you're a nobody! Then meekly ask for permission to correct the problem. When he gives it to you, begin to move toward him to correct it . . . then suddenly recoil and check in with him again. Is it really OK? He says yes; you move in; you recoil, asking him again if he's sure. Finally, gather the courage to touch this person, correct the problem quickly and then recoil, gushing with thanks.

The partner should play along with this, and gradually get irritated by this pest. Get the mustard *off* my shirt, for god's sake! Move it!

Here's an example:

"JOHN LENNON!!! Oh my GOD!!! You're John Lennon!!! Your music has totally changed my life. You saved my marriage with 'Imagine'!! I mean, I like the other Beatles, but you are . . . a GOD! I . . . uh . . . um . . . Mr. Lennon . . . um . . . there's . . . there's some pigeon doody on your collar. Would you . . . would you like me to get it off? I mean you don't have to! I mean, you're FAMOUS, and I'm just some geek from Royal Oak, Michigan." (*Lennon nods*) "Oh gee, thanks. I'll just wipe it, I'll just wipe it with (*backs off*) — are you sure!!?? Are you really sure. (*Lennon says, "Get the stupid poop off my collar."*) "Okay, sure, right away, I'll just . . . are you sure!?!"

(*Lennon: "Get it off!"*) "Okay, here it goes, here it goooooes . . . (*remove poop quickly and suck your finger*) Oh, thank you! Thank you so much!"

Use all the low-status tactics from the Status Dialogue exercise: giggle, fidget, touch your face, avoid eye contact, etc. And be extremely apologetic about invading your partner's space.

More Status Observations

Invading Someone's Space
A lot of status signals are universal like height, invading space with your voice, body, etc. But a lot of them are cultural and change from location to location. I was in a business conversation with an Egyptian who was about my age. Before long I found myself against the wall and couldn't figure out how I'd gotten there. I was then aware that he had been standing closer to me than I'd felt was appropriate for a business relationship, and I'd been stepping back to correct the distance problem. In short, he was invading my space, and subconsciously I wasn't going to lower my status by allowing him to. Then I wondered if he was coming on to me. But then his wife walked in. I was *completely* confused.

As I was explaining this to someone later who had traveled a lot he laughed. He explained that in different cultures the "safe" distance between two people varies. In Egypt the distance they consider normal we consider intimate. In short, I was being affected by what I interpreted as a status tactic that my partner was complete unaware of.

Eye Contact
I spoke earlier how a great source of comedy is to take an expected status and play the opposite: God as an idiot, or a baby smoking a cigar. In fact, so much TV situation comedy is based on this kind of reversed status: fathers who are idiots, and children who wisecrack like Walter Matthau.

This reversal of status can also be unsettling. Go back to the list of low-status behaviors and do them all with a partner with the following changes: instead of fidgeting your head, hold it steady and never break eye contact. The result is really pretty creepy: imagine a giggling, fidgeting bum who never takes his eyes of you wherever you go.

Obscene Words

One of the reasons that obscenity is high status is because the majority of obscene words consist of "plosive" constants; consonants that require a stoppage of air and then a release. They sound like a wind-up and then a punch, invading someone else's space. Think about the swear words you know, about the words used to put down minorities and ethnic groups: "wop," "polak," and "fag." The *sound* is aggressive and, consequently, invasive and high status.

Assignment: Experimenting with Status

When you're in conversation with someone, arbitrarily alter your status and watch the result. In part I, chapter 3: Make Your Partner Look Good, I talk about what a powerful positive reinforcement you give your partner if you nod while he's talking. When you're with a friend, try holding your head completely still for a while and see what happens. Then begin nodding and watch the change. (You should probably explain what you're doing afterward, since my experience has been that he'll find it very unsettling—it's that powerful.)

Class

[8] Status and Character Development

One of the purposes of this course is to give you improvisational skills that translate readily to scripted theater. In this class, we'll begin to use the four status states in short scenes to develop a wide variety of characters.

In addition, many characters are defined not just by the status they play, but by the status they are assigned by others. A butler entering a room alone is a high-status presence; for example, a status defined by his posture, his clothing, and his command of the space. But we know his low-status position the moment someone enters, throws him a command without looking at him, and proceeds to behave as if he doesn't exist, i.e., treats him in a low-status fashion. In fact, since butlers seldom have much to say in plays, this treatment by others is largely how his character is defined.

With this in mind, we'll end the class with an exercise called "Status Office Party" where your character is defined by the treatment you receive from your office co-workers.

Warm-up

- Physical Warm-up including Rubbing Butts Together (see description in Appendix 1: Warm-up Games)
- Blind Offers

Review Status Observations

Check to see who has brought status observations from outside. Don't just discuss or describe them, have the volunteer act them out as he's describing. The purpose again is to get it into the body. Then have the class point out what status tactics he's using.

If students are wondering what kinds of things you should be observing, here are some examples my students have brought in:

"I was walking home and we have this little side street with cobblestones, and the sidewalks are extremely narrow. I was on one side of the sidewalk, and I saw this really big guy taking up the entire sidewalk walking toward me. (*Standing up, she "makes fun" of this guy's size.*) Technically, I was invading his space as well, but I remembered our class assignment about walking while holding my head rigid and staring straight ahead. (See assignment at the end of this class.) And I thought, 'I'm going to do it to this guy.' So I start walking down the street, locked my head and stared straight ahead (*She does.*) and he literally not only moved out of my way (*showing us*), but also got down off the sidewalk and walked on the street. And I thought, 'Yeah!'"

Another observation:

"I was in South Beach and I was watching this guy trying to pick up this girl. This guy was like 6" 4" . . . he was big was standing talking to this girl who was lying on the beach topless. He'd talk and kinda giggle (*He demonstrates*) and ask her questions and she'd just give these one-word answers. (*Getting on the floor, he demonstrates.*) She just sat there watching him and he kept trying to talk to her and you could just see the fear in his face."

"What's going on status-wise?"

"Normally the guy would be high and the girl low but it's been reversed."

"How has it been reversed?"

"Sex. She's topless and it completely invades the space, the guy. It's her space. She's in control of it."

Another observation:

"I just realized now how low my status was this morning, and I feel really angry about it. I am not a morning person. So when things don't work out for me in the morning I can turn into the devil child. I woke up and I went to catch the bus, and I was tired. And the bus is there and of course it's starting to leave so I'm rushing after it. I'm kicking it (*he demonstrates*), I'm smacking the shit out of it. Finally it stops. And the bus driver literally does a *Terminator* thing with me (*imitates bus driver*), turns his head very slowly and stares at me through the door. And then pulls away. And I'm still kicking and screaming at the bus (*he does so*)."

"What raises the status of the bus driver?"

"He's physically higher than Bill."

"He turns his head slowly and stares directly at him."

"He's driving this huge piece of machinery."

"After staring at Bill, he drives off, essentially snubbing him."

"What lowers Bill?"

"He is doing high status tactics . . . raising his voice, invading space, kicking . . . but he's doing it to this huge indifferent piece of machinery, which makes him look in contrast like a yapping lap dog."

Two comments on this observation. First keep in mind that there are often two levels of status going on in a given situation: the level you are trying to achieve and the level the audience gives you. A dog yapping away is trying to achieve high status. The average person, on the other hand, treats it like a low-status annoyance. Often characters are trying hard to raise their status, like Annette Benning in *American Beauty*. But the audience gives her low status, partly because she's trying too hard. (By the way, I've mentioned this movie before . . . it's a fascinating study in status tactics and status transfers.)

Second, I could tell that at first this student was hesitant to tell this bus story because I suspect he was embarrassed by his behavior. But people come to the movies to watch this very thing. If you can not only accept this behavior in yourself, but also embrace it, it enables you to bring it to the stage as a performer or as a director. In addition—and this is one of the great benefits of being in the arts—I feel that embracing moments like these is the route to sanity. If you know that this is in you as it's in all of us, you simply see it as human—and people will turn to you for this wisdom.

Again, it's one thing to talk about status behavior and status tactics in class. It's something else entirely to take it into life and feel it in your body. It's like reading about swimming: you can talk about it in class and read about it forever. But until you've done it, you have no idea what it's like. The effects you create experimenting with status tactics in life, and the effects you're aware of in yourself created by other people's tactics—these are the same effects you can create in an audience by simply repeating those tactics.

Gibberish

One of the great ways to get life into an improvised scene is to hamper the ability to communicate verbally. Deprived of language, actors tend to get animated as they try to communicate with vocal tone, facial expression, gesture, etc.

We're going to be doing exercises now that involve gibberish, a way to limit your verbal skills. If anyone doesn't know what gibberish is, have someone demonstrate who does. In fact, I suggest the leader carry on a brief gibberish conversation with each participant as a warm-up.

There are two signs of good gibberish. First, if a seven-year-old walked into the room during the gibberish conversation, he should think you were talking a foreign language. If, on the other hand, you're just repeating, "Bassa, bassa, bassa, bassa, bassa, bassa . . . ," no matter how animated you are, no one would believe you're speaking a language.

Second, *listen* and respond. That is, be affected by the gibberish you've just heard. Often when two people are speaking gibberish they just make noises at each other, talking at the same time. *Look* like you're listening; that is, when one of you is talking, the other should stop, listen, be *changed* by what you've heard and then respond.

And part of listening and responding is to reincorporate what you hear. Take gibberish words your partner makes up and use them in *your* sentences. *"Taka pookie wanna bishow ma la pokopikina."* *"Pokopikina?! Tona koram ma la pokopikina!"*

Review the Four Status States

Review the aspects of unpleasant high status behavior. Then everyone should simultaneously strut about the room, creating the most arrogant unpleasant high persona they can, speaking all at once in gibberish. For the purposes of this warm-up, don't worry about listening and responding just yet.

Do the same for the remaining three status states, everyone wandering the room in that status state at the same time. For Unpleasant Low be sure to fall to the floor and vomit a lot and if the instructor "kicks" you (faking this with a foot stomp), thank him in gibberish. For pleasant high, direct eye contact and you might in fact join in gibberish conversation with people you meet, listening and responding at this point. And for Pleasant Low, everyone you meet amazes you, and if you touch or bump into someone apologize profusely.

Exercise: "Four Status State" Scenes

The instructor puts the four status states on a chalkboard and numbers them one to four. The participants count off one through four until each one has a number, corresponding to the status state that he's going to begin this exercise with.

- Now everyone wanders the space in silence, finding a body for this character based on his assigned status state. Exaggerate it. Imagine that Looney Toons is looking for a new cartoon character and they need the most extreme examples to base him on.
- Then on a signal from the instructor, everyone add a gibberish voice for this character. Exaggerate this as well as you continue to wander the room.
- Next, on the instructor's signal, find a partner and go for a walk together, carrying on a gibberish conversation . . . listening and responding, being affected by what your partner says.
- Then, the instructor calls out the name of two participants.

They could be two people already together, or two people he thinks would make an interesting pair. Everyone else immediately withdraws to the sides of the room as those two walk (or crawl, as is often the case with unpleasant low characters) and carry on a gibberish conversation.

• Finally, the instructor says "English!"

And they break into English, retaining the body and the vocal peculiarities they've developed as much as possible.

• However they must begin the English dialogue with the following two sentences:

"I like you."
"I like you, too, but we have a problem . . ."

• At this point, either one of them immediately identifies the problem.

It can be anything. "Your hair's on fire." "My mother died." "I walk funny." "I/you fart." "I hate peaches." The second person must immediately accept this offer and then the two work together to find a solution.
"I know I smell funny and I think it's time you gave me a bath!"
"I have a tub in my apartment. Let's go."
Once a solution is reached, they find a reason to leave and go. This whole scene needn't last any longer then 30–60 seconds.
I have deliberately chosen these two opening sentences to keep the scenes from just becoming arguments, which are deadly in improv—two people insisting they're right and refusing to budge without a playwright forcing them to move onto the next beat. Unpleasant status characters are particularly prone to arguing, or simply dismissing their partner, which ends the scene. With this scenario—*I like you/I like you, too, but we have a problem*—they have to work something out together.
Now repeat the exercise, and everyone moves on to the next number. Ones become twos, twos become threes, etc. Each creates a new character, then a voice, then a dialogue, etc. Repeat this exercise until everyone has had a chance to come to the middle and improvise a scene in English.

A Review

Think back on the first class, where I'm sure many of you were scared of improv, scared that you weren't going to be funny enough or quick enough or clever enough. Look back at what has happened in this class: I'm sure much of what you've created is hysterically funny, not because you're clever or quick or trying to be funny, but because you've created a dramatic tension as two exaggerated characters try to work out a relationship. All of these body types are in all of you.

Again, narrative improv is character humor, not joke humor. And as such it is so much easier than competitive improv. And, again, these skills you're developing here can be carried directly into scripted theater.

Exercise: Status Office Party

We're now moving from the farcical status exaggerations of the previous game to a more "realistic" use of status.

As I've said before, whenever we are face-to-face with anyone in life, we are using status and status tactics to achieve an objective. Also, our status is often defined by how we are treated by others. This is an exercise to help raise awareness of how we do it in our everyday lives.

The instructor will get a deck of cards and deal one to each participant, face down in his hand so that he can't see his card.

The premise of this game is that you're all at the annual office Christmas party. When the game begins, take the card, and, without looking at it, hold it on your forehead face out with one hand so that everyone but you can see it. Then mingle and chat with everyone else at the party as you continue to hold the card.

Treat people with high-numbered cards as high status and those with low-numbered cards as low status. For example, if you meet someone who is holding an ace, king, queen, etc., to his forehead, treat him like an executive: offer to get him drinks, flatter him, etc. Treat sixes through nines like middle management, and twos, threes, fours, etc., like waiters, filing clerks, etc.: ask them to park your car or send them for drinks or hors d'oeuvres.

And at the same time, try to figure out what number you are by the way *you're* being treated. Find the people with numbers that you think are close to yours and hang with them.

Now, in the beginning, since no one knows what number he himself has, an ace who doesn't know he's an ace may come up to you and ask if he can get you a drink. Raise his status: "Oh no! You don't have to get me a drink. Let's get a waiter," as you call a two over. Or a two may come up and be chummy. Walk away.

After a few minutes, the instructor should call an end to the game. And without looking at your card, form one line from one side of the room to the other, with aces at one end and twos at the other. As this line is forming, place yourself where you think you belong. Once the line is formed, look at your cards and sound off from the twos up to the aces to see how well you placed yourselves.

The instructor should then have people review what made them think they belonged in that particular position: how did people treat them, talk with them, etc. Pay particular attention to the people who seemed to place themselves in the "wrong" position. They didn't get it wrong. They're responding to whatever status signals they were given as best they can. Find out what those were and how they may have been misinterpreted. Like all exercises, this is a learning experience, not a test. It isn't about getting it "right." It's about making mistakes as you observe the signals coming your way and then clarifying afterward. It's about internalizing those signals and the feelings they created in you, and then later using them in a future performance to create similar feelings in your scene partner and the audience.

By the way, I think you'll find that people with cards numbered five through ten will have a difficult time ranking themselves. This is the same thing in most offices: middle-management people are very unsure of their status. They know who the CEOs are, and they know who the word-processing people are, but they are continually jockeying for position in between, always unsure of where their status lies.

You may also notice that the low-status people end up with two options. They are either terribly solicitous because they want to keep their jobs, or they band together, make fun of the people around them, and head out for a cigarette. Upper- and middle-management people never do this, but lower-status people often try to see how much they can get away with. This is the basis for so much of the humor in master/servant plays like those of Moliere. Servants sometimes feel so oppressed by being in such low-status positions that their only pleasure is in making faces behind the master's back. This creates enormous dramatic tension, of course, because they and the audience know that if they get caught at such high-status behavior, they get fired.

A Brief Tangent

Choreographer/dancer Agnes DeMille once said, "If you don't realize your creativity, it will never occur again in nature." What makes this so difficult, of course, is that there is no model for you. Whoever you are who's reading this book right now, you at your best are like no one who has ever existed or will ever exist. Exhilarating as that may sound, it can also be frightening because you can never know if you have finally achieved a standard. There is no standard for you. Saying the first thing that comes into your head, daring to be obvious is the courage that throws your uniqueness on new ground where it blossoms at that moment in a unique way. Saying "Yes! And . . ." encourages an equally frightened partner to do likewise. Making each other look good is the bonus of all communal art forms that reinforces that progress through communal validation.

As we struggle to discover who we are, we move through a society of rules, rules that aid us when we're younger to function and communicate successfully within that society. At the same time, these rules also ensure society's preservation: don't kill, don't steal, learn English so we can all communicate effectively; etc. But even in the midst of those rules you still have to come up with who you are. And the rules won't tell you. The community won't tell you. It can't.

You've seen something like this in this exercise. "Am I a six? Am I a nine?" In life, no one's going to tell you. No one knows. And I'm sure you've worked in situations with someone who might have a position equal to yours, yet comes across as much more high status than you. These people may start at the bottom, but you know when you meet them they really belong much higher. Something about them will carry them through. And you probably also know people in high-status positions who make you wonder how they ever got up there. Not that they necessarily should be in a lower position. But the status equated with their position isn't reflected in their behavior.

We struggle to establish who we are. It's a constant struggle. And that's the risk we take: stepping into this unknown, into the fear of becoming who you are. But this continually reveals and releases the uniqueness of yourself, these challenges you present yourself, knowing that only *you* are going to define who you are, step-by-step.

Assignment

As you're walking down the street, stand tall and lock your head, as if it were a camera and you were a tripod that had to keep it steady as you move. If anyone catches your eye, look right back at him or her until they pass. These are high-status tactics. You'll probably be amazed to find that *everyone* will move aside and give you space, even those who never make direct eye contact.

Class

[9] The King Game

As I've said, theater and improvisation are communal art forms. And the most exciting performers are those who honor this communal effort by keeping the creation in a constant state of flux, constantly surprised by their partners' offers and constantly changed by them. It's this willingness in all the participants to be changed that makes the event an organic expression of all of them, unique in that moment, and out of their individual control.

And in this light, there is no change more interesting on stage— in fact there is *nothing* more interesting on stage—than a status transfer. We're going to do a couple of exercises that focus on this.

Warm-up

- Physical Warm-up, including Blind Offers.
- Whoosh! Include assigning three people to do something, e.g., "Sing opera in gibberish," "Do the ducky dance." (See Appendix 1: Warm-up Games).

Pop Quiz:

- Which is better: high status or low status? (Neither.)
- Why do we use status? (Status is a tactic we use to get what we want, to achieve an objective.)
- Does anybody here use status in his or her daily life? (Yes, whenever you are face-to-face with anybody you are continually adjusting your status to achieve your objective.)

Continue to ask students to demonstrate status observations from outside class. Don't just describe them, act them out.

Status Transfers

Again, I feel that there is nothing more interesting on stage than a status transfer: someone starts high, someone low, and they switch. It can be rapid, as in farce, or take an entire play, as in many tragedies.

But status transfers only work when both parties are cooperating and transferring simultaneously. If two people are struggling for high status and both refuse to lower their status, you have an argument, which the audience will tire of very quickly. However, as soon as one person agrees to lower his status, backs down temporarily or gives in, the audience leans forward suddenly. Someone has been changed and they sense the plot suddenly advancing.

In scripted material, this is taken care of by the playwright. In improvisation, however, it's up to the performers to advance the plot, in this case to be sensitive to the beginning of a transfer on his partner's part, and to be changed by it by reciprocating accordingly.

The King Game is an exercise in status transfer, paying attention to your partner and willingly raising or lowering your status in response in order to make the scene work.

The King Game

Create a platform with a chair on top if it's possible. In our classrooms we usually have several black boxes; we put six together in two rows of three and add a chair, preferably one with runners as opposed to legs so that the legs don't fall through the cracks during the exercise. Or, if you have a stage, put a chair about three feet back from its edge and use the audience space directly in front of the stage as the "servant" area.

Do a quick gibberish review as a warm-up: the instructor should go from person to person carrying on a brief gibberish conversation.

The premise of the game is that this is a throne room. The first person to go, character A, is the king. He begins the game by standing on the platform in front of the throne and singing opera in gibberish at the top of his voice, throwing his arms up into the air and taking up as much space physically and vocally as possible. He should pitch his voice low: a bass voice is higher status than a treble voice.

The instructor then chooses character B at random from the audience and whispers in his ear a task that he, upon entering, must explain to the king and get permission to perform—again, all in gibberish. The task could be to serve the king tea, or to measure him for clothing. (See Appendix 2: King Game Assignments, for a list of tasks.)

Character B must then enter as low status as possible. He should crawl, and use a high treble voice as he tries to get the king's attention.

The king, upon seeing B, should be outraged that this scum has entered his space and should chew him out accordingly, trying to get him out of the throne room. B is persistent, however, still in a low-status way with his little squeaky voice, until finally the king lets him explain why he's there. (This is the beginning of the status transfer.) B does so in gibberish, acting out as much as possible to help the king understand that he wants to serve him tea, measure him for clothes, whatever.

Finally the king acquiesces, reluctantly, and sits on his throne, tolerating this idiot. Approaching the throne tentatively, B begins his task talking in gibberish all the while. He is very hesitant to invade the king's space and always checks in before doing so. At the same time, he should keep up the gibberish banter as much as possible, continually explaining what he's doing, telling the king how pretty he is, etc. The king mutters and grunts rejoinders.

Suddenly . . . B notices something truly gross or truly funny about the king: he smells, or his nose is six inches long, or his penis is tiny. B begins to giggle or show signs of disgust. The king catches him and asks, still arrogant, what the hell is going on. B apologizes profusely and tries to act as if nothing has happened. This moment of tension—accusation by the king and immediate apologetic denial by the servant—is very important and very funny as the audience watches the danger rise and fall gently a couple of times—B trying hard to control himself while A is suspicious, then calm once again.

But it's too awful or too funny and B begins gradually to lose it, laughing in disbelief or groaning in disgust. The king *demands* to know what's going on, and B shows him: takes lice out of the king's hair and shows him, or smells the king's armpits and makes a gagging noise, or indicates how tiny the penis really is.

The king continues to be outraged, but this condition is too much for B and he finds more and more lice, or compares his own penis, which is huge, to the king's, or smells the other armpit and it's worse.

Suddenly the penny drops and the king realizes it's true. He begins to shrink in humiliation, checks the problem himself and finds that it's worse than he imagined, and begins to cry. Now B is king and roars at A as he kicks him off the throne and yells him out of the throne room. A, whimpering, crawls out humiliated.

B now begins the scene all over again, only this time as the new king standing on the platform and singing opera in gibberish. The instructor finds a new servant, gives him a new task and sends him out. Continue this cycle until everyone has had a chance to participate, sending the original A in at the end as a servant to complete the cycle.

Once again, these are exaggerated status states. This is an exercise in going as high as you can go and as low as you can go. And like all farce, it's also an exercise in emotional extremes. If these scenes were real, they'd come across as terribly cruel. But if you take the emotions to extremes, the audience ceases to identify and is released to laugh at how ridiculous you are.

In addition, the crueler the king is in the beginning, the greater the release for the audience when the tables are turned. Take advantage of this when you're the B and satisfy the audience as your status rises by cruelly making the king more and more ridiculous: his smell is so bad that you throw up; find lice not only in his hair but all over his body; squeeze his zit until it explodes and knocks you over. Remember, vulgarity is a taboo that society imposes to keep us in our place. Farce defies this taboo, allowing the audiences to go places that they all know exist but that everyone is denying—like the elephant in the living room that everyone pretends isn't there. Break these taboos with glee.

Review

When it's over, check in: What were some of the things that people did to raise their status?

- They were physically higher than the servant.
- Spoke in a loud, bass voice.
- Made direct eye contact with the servant.
- Had rage and anger in their voices.
- When they yelled, their heads didn't move.
- Pointed.
- Stomped their feet.
- Didn't allow the servant to touch them.
- Invaded the servant's space.

And to lower their status?

- Crawled in, keeping themselves physically lower than the king.
- Had a high, squeaky voice.
- Avoided eye contact.
- Hesitated to invade king's space.
- Nodded head and fidgeted a lot.

I think you'll find this exercise outrageously funny. This is narrative improv, character-based humor, as opposed to gag improv, which is joke humor. Notice how easy it is to send the audience into gales of laughter without saying a single word in English, simply by making a strong character choice, committing yourself completely to it, and then responding cooperatively with your partner—being changed—as your mutual transfers advance the story.

Class

[10]   The Status Therapy Group

This exercise reinforces the four status states and gives you further opportunity to develop characters on the fly based on these states. As a professional whose job it is to reflect the human condition, you have an infinite number of characters within you. You can arrive at many of these as variations and gradations of the four status states.

I'm flying in a jet as I'm writing this. The movie showing is *View at the Top* with Gwyneth Paltrow. In the past, I have seen her play a character that lacerated her partner with high-status, laser-like precision. Although I can't hear the sound track of this in-flight movie, I'm very aware in this performance of a sincere, very vulnerable blonde bimbo . . . the antithesis of the previous role . . . simply through her pleasant, low-status behavior. She's creating this effect in me clearly not through the dialogue—I can't hear it—but because of what her body is doing.

In this exercise, exaggerate these physical and vocal extremes. Make fun of them. The more flexible you are jumping from extreme high to extreme low, both pleasant and unpleasant, the more versatile—and castable—you are as an actor.

Warm-up

- Physical Warm-up including Blind Offers
- Whoosh!

The instructor should review the three rules of improvisation, ask the class for any status observations they may have made outside of class, and have them act them out.

Next, review the four status states by repeating the review exercise described in the previous class.

Status Therapy Group

As we've seen, the basis for humor in narrative improv and the basis for a lot of humor in comedies, particularly farces, is character humor. Create a character with a driving passion and you can hold an audience for an entire play as they watch him batter himself against the world; whether he's saying things that are particularly funny at any given moment or not.

One of the purposes of this course is to help you create these characters by increasing confidence in your ability to discover things on-the-fly, and to get you out of your head.

In every scene you do, whether in improv or in a scripted play, the character has an objective. And in every *interesting* scene there is an obstacle to that objective. Analyzing that scene and choosing an appropriate objective ahead of time is essential.

But if you also analyze the scene and, in addition, preplan your behavior to achieve that objective, ("I'm going to be angry on this line; I'm going to start crying on this one"), the scene can feel to the audience like they're watching a list of your choices, a list that has no relation to the list of choices your partner has made. They sense a lack of connection between the two of you.

What they want to see is the two of you throwing yourselves into an unknown future, surprised by each other's reactions at every turn and risking failure on the fly as you instantly adjust your next tactic and *Say the first thing that comes into your head.*

As you are creating a character from scratch, so much of who he is can be discovered as a result of these spontaneous interactions with your partner. Instead of going into your head to analyze and create him, his wants, his desires, his physicality, etc., you can discover him on-the-fly by making one or two strong decisions about him and then throwing him against unexpected obstacles and seeing what evolves.

Status Therapy Group is a great exercise using status to do just this.

Everyone sits on chairs in a circle. The instructor is the leader of this particular therapy group, and in the course of the exercise gets each participant to introduce himself to the group four times as four different characters, each based on one of the four status states: pleasant high, pleasant low, unpleasant high, and unpleasant low. He does this randomly, interviewing student number one, who's chosen pleasant low, and then jumping to student number seven, who may have chosen unpleasant high, and so on.

To create these characters, begin by assuming the body posture of the state you've chosen. Let it invade the way you feel. You may choose a name and profession as you're waiting to be called on. Or I invite you to just find the body and wait until you're chosen to discover on the fly who you are, what you do, and what your problem is.

If you're the group leader–the "therapy" leader–you will carry on a brief conversation with each character, jumping randomly from one student to another. Ask the students who they are, why they're here, etc. Your position is very much like that of the expert's interviewer with two additions: You'll have to ask more questions as you help each "patient" discover who she is on-the-fly. And you should adjust your status to contrast with that of whomever you're speaking to: play high status for a low-status group member; low for a high.

For example, if someone introduces himself in an arrogant manner as the CEO of International Business Concerns, the therapist can be over-awed, look, look away, and apologize for the inferiority of the therapy group. If, on the other hand, the member crawls under the chair and cries because he eats dirt, the therapist can yell, shame him, and get the group to call him names. In short, whatever status the patient has chosen, help her drive it to the extreme. "You're a CEO! (*giggle*) I'm not even sure what that means . . . Are you comfortable? Would you like my chair?" Or, "You STILL eat dirt? Didn't you say you'd quit LAST WEEK!!!??? Everybody sing Bobby eats dirrrrt! Bobby eats dirrrrt!"

If you're a patient, take these cues. The therapist may be nasty with you . . . give him and yourselves permission to go wherever this exercise takes you. With the unpleasant high characters you create in particular, be sure to "Yes! And . . ." the therapist's offers. These particular characters can tend to say "No" to everything because they're arrogant. If, for example, the therapist asks what your problem is, don't say, "I don't have a problem." Tell him your problem, arrogant though you may be. "I'm fat." "Nobody likes me." "I eat too much Swiss cheese." Again, it makes no difference what the problem is. The humor here is in the character's passion about whatever you choose.

Now when you were originally working with the four status states, I gave you lists of some very specific things to keep in mind. However, for the purposes of this exercise, don't worry about executing everything on those lists in order to get it "right." Find a body posture, find a feeling of the status, then let the character take over and do whatever feels right. Forget the list of characteristics and let the leader side-coach you if he feels you're getting off track. He may remind you to "Yes! And . . ." or, if you're low, to look, look away, look back, etc. Leave it to him to cue you if needed. Just find the character and go with it.

Once you've done all four of your characters, get up and leave the circle so everyone knows that the game is winding up.

Here are example conversations:

"Hello there? Hi. What's your name?"

"F . . . F . . . Frank." (*he smells his fingers*)

"Frank! Frank. Hi, Frank. Frank? Are you smelling something right now, Frank?"

"Yeah."

"Yeah. What are you smelling, Frank?"

"Uh . . . I smell . . ."

"What do you smell, Frank. Tell the group what you SMELL, FRANK!"

"CA-CA!"

"YES! WHY DO YOU SMELL CA-CA, FRANK?"

(*Weeps in anger*) "Because I have bird ca-ca all over me!"

"YES! That's right, Frank! And why do you do that, Frank?"

"I don't know."

"YES YOU DO, Frank! Share with the group. Frank! Share with the group!"

"Because I LIKE bird ca-ca!"

"That's RIGHT, Frank. That's pretty disgusting."

"I know . . ."

"Yes, you know, FRANK. Now you just sit there and think about cleaning that ca-ca off or your body, FRANK."

Notice how the leader keeps going higher in status, driving Frank lower.

Here's another example.

"Hi there."

"Whassup."

"Uh . . . uh . . . uh, I'm, uh, your therapist. (*pause*) That's . . . uh . . . why I'm here."

"So?"

"Uh . . . well, I just thought, you know, I might be able to help you . . . uh . . . if it's OK . . . if you . . . if you would like to . . ."

"Does it look like I need help?"

"Well, I just . . . I . . . I mean, silly me . . . I just assumed that since you were in the group you were looking for some kind of assistance. What's your name?"

"Does it matter?"

"Yes, I'm afraid it does because I have to keep (*giggle*) a record."

"Buster."

"Buster. Um . . . Buster, what do you . . . what do you do for a living, Buster?"

"I bust people's asses."

"Oh! Oh! Ah . . . what, what causes you to bust people's asses?"

"Because I love it. I like to put people in pain."

"Uh . . . do you think you'd like . . . um . . . like to put, like, therapists in pain . . . and stuff?"

"If they talk too much."

"OK . . . OK . . . I'll just . . . when you feel like talking, just say something. Is that OK? Otherwise I'll just, like, move on."

Checking In

The above game is being introduced late enough in the course that everyone should feel comfortable enough with each other to go to these extremes. However, there are two things to keep in mind, which you, the instructor, should enforce.

First, it's worth reminding everyone at the end of class again about their promise: they may discuss what goes on in class outside of class, but they are never to name names. This is a class, a laboratory to experiment in, a professional situation, and not a social event. Honor it as such, and honor your fellow classmates as they achieve their own breakthroughs. Do this by making it clear that they can trust you with whatever startling discoveries or activities they release. If I'm making this sound serious, it's not meant to be. Again, an improv class should be infused with a sense of play. The ridiculousness we allow ourselves to display in such a class should be a source of explosive humor.

Taking Care of Yourselves

Beneficial as I feel any acting class can be for participants, this leads me to my second point. This course isn't intended to be therapy. As a result, any reasonably prudent and sensitive teacher should feel qualified to teach it, without feeling she needs interpersonal skills beyond compassion and support.

What you as the instructor are doing is "coaching." I make a distinction between "coaching" and "therapy" as I define the terms. With coaching, you and your student have a goal in mind. For example, you could be coaching someone to win an Olympic gold medal. The overall goal for the coach/student relationship in *this* class is to become a better narrative improviser. And this is achieved by working toward individual goals as they are described in each chapter.

The teacher's job is to help the student as best he can to achieve these goals. If, for example, a student has a problem giving up control in a scene and insists on driving it where he chooses despite his partner's offers, there are exercises like Word-At-a-Time story (described later in this course) that directly address this issue, helping the student give up control. That's what a coach does: figures out with the student what needs to be done to achieve the goal. You don't need a long analysis of *why* the student feels he has a control issue . . . because of his parents, because of his church, etc. That's therapy. And if these issues finally impede his ability to reach the chosen goals, then they must be taken up with a different professional.

There is no stigma to this. Like a lot of creative professionals, I had personal issues that impeded my advancement as an artist. As I worked them out outside of classroom/rehearsal situations, my work inside these situations progressed. But it wasn't appropriate for me to expect teachers or directors to have those answers for me. They were there to coach me.

So it's worth checking in at the end of broad exercises like this to make sure that no one is feeling in any way uncomfortable, losing the desire to reach the goals set in this course.

If you're a student and invited to report, be honest about this. We are directly addressing taboo areas. And we're doing this for a reason: name a taboo and you have a subject for a movie or a play. And you can star in it, just as everyone else can. But at the same time, give yourself all the permission in the world to address these taboos at your own pace.

On the one hand, stretch yourself. Remember, you have two moralities: those things you permit yourself to do in life, and those you permit yourself in the arts. Both need to be honored. But they aren't the same: because I may eat dirt as a character doesn't mean I am only "Dan Diggles: Dirt Eater." And if the class is playing by the three rules, they're going to applaud you as you break through taboos.

On the other hand, if you find yourself experiencing a sense of shutting down rather than opening up, speak up. If you don't take care of yourself, you can't reach your goals. And, equally importantly, you can't take care of the group. You're always and finally the best judge of what's best for you. Help your teacher help you.

Class

[11] Status Soap Opera

Again, there is very little that is more interesting on stage than a status transfer. However, as we explored in the King Game this does require that both parties be willing to raise and lower their status reciprocally, sensing changes in their partner and complementing them by doing the opposite. If you see your partner going up, you go down and vice versa.

For many people, lowering status is equated with losing. But your willingness to both raise and lower your status guarantees that, whatever the *character* you're creating may gain or lose, you, the *performer*, will always win because you immediately charge the moment with dramatic advancement.

The following exercises help you practice raising and lowering status in order to create this sense of drama.

Warm-up

- Physical Warm-up including Blind Offers
- Kitty Wants a Corner. (See Appendix 1: Warm-up Games)

As in previous classes, review the three rules of improvisation. And ask class for any status observations they may have made outside of class and have them act them out.

Status Confessions

This exercise is a preparation for the Status Soap Opera exercise that follows.

Everyone sits on chairs in a circle. Each of you will carry on a conversation with the leader. Choose a very high-status persona: principal of a high school, a CEO, God, Miss America. It can be pleasant or unpleasant. If you're unpleasant, don't be defiant or hard to get along with; be cooperative. When the interviewer addresses you, tell him who you are. The interviewer should address each character in a pleasant, relatively low-status "talk show host" personality. Smart but low key, like a PBS interviewer.

In the course of this conversation, this high-status character you've created should make a very low-status confession, beginning a status transfer as the interviewer goes up and you go down. Then gradually reverse the transfer as you raise your status again and the interviewer lowers his.

Here's an example. The interviewer begins:

"Hi. How are you?"

"Hi. Fine. I'm very fine."

"What's your name?"

"I'm the President of the United States of America."

"OH, WOW!"

"Yes, I'm newly elected. President Corbin. And I'm glad to be here because I just love everything that's happening in America, and particularly here at Baldwin Community College. In fact, I want to make this sort of a bright light in all the academic activity that's happening in America. Because I think it is one already."

"Well, thank you! That's just wonderful."

"Uh . . . personally . . . um . . . I can't spell. In fact, (*giggle*) to be honest, I can't write."

"Well, uh, gosh. That's gotta be kinda hard being President."

"Well, yes, it is. In fact, the reason I'm here is . . . I'm sorry, your name?"

"This is the Rob Peterson talk show you're on, Mr. President. I'm Rob. 'Duh!'"

"Oh yes, silly me. Well, uh, I can't read either . . . and I wanted to ask you if you could read this . . . stuff that they gave me."

"Well. That's not really my job, is it?"

"Well, I'm the President, and I would really appreciate it. And, I could, you know . . . make it really difficult for your parents."

"Oh."

"I have their number. I mean, someone else wrote it down because I couldn't. But it's in my cell phone and all I have to do is push a button and . . . pffft!"

"Well, we can work this out I'm sure . . . uh . . . Mr. President."

"I'm reaching for my cell phone right now."

"Why don't you just hand me that material and I'll see what I can do. Hm, this looks really interesting!"

Again this is an exercise in voluntarily lowering your status. There's a tendency for improvisers to want to remain high all the time, and when two people do this, it simply results in an argument that goes nowhere dramatically. You'll notice in the above example, however, that the status transfers create a developing story that goes somewhere. Your willingness to lower your status gives you enormous color on stage. In addition, your ability to sense a status change in your partner and to raise or lower yourself in a complementary fashion results in a story that grows and develops, and that makes your partner look good.

Here's another example, which shows more prompting from the interviewer:

"Hi!"

"Hi."

"What's your name?"

"Steven."

"Steven! It's a pleasure to meet you. What brings you here?"

"Well, I'm the reigning Miss America."

"OH, MY GOD! YOU ARE!! I didn't recognize you with your short hair! That's fabulous! And you've been reigning for how long now?"

"It was just a couple of months ago."

"Uh huh! Uh huh! And what's it been like for you?"

"Well, people recognize me in the street. And everyone is telling me how beautiful I am."

"You are. You are one of the single most beautiful people I have ever met."

"Thank you."

"It's true! It's true! And you're kind. All those good works you've done. I've read about it."

"Thanks."

"However, there was an incident last week that the papers kind of hushed up?"

"Yeah? So?"

"Well, that's OK. What was it?"

"Well . . . I . . . I really enjoy peeing on myself."

"(*pause*) I'm sorry. I must have misunderstood. I thought I heard you just say that you enjoy peeing on yourself."

"That's what I said. I'm . . . I'm sure you'd enjoy it too (*long pause*). I'm peeing now."

"I was wondering. And it isn't like something you can't control. You actually enjoy this (*pause*). Oh, dear god. You enjoy pissing on yourself. And . . . how often to you do this?"

"Three times a day. (*"Go lower. Start crying."*) I peed when they crowned me and now it just, you know, reminds me . . . makes me feel loved."

"So the reigning Miss America pisses on herself. Is that correct?"

"That's right! Miss America! I know it sounds terrible, but now I understand suffering! In fact I'm taking all my millions and donating them to the Institute for Bladder Control in Sweden. And when my reign is over, I'm going to tour European countries and the entire Middle East and help lower-class women who are ignored come to grips with their own urinary challenges!"

"Wow. All that money?"

"What is money? It's a means to an end."

"Miss America, you're amazing!"

With this exercise as with previous ones, exaggerate the status. Go as high as you can go and then as low. And the interviewer should help drive you higher or lower with side-coaching and his own status choices.

Status Soap Opera

The instructor sets up a hospital waiting room with a couple of seating areas. I put a table with a chair next to it on one side, and three chairs in a row as a couch with a low coffee table in front of them on the other. Then put three to five props around the space, props that could be used for what they are or that could be described and used as something else. A pen might be used as a pen or as a thermometer; a soda can could be a soda can, a urine sample, etc. These descriptions and uses will spring out of whatever the action is during the exercise.

You'll be performing a soap opera: *Municipal Hospital.* And, like the King Game, it's done in the round: there are always two people on stage and, as one character leaves, another enters, until everyone has had a chance to perform. The first person to leave the first scene becomes the final person to enter in the last scene, completing the circle.

Character A begins on stage alone. He assumes a low status posture: sitting and fidgeting or crying, etc. Character B enters high status. When he sees A, he approaches him and introduces himself, making clear to performer and audience alike who he is as quickly as possible:

"Hello, I'm Dr. Forbes. I've been operating on your mother."

Or:

"They called for a janitor. Who's responsible for this mess on the floor? You?"

If character A, the low-status player, isn't identified by character B during his own introduction, then A should identify himself as quickly as possible.

In response to the first offer above, for example: "Thank you, Dr. Forbes. I've been waiting for hours, but everyone says she's in the best hands."

Or in response to the second offer: "Yes. I'm here for a stomach ailment and I'm afraid I threw up. Jaimie? Oh my gosh, it's me, Mrs. Marsh! Your second grade teacher!"

As in all improvised scenes, be specific, use the environment, and be descriptive in what you're doing to cue your partner:

"I'll just get some coffee from this machine."

"HERE'S my urine sample! I've been looking for it everywhere!"

And for those of you waiting to go on, pay attention to all of these environment offers and use them if you can in your later scenes. If a soda can is a urine sample, it's a urine sample through-out the exercise. At the very least don't violate the environmental offers; don't walk through the coffee machine.

Now a conversation ensues, in the course of which character B, who has entered high status, makes a low-status confession:

"I dropped your mom's brain (*starts weeping*) and they kicked me out of the operating room. And this hospital is named after ME!"

Or:

"I'm a janitor now. But I used to be a neurosurgeon."

At this point the status transfer has begun, and character A should balance the transfer by finding this information either terribly funny or completely appalling.

"I'm sorry. You dropped my mother's brain? Is that what you said? Dr. Ronald Forbes, founder of Municipal Hospital and you DROPPED HER BRAIN?? What do they call you? BUTTERFINGERS!?"

"YES!!! (*weeping*) I am sooo sorry! Butterfingers Forbes on another bender!"

"YOU'RE DRUNK?!? Oh my god! (*rises*) YOU'RE the one who's ruined this hospital with malpractice suits!"

"Yes! (*falls to the floor and crawls*) PLEASE! PLEASE! Don't sue me. My wife just left me and I'll have nothing!"

"I'm calling my lawyer right now."

Character A exits, high status now, leaving a low-status B on stage. The class instructor now sends in another character. The teacher shouldn't let a student know that he'll be up next ahead of time; just tap someone on the shoulder at random and send him in. Again, if you know that you're going on next, the tendency is to stop listening and start planning.

At the same time, as you're waiting to go on, watch what's happening closely and have a couple of characters in mind that complement the action. For example, you could be someone from the operating room with a brain in a pan; you could be the mother; you could be the doctor's wife. This is reincorporation, one of the most satisfying elements of storytelling. Audiences love it when someone they've heard mentioned earlier shows up later. Or when someone arrives after a while looking for the urine sample someone else has identified earlier.

By the way, if the instructions to this game begin to confuse you as you're waiting to go on, all you really have to remember is to enter high status. I think you'll find that the scene takes care of itself. If you forget to make a low-status confession, the instructor will side-coach you.

The new character enters high:

"Dr. Forbes! It's Nurse Jensen from O.R. and this brain has to go back in immediately!"

The character on stage is still low from the previous scene:

"Oh, god (*he crawls over and hugs her legs*). Don't make me go back in there. Every time I look at your youth and beauty, I think of all I've lost, my drinking problem, my wife . . . and my hands begin to shake."

"You like me? (*giggles*—status transfer begins) I'm just a fat nurse with pimples. NO ONE likes me."

"Well, yes, you are fat (*he begins to rise*). And if we went out, you'd have to cover those pimples with your operating mask."

"Oh, Dr. Forbes (*drops the brain*). Oh! I dropped the brain (*scrambles on the floor to retrieve it*). All these years I've stood next to you blotting your forehead . . . and here, look! (*reaches into her cleavage*) I'VE SAVED ALL THE TISSUES!"

"YOU'VE BEEN CARRYING SWEATY, GERM-COVERED TISSUES INTO AN OPERATING THEATER ALL THESE YEARS! No WONDER you have pimples! GIVE me that brain! I revile you, and all the crap that's gathered around my wasted life. I may have one good operation left in me, but, by god, I'M GOING IN!"

And he exits.

Review

When this is over, the instructor should use the remaining class time to review:

- What tactics were used to raise and lower status throughout *Municipal Hospital*?
- What aspects of the environment were added to by the performers and were they honored by subsequent performers? (If you didn't honor something, don't feel you got it wrong. Feeling that way isn't your job. Simply make a plan to be more observant next time. *That's* your job.)
- What are some examples of reincorporation?

Class

[12]   "I Love You" Scenes with Status and Status Dialogue

At the beginning of this course, we were building exercises that incorporated skills learned in previous classes. We put that on hold temporarily to introduce the concept of status.

Now we'll add status to the "I Love You" scenes with expertise you were working with earlier.

This is followed by an optional demonstration called "Status Dialogue," one that emphasizes how status work can thoroughly alter the meaning of any scene.

Warm-up

- Physical Warm-up including Blind Offers
- Kitty Wants a Corner

"I Love You" Scenes with Expertise and Status

Review the format of "I Love You" scenes with expertise. You're going to do another round, this time adding status.

Just as in the first round of this game, character A should launch into his monologue about how much he adores his expertise—bowling with monkeys or flossing with barbed wire. Remember to make this an anecdote, a story he relates about his earlier life. This time, however, in the course of this story, he should raise his status as he does so, standing, taking space, heralding his passion. Character B, in the meantime should lower his own—compared to A's expertise, he is nothing. If you are B you should sit, maybe on the floor; cry if you feel like it. Contract in disappointment with yourself as your admiration for A overwhelms you. And while A is going on, add rejoinders like, "You are so amazing!" "I always admired that in you," raising A's status as you continue to lower your own, etc.

Then, when you discover your expertise and launch into your enthusiasm, begin the status transfer as B goes up and A goes down.

And, finally, bring the scene to a conclusion by finding a reason to leave.

After each scene is over, the instructor should bring the two performers on stage and ask them and the audience to review the status tactics each used throughout the scene: how did they raise their status; how did they lower it. And once again, this can be terribly repetitive, "He stood up." "He filled the space by walking around." "She also stood up." Like all skills, the more you repeat the basics, the more they become a part of you.

Status Dialogue

This is an optional demonstration of the use of status work in scripted material. As a demonstration, you only need to do the exercise with two couples to make the point to the entire class.

You can radically alter the meaning of any scene, simply by altering your status. Of course, in scripted material your job is to make appropriate status choices that would result in a scene in line with the playwright's intentions. Because the following scene is neutral, however, and not from a play, you can use it to see how effectively you can bend the meaning of any scene to fit those intentions by changing your status.

Here's the scene:

A: Hello.
B: Hello.

A:	Do you come here often?
B:	I beg your pardon?
A:	Do you come here often?
B:	Yes. Do you?
A:	I beg your pardon?
B:	Sorry.
A:	I like you.
B:	What time is it?
A:	One o'clock.
B:	When is he coming?
A:	Who?
B:	Frank.
A:	(*grunt*)
B:	Do you still like me?
A:	Good-bye.
B:	Good-bye.

The Exercise

Put two chairs face to face and seat actors A and B, each holding a copy of the script. The audience is asked to imagine that they've just turned on the TV in the middle of a program and have no idea what this scene is about. When the scene is over, they're to report back as to what they thought they were watching.

If you're the instructor, kneel in front of the two actors facing them, your back to the audience. Just as the scene is about to begin, (*Curtain going up. Lights!*) give actor A a thumbs up or a thumbs down with your right hand held close to your body so the audience doesn't see. Thumbs up means begin as high status; thumbs down, begin as low. Do the same for B. It can be the same status signal as A, or the opposite. As the scene progresses, change either signal, causing the actors to change their status. Usually one change is enough for a scene this short. You can also prompt either actor to exaggerate his status even more by moving your thumb up higher or lower.

At the end of the scene, ask the audience if they'd seen this scene on television without knowing the program, what would they assume they were watching? What would they assume the scene was about? The kind of answers you're looking for are: "*Two sorority girls in love with the same guy, Frank.*" "*B has a crush on A.*" "*Two druggies in rehab.*" You're not looking for these specific answers, but answers like these that describe the relationship between the two people and possibly where it might be taking place.

Then do the scene again, this time giving different status signals to the same two actors. And again, ask the audience to report on what *this* scene was about. Bear in mind that these are exactly the same two people as the previous scene saying exactly the same lines. And yet the relationships, the whole mood of the scene, has been changed. If you have time, repeat the exercise with another couple.

As I've said, status work is an extremely powerful tool and with it you can change the meaning of any scene, or use it to amplify the playwright's intentions in a subtle and highly effective way.

[13] No You Didn't

We're now going to move into a series of exercises that increase our sense of spontaneity, risk-taking, and story-telling. At the end of the course, you'll begin to combine these skills with those we've developed in the "I Love You" scenes as you apply them to Neutral Scene work.

Neutral Scenes as I've employed them are short scripted dialogues that may involve a conflict, but are vague as to the character's descriptions, relationships, and the environment. By applying the skills learned so far, you will elaborate and amplify these ordinary scripts into scenes that are as theatrically and dramatically interesting as possible.

In all scripted theater, you must stay true to the playwright's intentions. But by using the skills acquired in this course as you'll be applying them to neutral scenes, and by trusting your own sense of spontaneity, you can transform a character and a performance into something that is both true to that playwright's intention, and yet a vivid expression of the unique voice that is yours, the voice that will get you hired.

A Note About Warm-ups

Up until now, for each class I've assigned a game for the pre-class warm-up games, which have included "Whoosh!," "Blind Offers," and "Kitty Wants a Corner." Again the purpose of these games is to have fun, to lose face as a group so that no one's presence is perceived as judgmental or threatening, and to bond in preparation for participating in a communal art form.

Play each game often enough for everyone to get a feel for it, but not so often that it ceases to be challenging. There should always be the risk of failure, creating that "moment of theater" where someone is tottering on the edge before flinging themselves forward. When this is no longer the case, introduce a new game.

I've included alternate games in Appendix 1: Warm-up Games. I will continue to suggest warm-up games from this list as this course progresses, but from this point on, use your discretion. Continue games as long as you feel they are useful; introduce new ones when you feel they are appropriate.

Be particularly sensitive to students who tend to disconnect from whatever energy the game is generating. "Whoosh!," for example, should go faster and faster, getting away from the students. If, on the other hand, someone is quietly muttering "Whoosh" when it's his turn and lamely moving his fingers to the side, this building energy hiccups and has to start over. The student could be tired, bored, resentful. For whatever reason, however, it's important for you as a coach to make it clear to him that the reason for the warm-up is to help him leave all these concerns and issues outside for the duration of the class and join in the communal effort. That's the job of everyone present.

Be careful about handling this in a shaming or critical manner. Chances are this explanation won't solve the issue immediately and he or she may simply close down even more for the moment, feeling singled out or misunderstood. But handling it with kindness and reason can help the student gradually shift into a more cooperative frame of mind. At the next class, as a reminder to this student but without singling him out, make a general announcement about the importance of losing oneself in the game energy before you begin the warm-up.

Warm-up

- Physical Warm-up
- Bunny. (See Appendix 1: Warm-up Games).

No You Didn't

In describing the Expert's Game, I discuss how there is this wealth of random, creative material in our subconscious with which most of us are out of touch. I suspect that one of the jobs of our conscious brain is to quell the subconscious while we're awake so that we can focus on and cope with what's immediately surrounding us. On the other hand, your subconscious is rich and unique and more *you* than anything clever you can imitate.

There are all kinds of acting exercises designed to help get in touch with this subconscious. "No, You Didn't" is a particularly good one, designed to help you by-pass the "clever" censor who watches everything you do and to short-circuit you into more truly obvious and spontaneous choices.

The Rules

The instructor chooses a student at random, sends him to the front of the classroom, and tells him to "Tell me a story about . . ." anything: plastic wrap, Queen Elizabeth, Vaseline, peanut butter. Like all other offers, make the subject matter simple. Tip for the instructor: If you're going dry for ideas, say the first thing that comes into your head by looking around and suggesting something in the room such as a fire extinguisher, a water bottle, a window, or something someone is wearing such as a baseball cap, an eyebrow, etc.

As the chosen player, you will then launch into a monologue. Begin the monologue by making a strong emotional attitude toward the subject matter: "I LOVE plastic wrap!" or "I HATE plastic wrap!" And then explain why. To illustrate your passion, as quickly as possible start telling a story from your past about your relationship with plastic wrap. If you're having trouble making the transition into this story, just say, "One day . . ." or "When I was a kid . . ." and the story will begin. Act this story out, being as physically animated as you can. In short, commit yourself whole-heartedly to your passion for plastic wrap and the need you have to make this story as clear to the audience as possible by animating it.

However, during this story, the instructor will interrupt you throughout and say, "No, you didn't," or a variation on that phrase, contradicting whatever you've just said. You immediately realize that he's right (say, "Yes! And . . .") and without missing a beat you correct yourself with enthusiasm by changing your statement and then continuing the story.

The instructor can also prompt the storyteller for specifics, "Who did you meet?," "What did he do?" And occasionally he'll make suggestions:

"Cry!"

"Show us how happy you were."

"She had a speech impediment. What did it sound like?"

Again, immediately accept the offer and respond to it.

Here's an example. The instruction was, "Tell me a story about hair."

"I HATE hair! When I was really little, my mother always cut my hair. (*No she didn't.*) My mother NEVER cut my hair until I was two years old. (*That's right!*) And it grew really, really long, and really, really gross. (*Show us how long it got! And what did you do with it?*) She used to dye it. All the time. And I used to play with it. (*No you didn't.*) I used to braid it really elaborately like this so I looked like Princess Leia, and I used it as a jump rope, and I'd hold it up like this like a really scary antenna. And all the kids at school used to laugh at me because it really smelled bad because I never washed it because if I washed it, it would ruin the texture and mom would get really upset. (*So one day . . .*) So one day on my way to school I was passing a grocery store and there was this tiny pair of scissors in the window. (*It wasn't scissors.*) No actually it was one of those old-fashioned razor-type things that you . . . (*No it wasn't! Remember what it was?*) It was an old woman who ate hair. (*That's right!! And her name was . . .*) Her name was Bertha. (*Go! Go! Go!*) And I said, 'Bertha, I know that you eat hair. And my hair is so long you should take it on.' Then she said, 'Yes.' And she was ecstatic. (*And what did she do?*) She ate it. (*That's right!*) She started at the bottom and she worked her way up. (*Show us what she looked like.*) (He eats hair making a garbling noise.) She was so scary. Because she made this noise and my hair was so long. (*And she had a foreign accent. What did she sound like?*) She said, 'AAACH yooour hairrrr is so BOOOOOTIFUL, I LOVE you.' And I said, 'Bertha! Keep eating! Keep eating!' (*But she went too far!*) She went too far, and she started eating my scalp. (*Go!*) And I went,

'AAAAAAAAAAAGHHH!' She was like a vampire, and she kept eating and eating and eating and she ate my ears, oh, god (crying) she kept eating and eating. (*So what did you do?*) I screamed! (*No you didn't.*) No I didn't. I LIKED it. (*Yeahhhh!*) I said, 'Bertha! Keep eating!' And she kept eating. But you know what? She got too full. Then she threw up. Yeah, it was kind of bad. (*What did you do?*) I laughed."

As demonstrated above, as the instructor contradicts, side-tracking the story, he should instantly reward the performer for the new choice with, "Go!" or "That's right!" When most people who are playing this game for the first time are contradicted, they often need to be reassured that their new choice is the "right" one. Actually, the instructor is rewarding them not for the "rightness" of a particular choice, but simply for making one that's different. It can take a while for the performer to get a feel for this: that any choice is fine as long as it's random and unrelated to the previous one.

In addition, one of the purposes of this game is to spur you on to make choices that are more and more outrageous and to do it with conviction, raising the stakes higher and higher. *We* know you're in trouble and *you* know you're in trouble, and the class generally falls about laughing as you grasp at straws and then fling yourself forward with conviction. So, if the performers choices are consistently safe and sane, it's the instructor's job to steer you toward raising the stakes. "So we sat and chatted." (*No, you didn't.*) "No, we ordered lemonade." (*No you didn't.*) "No, we danced the lambada on the table top." (*Right! Go!*)

The instructor should not offer specifics: "No, you didn't! You had a gun!" The instructions should be open-ended so that the performer has to make a choice on the fly. "She had a French accent" is specific, but the following question . . . "What did she sound like?" leaves it open-ended.

If, on the other hand, the performer is on a roll and outrage is already building on outrage, let him go and don't interrupt him. Here's an example. I asked this student to tell me a story about high school:

"I LOVED high school! (*No, you didn't.*) I HATED high school more than life! I had the worst fucking teacher. I stayed up all night writing this extremely long paper for him. My final essay of the year and I turn it in and he looks at me and he goes, 'This is complete crap!' (*That's not what he did.*) He said, 'This is the most wonderful paper I've ever seen. (*That's right! That's right!*) So I thought, 'What the fuck!' (*And what did you do?*) So I said, 'Do you want to go get lunch?' So we went and we got lunch. (*That's right!*) So we walked into the cafeteria and we sat down and we ate a pizza. (*No, it wasn't pizza.*) We were eating fried chicken. (*No, it wasn't fried chicken.*) We were eating eel. (*No it wasn't eel.*) We were eating really big cans of garbage. (*That's right!*) And I got really sick and . . . (*No you didn't!*) I LOVED eating garbage because it was like manna in the desert that we were just reading about in CCD class. (*Yes!*) So I rang my little dingy bell that I just happened to have in my pocket and yelled, 'MORE GARBAGE! MORE GARBAGE! FEEEEEED ME!!!' (*Oh, my god!*) And the teacher got really angry . . . (*No he didn't.*) He kissed me. (*No he didn't. You remember what he did.*) He pulled out this bullhorn and screamed, 'Release the garbage trucks!' And these big yellow garbage trucks that were parked outside backed into the cafeteria wall and knocked it down killing hundreds of children! (*Oh, no!*) But I DIDN'T CARE! I grabbed the garbage, old slimy Snickers wrappers and yogurt containers and dead squirrels, and I stuffed them down my throat! And my teacher, whose name was Mr. Snickers, pulled a funnel out of his pocket, rammed it down my throat and rammed garbage down it screaming, 'I LOVE YOU!' Slam! 'I LOVE YOU!' Slam! 'I LOVE YOU, YOU STUPID STUDENT!' And I blew the garbage out of the funnel and screamed, 'THIS IS THE WORST FUCKING TIME OF MY LIFE!' (*That's not the way you felt.*) I said, 'THIS IS ACTUALLY QUITE EXCELLENT!'"

Note that as the student was on a roll, becoming more and more outrageous, pushing the edges of his taboos, I let him go without interruption.

Some Things to Keep in Mind

The purpose of this game is to give you no other choice but to grab at whatever arises from your subconscious. This is this vivid, rich source that is unique, that you *can* tap into and that is the result of a life that you've led, that is individual and uniquely you. You *can't* plan ahead in this game. You're desperate up there so you immediately grab the most obvious thing your subconscious can supply, a unique offer that can only come from your brain. And accepting that obvious thing that comes to your brain, as I've said before, is the first step toward becoming the unique voice in the arts that you already are.

This includes possibly saying something someone said in a previous scene, if that's the first thing that occurs to you. If someone has said *garbage* in this scene and that's what you're thinking, say it. It makes sense that that would be the first thing that comes into your head. You will, on the other hand, tell a totally different story as you use it.

Don't worry if the story takes you way off the subject matter you're originally given as an offer. The subject matter is given just to get you started.

Also, it's important that the story you launch into to illustrate your passion of this subject matter be from your past, not from the present. A story from the past already has a beginning, middle, and end. A story about the present may leave you wandering as you tell it because there's no conclusion yet.

One trap when you're contradicted with a "No, you didn't" is to stay safely where you are simply by doing a variation on what you said. For example:

"I took a sausage that was twelve inches long . . . (*No, you didn't.*) No, I took a sausage that was eighteen inches long . . . (*No, you didn't.*) No, I took a sausage that was two feet long . . ."

Forget the sausage. Grab something totally new out of the air:

"I took a sausage that was twelve inches long . . . (*No, you didn't.*) I took a big red spaceship . . ."

The whole idea of the game is to continually throw you back to square one where you have to start all over again without time to plan, and then fling yourself forward yet again into the unknown future with enthusiasm. Again, this is "the moment of theater," when the audience knows you have no idea what's going to happen next, and yet you throw yourself forward. And no matter how scary that moment is, if you proceed, you will always succeed as an entertaining and interesting performer. Again, this is a class about getting comfortable with being uncomfortable.

A Reminder . . .

Remember the promise you made earlier in this course: What goes on in this class, stays in this class. You can talk outside of class about the scene where a teacher rams garbage into a student using a funnel. In fact I think you'll be astonished at the number of people who hear these stories and wish they were taking the class. But never identify who said it. "Bill did this scene where . . ."

In fact, I invite the instructor to remind everyone of this promise at the end of every class. You're going to bring things up that part of you may be ashamed of, part of you will be shocked by, part of you doesn't really want to share in front of all these people. But by doing so, you're learning to embrace and trust *all* the color that is you. And it's this panorama of you, including outrageousness in this case, that makes you unique. And that's what people pay to come watch you do. Because *they* all feel these things. *They* all know these things.

However, by talking about someone else outside of class, you may be reporting something without someone else's permission that they're not ready to have shared with the general public. You will have broken their trust and they will shut down.

Remember, when people ask me "Am I a good improviser?" my immediate response is always "Do people want to play with you?" Make certain everyone around you feels safe in your presence, trusts you, and looks forward to working with you. This is more than just being nice. If people feel this way about you, they hire you.

You may find that your scenes are vulgar. Excellent! I'm not saying that being vulgar is the secret to good acting. I *am* saying that taking the risk of going into territory that is risky for you, scary for you, makes you an exciting person to watch. And vulgarity is one place to practice *because* you may not want to go there necessarily.

But there are all kinds of additional places that are risky for us. Falling in love is risky: really feeling that you're not going to get what you want from someone you're willing to abase yourself in front of. Asking for a raise is risky. Every time I have to negotiate a fee for teaching a workshop, for example, I feel like such a fool while everyone else in the business world, I'm convinced, is so adept. Telling your parents you're dating the wrong person is risky.

At the same time, remember what I said about the two moralities you hold simultaneously as an artist: those actions you permit yourself to do in life and those you permit yourself to do in the arts. They both require constant examination and both must be honored. Just because you do something in one, doesn't mean you need to do it in the other. Being vulgar in class doesn't mean you are required to do so in life or else you'll be a bad artist.

And vice versa: because you don't let yourself do something in life doesn't mean you shouldn't let yourself do it in the arts, or in this classroom. This is the morality strangers pay to come pay attention to, to come watch you expose . . . whether it's vulgarity or tears or any of those things that we're afraid to reveal, that we may be ashamed of. Or that we feel will reveal us as "crazy." Everyone feels this way. How refreshing to see someone else, like us, admit it.

. . . And a Review

I think you'll find that you will create some wonderfully funny stuff with this exercise. Now I invite you at this point to remember what you were feeling when you first joined this class. Probably your experience of improv, either performing or watching, had been gag improv: people who were coming up with incredibly clever, witty things. And that's what's so frightening for new improvisers.

On the other hand, look what you've done in this class today. By getting emotionally and physically involved, by committing yourself passionately to your feelings, and then by getting way ahead of yourself, hysterically funny things happen. *Not* because you were trying to be funny or witty or clever. But because you threw yourself forward into an unknown future. This is a rich, rich source of comic material. It's comedy coming for character work. And this skill is very readily carried to scripted theater.

Word-At-a-Time Stories

You are now going to play the hardest improvisation game I know.

I also feel it's one of the best improvisation games ever invented, for three reasons. First, it's a great performance game. Second, it's a great learning tool because it only works when both partners are rapidly applying all three rules of improvisation. When it breaks down, it's usually because someone isn't following a rule.

And third, when it does work, I've found it to be one of the most exhilarating things a performer can do, because the two of you will rapidly create something that's bigger than both of you, a theatrical event that seems to have taken on a life of its own.

When you do the first round of this game, it's going to be very hard. My advice, knowing that this will probably be the case, is to lower your expectations immediately. Knowing that there's a good chance that you're going to fail, you now have nothing to lose. In fact, this is the best attitude to take into any exercise that you've never done before in this course.

As I've said, each improvisation game requires new skills or a new combination of old skills. It's a little like swimming for the first time. You jump in the water and there is no earth beneath your feet. You have to learn new ways to organize your body in order to stay afloat, advance forward, etc. Once you've learned the skills, however, it seems like second nature.

Stumbling through an improvisation game the first time doesn't mean you're a bad improviser any more than your first floundering in the water means you'll never be a swimmer. This course, like all performance courses, is about getting it into your body. You have to jump in the water and flail around at first or you can't acquire the skills.

Warm-up

- Physical Warm-up
- Bunny

Word At-a-Time Story

Two people ask the audience for a dangerous location. It really makes no difference what the location is: it could be a jungle, it could be a pillow factory. Whatever it is, the improvisers are going to *make* it dangerous.

You're going to go on an adventure in this location. You're going to meet terrible danger. And you're going to conquer it. As you're acting out the story, you're going to be narrating it as it's going on, telling the audience what you're doing as you're doing it. And you tell this story by taking turns speaking alternately . . . one word at a time.

Here's an example taken from one of my classes. The dangerous location was a river. One of them immediately started paddling a canoe and the other jumped beside her and did the same:

"(*student A*) Paddling . . . (*student B*) down . . . (*student A*) the . . . (*student B, etc.*) . . . river . . . we . . . were . . . scared . . . by . . . the . . . big . . . Nazi . . . named . . . Jill. We . . . tried . . . paddling . . . faster . . . backwards . . . then . . . we . . . hit . . . the . . . Nazi . . . and . . . screamed . . . (*unison*) AAAAAAARGH! . . . and . . . took . . . our . . . machete . . . and . . . we . . . sliced . . . his . . . nuts . . . off . . . He . . . hopped . . . up . . . and . . . down . . . despondently . . . until . . . we . . . got . . . bored. So . . . we . . . smacked . . . him . . . with . . . our . . . paddle. We . . . discovered . . . that . . . he . . . was . . . dead . . . So . . . we . . . paddled . . . slowly . . . down . . . the . . . river . . . singing . . . Aida."

Throughout this scene, they were racing up and down the class-room acting it out, eyes focused on each other at all times and mir-roring each others activities, screaming, slicing, beating, shaking the blood off their hands, paddling.

Again, this game will be difficult the first few times you do it. But as you eventually develop a feel for it and the skills, it will look and feel like mind reading.

Clearly, you have to give up the future. You have no control over what's going to happen because one person may be thinking he's pick-ing up a paddle but when it's time to name it, it may be his partner's turn and he says "machete." (*Say the first thing that comes into your head.*) So it's now a machete for both of you (*Say "Yes! And . . ." to all of your partner's offers*). Your partner may be just as surprised as you that "machete" just came out of his mouth, but you immediately use it with a smile and without hesitation to spay the Nazi (*Make your partner look good*).

General Rules

There are some general rules for this game that help make it work:

- Try to begin as many sentences as possible with present par-ticiples, that is, verbs ending in "ing." And act them out as you do: "Walking . . . through . . ." as you both mime walking; "Climbing . . . up . . ." as you both climb; "Dancing . . . seduc-tively . . ." as you dance, etc.
- Always tell the story in first person plural: "Walking through the woods, *we* were singing . . ." or "Dancing the Macarena, *we* were approached by . . ."
- The conflict in the story should never be *between* the two of you. The danger comes from outside, and the two of you work as a team to conquer it.
- If you're in the middle of the story and there is no conflict, the solution is very simple: One of you says the word, "Suddenly . . ." and danger will arrive. You will discover it and describe it later as it's happening.
- Get a feel for the balance required in this game, of mutual give-and-take.

There's a danger that you may let your partner take over. And there's a danger of doing just the opposite and trying to take over yourself.

What you'll find is that neither one of these choices work. Like volleyball, you have to be there to receive the ball your partner throws your way—accepting his offer immediately—and then bat it back with equal energy.

- Before either one of you says a word, start doing something physical. Dance, walk, crawl, apply makeup, anything that may seem appropriate for the dangerous location you've been given by the audience.

If it's a river, one of you can immediately start paddling or swimming or rowing or fishing or skiing, etc. And as soon as one begins, the other should do exactly the same thing, eyes on each other. You'll have no idea why you're doing this. Give up control; you'll soon find out why.

- And keep your eyes on your partner at all times.

Although you're narrating the story for the audience, don't look at them. Stay locked on your partner, so that you can pick up physical and vocal cues and mirror them.

- Mirror each other in everything you do.

If one of you starts walking, the other should also walk immediately. If one of you reaches for something, the other reaches too. If one of your voices gets loud and frightened, so does the other. The more in synch you are physically, the more in synch your offers become. When this game is on a roll, you'll feel and act as if you're one mind and one body; physical imitation helps nudge you in this direction.

- Make physical offers before you know what you're doing.

Reach into your pocket and pull something out without knowing what it is. And if your partner reaches into his pocket, don't feel you have to guess what he's reaching for and give him the "right" answer. "Reaching into his pocket" is all that he's offering; name the reason yourself: a knife, a banana, a penny. Your offer will always be "right." Start climbing; your partner will mirror you and shortly you'll find out where you're going. Cry, laugh, yell; your partner will mirror, and again you'll find out why in a moment.

The first few times you do this game, it will feel like you're hic-cupping through it with long pauses as you search your partner's eyes trying to figure out what word he's expecting next. This is actu-ally a good sign because it indicates you're trying to give up con-trol. But it's also a variation of The Improvisational Cylinder of Panic. In this case, however, instead of going up into your own head you're trying to go into your partner's.

You can't. Nothing passes from person-to-person at that level. If instead you make a blind physical or emotional offer . . . reach for something or start crying . . . you'll be amazed at how rapidly you begin to sense in unison where the story is going. Physical activities and emotions help narrow down the choices. That is, if you're reach-ing up high for something, the next word isn't going to be "kissing" or "sleeping." If you start crying, your partner probably won't say "giggling." By mirroring physical and emotional choices, you're cor-ralling each other into a limited, shared direction.

- You can run from the danger temporarily if you want, but you *must* turn back and conquer it.
- Avoid using the word "decided." "The . . . monster . . . ap-proached . . . so . . . we . . . decided . . . to . . . shoot . . . him . . . with . . . our . . . fingers . . ."

Using the word "decided" is a way to delay taking action and keeps you safely in your head. Instead say, "The monster approached so we shot him with our fingers." Use action verbs. Again, if you say the first thing that comes into your head you will get yourself into trou-ble. Guaranteed. That is the moment of theater: the moment you face an unknown future, risking failure and then leaping forward. We hesitate to do this in this game at first without "checking in" with our partner to see if it's OK.

But all you're doing is shifting the responsibility of making an offer to his shoulders, which isn't serving either one of you. His job is to "Yes! And . . ." your offer, keeping the momentum of the story going. You're only hindering him, yourself, and the story by not making clear, action-based offers. On the one hand, your desire to stay safe is absolutely understandable; we all want it. But on the other, no one's going to pay money to watch you be safe. The audi-ence comes to the theater to watch you jump in the water and flail, eager to see if you sink or swim. Make your partner look good by

"Yes! And . . ."–ing his startling offers with glee, and engendering his trust. He'll do the same for you, and then this risk-taking becomes a party and you will *always* succeed.

- If you start laughing at what you're doing, you're out of the story.

Laughter is a way to stay safe. Feel the emotional mood of the story, share it with your partner, and stay there. If you're happy, be happy together; if it's spooky, be spooky. Creating and sharing an emotional mood is, again, a way to bring the two of you together as one mind.

- Finally, keep in mind once again that this is the hardest game I know.

Give yourself plenty of permission to fail and keep going. You'll find that it gets easier and easier. When it's working, it's exhilarating. For me, Word-At-a-Time stories are the ultimate experience of playing by all three rules of improv.

Slaughter Duets

The bolder the physical choices you make in these Word-At-a-Time scenes the better. Spaying a Nazi will probably surprise both of you; the action is enormously dramatic *and* the audience knows you've shocked yourselves *and yet you keep going forward "helplessly"* into the future, creating a roller-coaster effect. People at amusement parks pay a lot of money to roar out of control down ever-more elaborate roller coasters just for the thrill. You can give yourself this thrill and the audience a vicarious one by making bolder and bolder offers and then pitching yourself forward.

Consequently, if after three or four of these scenes in the class they are still fairly tame, the instructor should introduce a round of Slaughter Duets. This is an exercise in giving yourself permission to be outrageous. (The entire class should do this exercise at the same time.)

Find a partner and stand facing each other. Then take turns finding more and more elaborate and inventive ways to kill each other:

machine guns; drive over him with a Mac truck bumping up and down over the body; your lawn mower goes out of control; strangle him with your dental floss. And if you're the one being killed make lots of screaming, horror noises, and blood spurting noises as you collapse to the ground. Try to crawl up the wall screaming to get away, then fall with an audible splash in the pool of your own blood.

Then both of you stand up, shake hands and say, "Thank you." Then it's the other person's turn to slaughter. Kill elaborately; die elaborately; then say "Thank you." Go back and forth this way a few times.

While doing this, never manhandle your partner. You never have to make any physical contact at all in this exercise. If you're strangling, keep your hands slightly away from his neck. As soon as you take control of someone's body, you begin to lose his trust. This isn't about slaughter, it's a *show* about slaughter. Let him act his part in this show under his own control.

This exercise should help free up your sense of spontaneous risk-taking. It's a lot easier to pull an Uzi on an old lady in your Word-At-a-Time story without worrying how your partner may react if you've already seen him dismember you with an eggbeater. After you've done this exercise for about five minutes, continue the Word-At-a-Time stories.

[15] Story Structure

I've made a distinction in the beginning of this book between gag improv and narrative improv. When done well, both are excellent forms of entertainment. As I've said, however, gag improv is more difficult and can be highly competitive. And few of the skills that are emphasized translate well into a cooperative art form like theater.

Narrative improve is relatively easier than gag improv. It is character based, and as such audiences will stay with you longer without feeling the need for a quick laugh as they watch the character grow and develop, facing challenging situations.

Part of what holds them is the story that unfolds as you, the improvisers, build offer upon offer as you "Yes! And. . . ." each other. This is one aspect of good storytelling.

We're now going to work on additional storytelling skills, simple elements that give a story structure, a "skeleton." Keep this structure in mind as your story unfolds and it guarantees a satisfying story or scene every time: with a beginning, a conflict, and a resolution.

Simple as the structure we'll discuss may appear, I'll illustrate it's power below by discussing the effect of similar "hidden" structures in other art forms.

Warm-up

- Physical Warm-up
- Sound Ball. (See Appendix 1: Warm-up Games.)

Song Structure

There is a style of song called the "tag-line" song. "Somewhere Over the Rainbow" is a good example. In it's simplest form, a tag-line song starts with a four-line verse that includes the tag line, which in this case is, "Somewhere over the rainbow . . ." And in this four-line verse, the second line of the song usually rhymes with the fourth line.

The second verse of this song also includes the tag line "Somewhere over the rainbow . . ." and though the subsequent lyrics are different than the first verse, the melody is exactly the same.

Then there is a "bridge" where, in this particular song, some day she wishes upon a star. The bridge melody is usually less interesting than the verse. I say it's less interesting because in the plan of the tag-line song, the bridge is often just a delaying tactic that builds to the climax: a reincorporation of the tag-line verse. You've already heard this initial melody often enough (twice) to remember it, and there's something very satisfying to hear it brought back.

This is the logic of the tag-line song. It's also known in the music world as the "AABA" song, where verses one, two, and four are the same and have the tag line—the "A" verses—and verse three is dif-ferent—the "B" verse. Other examples of this song are the Beatles' "I Saw Her Standing There"; Billy Joel's "I Love You Just the Way You Are"; "Wouldn't It Be Loverly" from *My Fair Lady*, etc.

Not all songs are tag-line songs, but a huge number of them are. Why? Because audiences find the very structure of the tag-line song very satisfying, a structure that amplifies whatever the music and lyrics may be.

Symphonic Structure

Here's another example of structure:

As symphonies evolved, they started as suites of dance music composed for court occasions: gavottes, minuets, sarabandes, etc. As time passed, however, people came just to listen, not to dance, and their attention span was longer than just a turn around the dance floor. Individual movements or "dances" got correspondingly longer, though the number of movements became fewer. And eventually another "structure"—in this case a symphonic structure—was arrived at that a listening audience found, and still finds, very satisfying. This is usually in three movements consisting of a broad, opening movement, a slow, either sweeter or sadder second movement, and a rapid or majestic third movement.

Not all symphonies follow this structure just as not all songs are tag-line songs. I'm going on about this, however, to point out that there are certain structures that appeal to audiences—in these cases the tag-line structure and the symphonic structure. There's something about them that feels "right" and "complete."

You have a feel for structures like this from a very early age. Tell a seven-year-old the following story:

"Once upon a time there was a little girl named Olga who lived in the woods with her grandma. And every day, they went to the woods to pick strawberries. One day, they opened the door of their cottage and there stood a huge wolf with a bazooka. The end."

"No!" the seven-year-old will say. I think you can predict that with a degree of certainty. Now, a one- or two-year old might let it go as just one more confusing thing in a confusing world. But by the age of seven, a child *knows* that the structure isn't complete. They want to know: what happened next?

This may all seem obvious. But here's my point: ask someone to improvise a monologue or tell a story and often they'll stumble, make up something terrible that even a seven-year old would find unsatisfying; or else he'll just seize up. On the other hand, start with a shape, a story skeleton that the audience already finds satisfying, fill in the blanks, and you will always tell a satisfying story.

The Four-Part Story

We're going to be working on scenes where you'll be improvising monologues. I'm offering the "Four-Part Story" as a structure to hang those monologues on. Use it, and you will always tell a story that has a beginning, middle, and end; incorporates a dramatic build; and satisfies an audience.

This isn't the only structure for storytelling, just as the tag-line structure isn't the only one for writing a song. But it's a simple, though fairly universal, structure. In fact, our improvisation company used a variation on it as a basis for all our improvised one-act musicals. Stay alert to it as you improvise and you'll automatically be ushered through one satisfying story after another.

The Four Parts

The four parts of a four-part story are the following:

- The Platform: What is life like every day? This section should include the phrase, ". . . and every day. . . ."
- The Event: What makes today different than every other day? This section usually starts, "But *one* day. . . ."
- The Resolution: How is that dealt with? This resolution can be successful or unsuccessful; the audience just wants to know how it was resolved.
- What is life like from that day on?

Four-part stories can be as short as a monologue or as long as a novel. Here's an example of one told in four sentences, one sentence for each part.

"[*Platform*] Once upon a time there was a little girl named Olga who lived in the woods with her grandma, and every day they went to the woods to pick strawberries. [*Event*] One day, they opened the door of their cottage and there stood a huge wolf with a bazooka. [*Resolution*] As he pulled the trigger, Olga and her grandmother stuffed their baskets up the barrel, causing a backfire that blew the wolf into a million pieces. [*What is life like from that day on?*] From that day on, Olga always peeked through the mailbox before she opened the door."

Here's an alternate "Resolution" for the same story:

"[*Resolution*] He pulled the trigger, making grandma faint, as he'd intended, and he promptly ate the little girl and left. [*What is life like from that day on?*] From that day on, grandma locked the door and never went berry picking again."

Again, you can give the audience *any* resolution and they'll be equally satisfied. But fail to give them all four parts and they'll know something is wrong.

Reincorporation

There is one more element to good storytelling that we're going to add here, and that's reincorporation. I mentioned it earlier in the tag-line song where verse three is a reincorporation of the melody and structure established in verses one and two. This too is deeply satisfying to an audience, and I can't exaggerate its effect on them.

It's very simple: If you mention something at any time during a story, mention it again later on.

You can bring grandmother back to the same cottage in the woods she left that morning. Or it can be as simple as carrying a soda can into a scene you're improvising, which you put down and ignore, and then at the end return to pick up. An audience will think you're brilliant. If someone mentions Detroit, bring Detroit into conversation again later; if someone goes to the counter and mimes pouring a cup of coffee, go back later for more, for cream, whatever.

Remember, an improviser is like a man walking backwards. You don't know where you're going, but you know where you've been. And as you "walk backwards," offer by offer, you will gradually leave behind a groundwork of history, relationship, location, plot elements, etc., as the framework of the scene begins to structure itself. Remember these. First, they are the footholds that propel you into the future. And second, reincorporating any of these elements is one of the delights of watching narrative improv . . . which, again, is simply good storytelling.

I've already talked about reincorporation in the Status Soap Opera game. Perhaps you've already seen in that game how delightful it is when someone mentions a girlfriend, and then three scenes later she shows up. Or when someone new picks up the can that was identified as a urine specimen ten minutes ago with relief because they'd been looking for their urine sample. Like so many of the elements of narrative improv, things that amaze the audience and look terribly clever are often as simple as saying the first thing that comes into your head or, in this case, simply remembering something and bringing it back.

Exercise 1: The Four-Part Story Structure

You're going to tell a series of four-part stories as you sit in a circle. The first person will do the platform of the story, the next person the event, the third the resolution, and the fourth, what life has been like from that day on.

The instructor gives a subject matter to the person on his right, "Tell me a story about a button." Like all other offers, the subject matter should be simple, something in the room (a window), something someone is wearing (a baseball cap), etc.

That person starts by announcing what part of the story he's going to tell, and then does so. "This is the Platform, what life was like every day. Once upon a time there was a button that lived in a drawer. And *every day* [my italics] he told all his fellow buttons how much he dreamed of seeing what life was like on the outside."

The next person:

"This is the Event, or what makes today different than every other day. But one day, as Mr. Fisk was fumbling through the drawer looking for something, he accidentally knocked the button out of the drawer and onto the carpet. 'Look out world! Here I come!' cried the button."

Next:

"This is the Resolution. But Mr. Fisk's dog Rover came and ate the button and he was never heard from again."

Next:

"This is what life was like from that day on. So all his friend buttons huddled in the corner and vowed never to see the light of day. The end."

Give the next person in the circle a new subject matter and continue this until everyone has gone twice. There's a tendency to forget announcing what part of the story you're about to relate. Remind each other to do so. This helps reinforce the structure in everyone's brain.

What you're doing is to drilling these four parts so that the shape becomes instinctive. Then when it's time to improvise a monologue and you don't feel it's going well, you can correct it on the fly: "I have a platform but no event." "I have an event and another event and another event, but there's no resolution." "This is going on and on. I can bring it to a conclusion by saying what my life has been like every day since then."

Another way of looking at the event, or what makes today different than every other day, is something happens in the story that raises a question. And then the resolution answers that question. When the wolf appears in the door with the bazooka we want to know, "Did grandma and Olga make it out alive?" The resolution tells us.

Exercise 2: Four-Sentence Monologues

Do another round of four-part stories, this time as four-sentence monologues. After each monologue the next person in line should analyze the previous monologue, breaking it into the four parts, before he begins his own. The instructor should facilitate this by asking specifically, "What was the platform?," "What was the event"?, etc.

I asked student number one for a monologue on ChapStick:

"Well . . . every day I use a grotesque amount of ChapStick. But one day I opened my medicine cabinet and realized I didn't have any. So I screamed and cried in pain and went to the Rite Aid and bought some more. And every day after that I would keep gigantic vats of ChapStick and Vaseline under my bed."

I asked student number two:

"What was the platform?"

"He always uses grotesque amounts of ChapStick."

"What was the event?"

"He ran out."

"Good. What was the resolution?"

"That he went to Duane Reade and now he has all the ChapStick he needs."

"No. That includes what life was like from that point on. At this point, just tell me how he resolved it. He went to Duane Reade and . . ."

". . . bought more ChapStick."

"Good. And what was life like from that point on?"

"Now he always has wads and wads of ChapStick."

The more you drill this shape, as I'm asking you to do with these exercises and the following one, the more second nature it becomes. Obvious as it may seem now, it isn't a shape one normally reaches for when asked to improvise a story. When you do, however, the story is easy.

Exercise 3: Pop-up Story Book

The premise of this game is that you, the narrator, have come to tell a story to a kindergarten class . . . "Uncle Danny's Story Hour," or whatever you choose to call yourself. And you're going to tell the story in four parts: Platform, Event, Resolution, and what life was like from that day on.

Before you start, two volunteers lie down behind you on the "stage" with their feet toward the audience. Introduce yourself:

"Hi, kids! Welcome to Uncle Danny's Story Hour!" . . . at which point everyone should applaud.

"And what would all of you want to hear a story about today!?"

The audience gives a suggestion: marshmallows, orange juice, teachers, etc.

"Marshmallows! Wonderful! Okay! Would you like to see what life was like every day?" [This is Part One: the Platform.]

Everyone responds with enthusiasm. At this point cross to the left side of the room, and bend over as if you're lifting the page of a huge book that's lying flat on the floor. Bring yourself upright and haul the page across to the right side of the room as you make a page-turning noise and then drop it. While you're doing this, the two volunteers should "pop-up" as if they're part of a pop-up story-book, strike a pose and freeze.

It makes no difference what the poses are. Your job now is to use those poses as inspiration to begin a story about marshmallows. This again is page one, what life is like every day.

"One day there were two marshmallows, Goatie and Piggie. And *every day* they did aerobics in the front yard of their gingerbread house. Do you all want to see what happens when I pull this tab?"

The audience responds with enthusiasm. You then grab a big, imaginary paper tab and as you pull it toward you, make a sound that goes up the scale. Pause. While you're doing this, the marshmallow people should move into a new pose. For example, they may be doing something aerobic in this case since you've cued them that way. Then push the tab back into place making a sound that goes down the scale. They return to their initial positions. Do this a second time. As I've suggested, make vocal sounds as you do this and as you turn each page because the volunteers may be in a physical position where they can't actually see you pull the tab or turn the page. The sounds cue them.

Then ask the audience:

"Do you want to see what made today different than any other day?" [Part Two: the Event.]

Again, wild enthusiasm. Race across the room, grab page two, lift it and cross back to the other side. The pop-up characters now strike a new pose. Based on this new pose, create part two . . . the event.

For example, one may be posed like a dancer and the other may be facing him making a face.

"One day, Goatie announced that she was tired of living in a gingerbread house and she wanted to be a classical ballet dancer and tour the world and be famous. Piggie was pissed. Want to see what happens when I pull this tab?"

. . . and as the tab is pulled one way, Piggie rams his head into Goatie, then back to original positions when pulled the other way, back and forth again.

"Do you want to see how they solved this problem? [Part Three: Resolution]"

Cheers. Repeat page turning as volunteers strike new poses, such as, Goatie on the floor and Piggie standing with foot on Goatie's stomach.

"Well, Piggie knocked Goatie down and cried out in victory that no brother of his was going to make a fool of himself in a tutu, while Goatie died from internal hemorrhaging. Want to see what happens when I pull this tab?"

Pull, return, pull, return.

"And now, do you want to see what life was like from that point on?" [Part four.]

Enthusiasm. Cross, turn page, new pop-up poses, such as, Goatie standing with arms spread and Piggie hugging Goatie's ankles.

"Everyday, Piggie embraces Goatie's feet, whose body he has mounted in the den. And he vows never to use his head as a battering ram again. Want to see what happens when I pull this tab?"

Pull tab, etc. The End.

Now, before the next narrator begins his pop-up story, have him break the preceding story down into the four parts, naming the section and then describing what happened during it. Then it's his turn, get two new volunteers to lie on the floor, and so on.

Class

[16] "It's Tuesday!"

Start this class with Slaughter Duets (see Class 14) as a warm-up exercise to get you familiar once again with making big choices and raising the stakes. You're now going to combine these big choices with "I Love You" scenes and your four-part storytelling skills to improvise monologues.

Warm-up

- Physical Warm-up
- Slaughter Duets

It's Tuesday!

Two people set up the scene as you've done in the past with the "I Love You" scenes: get a location that can be contained on the stage (e.g., "a throne room" as opposed to "a castle," or "a bistro in Paris" as opposed to "Paris"). At the start of the scene, the two characters enter and see each other and there is enormous electricity between the two because they've worshipped each other in the past without revealing it, etc., and they carry on a conversation.

However, in the middle of this conversation one of them says something perfectly ordinary that triggers a *huge* emotional reaction in the other person. This reaction is so unexpected and overwhelming that he feels obliged to explain himself, and launches into a four-part story about his past.

This game is called *"It's Tuesday!"* because it's that kind of bland statement that triggers the reaction.

"It's so great to see you. My week has been so scattered. What day is today?"

"It's Tuesday."

"OH MY GOD!!!!! TUESDAY!!! . . ."

And the monologue begins. As an actor, you should have no idea why you're having this emotional reaction when you begin. Just do it: scream or laugh or cry or collapse to the floor or fling yourself against the wall and scramble to get away, etc. And then go into motormouth, creating a monologue that includes this explanatory four-part story from your past and contains an ". . . and everyday . . ." statement, a ". . . but one day . . ." statement, a resolution, and a description of what life has been like since then.

Now, this monologue must get so emotionally extreme at its climax that you have to clap your hand over your mouth suddenly to contain yourself. Then, once you've pulled yourself together, gradually close the monologue (usually with the ". . . and every day since then . . ." fourth part of the story). The two of you come back to terms with the present moment. And then you continue the conversation.

If you're the other performer, during this monologue your job is the same as the interviewer in the Expert's Game: throw focus, nod, and throw in little rejoinders like "Oh, my god!" "I'm sooo sorry," etc., anything to stay connected with the scene and to keep your partner going without interrupting the flow of the monologue. And, again, even if you don't feel connected because you're scared or distracted (which can happen and is perfectly understandable), deceive us with your voice and your body. The audience only knows what's happening on stage because of what your voice and your body are doing, whatever you may be feeling. You may feel frightened or detached, but lean into your partner, touch him sympathetically, keep your eyes locked on him . . . and we the audience will install compassion into your performance.

Once your partner's monologue is over and you're back in conversation, however, it's now your turn to take something inane offered by this partner and launch into your own "It's Tuesday!" monologue.

"What do you usually take on your hot dog?"

"Mustard."

"MUSTARD!!! OH DEAR GOD!!! YOU SAID 'MUSTARD'!!! . . ."

By the way, though we've worked with status a great deal in this course so far, don't worry about it for this exercise. Just focus on the rules of the "I Love You" scene with this added four-part monologue and ignore status work for the time being.

Here's a sample scene. The location was a "Jumbo Bagel store." Without discussing with each other, the performers pushed furniture around into some formation, knowing as per instructions that as the scene progressed, they would figure out what it was. As actor A entered, B spoke from behind a "counter":

"Hi. Welcome to Jumbo Bagel."

"I'll take a sesame bagel with cream cheese . . ."

"Oh, my god! Phillip!"

"Bill? Oh, my god!!!" (they embrace)

"Where have you been?!"

"I just moved here!"

"The last time I'd heard you'd gone off to Africa and then we never heard from you again!"

"Yeah . . . I went on a big-game hunt, shot a tiger . . ."

"And we'd all thought you'd died! Gosh, it's so good to see you again!"

"What are you doing here?"

"This is my place! I gave up college. I couldn't get through. I mean, you remember, when I was a sophomore how much trouble I was having. Couldn't make any sense out of calculus, for god's sake. Sit down! Sit down! Let me get you something! What would you like?"

"Um . . . orange juice?"

"AGH! (*starts to tremble*) Oh, god! (*collapses behind the counter*) Oh, god! I'm falling apart! I'm sorry . . . What did you just say? Orange juice?"

"Yeah . . . you know, orange juice . . ."

"OH, GOD, NO! I'm sorry! (*sobbing*) *I side-coach* (*"Go! Go!"*) The reason I left college, the real reason, had nothing to do with calculus.

Every day I used to go to the cafeteria and I used to (*sob*) ask for a glass of orange juice. And there was this little Swedish guy that worked behind the counter who was a midget . . . you could barely see him (*gasping for breath*). And every day I used to yell, 'Hellloooo! Is there anyone BACK there?', you know, as a joke. And so one day, he was so sick and tired of me, Mr. Tall Guy making fun of Mr. Little Guy, that he yelled at me in his stupid Swedish accent, 'I'm-a gonna give-a you some-a orange juice!' and he leapt up on the counter with a glass of orange juice and he STUFFED IT DOWN MY THROAT! ("*Make it worse!*") Well, I grabbed that little Swedish turd by his little Swedish ankles and I BEAT HIS HEAD AGAINST THE TRAY RAILING AND I CRACKED HIS HEAD OPEN AND HE DIED!!! (*Claps his hand over his mouth.*) And every day since then . . . I . . . just . . . can't have it around my . . . shop. You can have anything. Just . . . don't . . . say . . . (*whispers*) 'orange juice.' I'm sorry. I'm really sorry. Uh . . . uh . . . are you still big-game hunting?"

The scene continues, then this character makes a bland statement, the other launches into his "It's Tuesday!" monologue, then comes back down. Finally, the two of them find a reason to leave and the scene is over.

Now the first time you do this, you may find yourself distracted as you try to remember the four parts of a four-part story. Doing the three previous exercises in this class should make it easier. And if you're the instructor, side-coaching here is extremely helpful. If someone is having difficulty with the story thread, prompt them with ". . . every day . . . ," ". . . one day . . . ," ". . . how did you deal with it . . . ," etc. For those of you who are being coached, stay focused on the scene and your partner. Side-coaching doesn't mean you've failed. You're learning in the best way . . . by *doing*. Side-coaching is a way to help keep you on track as you career forward and get a feel for this skill.

Before the next two performers begin their scene have them each analyze one of the monologues from the previous scene, breaking them down into the elements of the four-part story. Keep in mind that there may be some disagreement as you analyze a particular story. For example, was this element the beginning of the resolution, or was it part of the event with the resolution coming later? This kind of discussion is important because it gets everyone thinking in terms of the four parts. However, don't worry about getting it "right."

And don't worry about doing a fabulous monologue. What's important here is internalizing the four-part structure. As it becomes part of your vocabulary, your stories will only get better and better.

Revealing Yourself

This is a good time to discuss one of the initial fears of most people facing a class in improv: the fear that you will reveal yourself.

You will. As you lay the foundation of these scenes in your joyful meeting and your opening conversation, and launch yourself into a huge emotional reaction without any idea why, and then try to apply structure, in this case the four parts, to a frantic story, informed in part by the Slaughter Duets you did earlier . . . you have no time to be clever. The only place you can go is to your subconscious, grabbing at the first thing that comes into your head. And as I've said earlier, you'll end up telling a story that no one else could tell because no one has lived your life. It may shock you. I certainly hope at the very least that it surprises you. Again, I'm not insisting that violence and vulgarity are the signs of a good improviser. But I am saying that breaking through any cultural taboos, of which violence and vulgarity seem to be the easiest, gives you an experience and wisdom that others will come to witness who are afraid to do the same. You don't have to behave like this in your private life. That's a separate, sacred morality. But as an artist, it's what people come to you for. It's part of your job.

. . . and Your Promise

At the same time, remember your promise to each other. You can talk about what goes on in class outside of class . . . but do not name names. Take care of each other: Make your partner look good.

Class

[17] Union Jack

Now that students in this course are being encouraged to make bigger and bolder choices, it's important to heighten their sense of how their choices can either contribute to or distract from the overall effect of the scene.

Union Jack is a powerful and unique exercise in developing an awareness of stage presence: the feeling of the stage picture the audience is alert to at any given moment, and the part you play in it.

In the Expert's Game, the Expert's chair was an exercise in taking focus. The Interviewer's chair was an exercise in throwing focus. Union Jack takes this a step further, as the performers slide back and forth between taking and giving focus, from foreground to background, alert to the event, the "dance," that they are creating, and the part they play in it. If you have the time to include this and a large enough space to do it in, I highly recommend it. If not, however, feel free to move on to the next chapter, as the course as a whole is complete without it.

Taking and Throwing Focus

In the chapter Make Your Partner Look Good, I talk about the importance of knowing how and when to throw focus. Whenever you're on stage, you must be aware of the part your character is playing in the stage picture at any given moment, take focus when appropriate, and throw the audience's focus of attention elsewhere when that's appropriate.

Communal artists like actors and improvisers must commit themselves to losing themselves in the process of creating a theatrical event; to contributing in cycles of moving forward to become the "figure" of audience focus when the creation demands; then receding into "ground" that supports the moment and the other actors, making them look good. And when you can do this on the fly, as you are required to do in improvisation . . . alternately moving forward and receding . . . this recruiting of individual egos in creation of a greater stage picture is breathtaking to watch.

I repeat: dancers develop this sense of stage picture and the part they play in that picture very early in their careers. If they've ever danced in an ensemble, they develop a keen sense of what the picture is that the ensemble is creating at any given moment and what part they play in that picture. They can even sense what's going on behind them, moving on cue like a school of fish. Actors must develop this sense of ensemble. It can be difficult to learn, however.

Extending Your Sense of Self into Space

When people who are just learning to drive park a car and gently bump into something, they may look startled and they'll certainly feel concern. However, when long-term drivers bump into something, they actually wince. It's as if the object has struck *them*, not just the car.

Jonathan Miller, in his book *The Body In Question*, talks about how we extend our sense of self into our bodies and into the space around us. As an infant develops, he extends this sense of self gradually into the extremities of his body. At first that "hand thing" that comes into view in the crib, for example, is simply a curiosity. As he learns to manipulate it, incorporate its sensations into his perception of his surroundings, and then gradually uses it to manipulate those surroundings, he extends his sense of self *into* it. This concept of *extending* our sense of self into our limbs, etc., is emphasized if we ever lose one. Patients who undergo amputation still *feel* the hand. And they've shown that this is more than just stimulation of the remaining nerves. They actually have to *unlearn* that hand and learn the new limit to their physical self in space.

That long-term car driver I mention in the example above has, in addition, extended that sense of self into the boundaries of his car, which is why he actually winces when he hears that thud. Actors must learn to extend that sense of self into the entire stage picture.

In scripted theater, the director is largely responsible for that stage picture. As an outside eye, he can tell individuals how to adjust. And all an actor really needs to be aware of is the energy he's creating where he stands, in his chair, on the platform, etc. A really good actor, however, can sense the energy in the entire stage space and how his work is affecting it, like a dancer, aware of all that's happening around him.

How do you learn this? And can it be taught?

Union Jack

Union Jack is an exercise that addresses this issue. Our improvisation company was taught the exercise by an improvisational dance troupe in New Zealand when we were there for TheaterSports competition. And I've found it to be the most effective exercise I know in giving performers an awareness of how their presence is affecting the stage space.

This exercise is as much for the observers as for the performers. The class should take turns being both. Once an individual has had a chance to perform *and* observe this exercise, I've found the subsequent episodes to be even more effective. On top of this, it creates, in its simplicity, some of the most exciting theater I've seen.

Preliminary Exercise: Bus Stop

Bus Stop is a shorthand exercise that quickly introduces the concepts in Union Jack.

The scene is about four people waiting at a bus stop. Take four students aside where the rest of the class can't hear your instructions. Number them one through four. Tell them that when the scene begins, they should all be in line, right to left, facing the audience, standing in a neutral manner: arms at their sides; no facial expression. Then tell them what to do each time you clap your hands (listed below).

Then have them line up in front of the audience. Tell the audience that these are four people waiting at a bus stop. Wait at least fifteen seconds in silence as the four stand in neutral attitudes. This moment of silence is important, as it fills the space with a sense of theatrical anticipation. Then clap six times, pausing about five to ten seconds between claps. On each clap, the four do the following:

- Clap 1.   Character four should act natural (fidget, look at her nails, something simple) while one, two, and three remain neutral.
- Clap 2.   Two screams. One, three, and four don't change (four continues acting natural, one and three neutral, etc.). Two continues to scream until . . .
- Clap 3.   One, three, and four look at two, who stops screaming.
- Clap 4.   Three laughs.
- Clap 5.   One, two, and four look at three.
- Clap 6.   All look to the left.

When it's done, ask the audience where their attention went on each clap, and why. Why did they look at four on the first clap? Equally importantly, why *weren't* they looking at one, two, and three? This is an exercise in throwing audience focus. One, two, and three's job on the first clap, for example, was to make four look good by not drawing attention to themselves.

Pull the four performers aside again and add the following instructions. Then repeat the exercise from the first clap.

- Clap 7.   One looks right.
- Clap 8.   One looks forward and three steps forward.
- Clap 9.   Three and four sit and look forward.
- Clap 10.   One collapses.
- Clap 11.   All look at one.

Again, ask the audience where their focus went, and why. This may seem like a simple exercise and that the answer is obvious: they looked at what was most interesting. What's important to investigate is what *made* it interesting. And what made the others *un*-interesting. At each moment a stage picture is being created. And each performer is either drawing focus or throwing focus. Being unique draws focus; it can be thrown by directing your energy toward the new point of focus, or by doing what the majority is doing and blending into a background "noise." Or simply by doing nothing.

Union Jack: How to Play

Union Jack requires a large space, the larger the better. Most classrooms are too small. A stage, a gym, or any large empty hall is ideal.

Using masking tape, mark out a British Union Jack on the floor (see the illustration below). These lines of tape will be paths that the performers are restricted to walk on during the exercise. Mark out a rectangle on the floor using as much of the room space as possible. Leave about three to six feet clearance from the walls and, if you're in a room and not using a stage, enough clearance at one end for the audience. Then lay out two diagonals joining corner A to corner E, and corner C to corner G. Finally, lay out two more paths joining the midpoints of the two parallel sides, B to F and D to H. (NOTE: Be sure to use tape that won't leave marks on the floor when you take it up after the exercise.)

Union Jack
layout

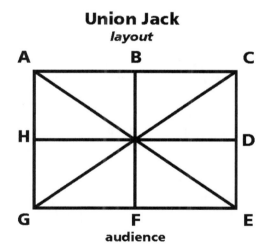

audience

The maximum number of performers in the exercise is eight. Try not to use any fewer than six. Place a performer at all eight points on the perimeter of the layout indicated above, A through H (or on six or seven of the points if that's the number of performers you're using).

These are their instructions when the exercise is in progress:

- You must stay on the tape lines.
- You may walk or run forward; you cannot walk or move backwards.

- You may laugh.
- You may scream.
- You may fall. This collapse should be natural and neutral, and your body *must* end up along the line of the tape.
- You may stand still.
- If anyone is standing in front of you, you may not walk around him or her. For example, if anyone is standing in the center, he effectively blocks all traffic through the center.
- You must remain *neutral* at all times when either moving or standing still: no character walks, no facial expression, just easy, natural movements. Think of yourself as a sort of neutral human clone, without personality. No acting. But keep it easy and loose. Don't behave as if you're participating in some great drama or as if you're a robot.
- Keep changing dynamics—fast and slow.
- This is very important: Pick up on offers. For example, if someone laughs, laugh. If someone is running, run. Don't try to be original. Look for patterns you can repeat. If you find yourself face-to-face with someone, stay with him. If you find yourself running, run a lot. *NB, repetitive patterns don't have to be broken.* Keep it up and it will evolve into something else on its own.
- If someone works well with you, stay with him. If relationships establish, retain them or bring them back. A two- or three-person pattern, if good, might be maintained throughout the entire sequence.
- Remember to be playful.
- Take your time. You don't have to use the vocabulary up all at once. You may never scream; you may never run; you may stand still during the entire episode and do nothing.
- You can make an offer over and over if you feel it's right.
- Laugh and scream spontaneously; don't force it.

The first round for each group of participants should last five minutes. Again, ask for complete silence in the space and let everyone stand neutral for at least thirty seconds before saying "begin."

When five minutes is over, ask the audience what they saw, what stories they were inventing about the performers as the game progressed. Since the audience is given so little information—laughter, running, stillness, screaming—it's amazing how their minds will work overtime to invent stories, relationships, etc. Then switch: audience become performers and vice versa. Another five-minute round.

You may find during this first round that the effect is largely chaotic with just a few moments of theatrical interest. Each performer will want to try everything . . . laughing, running, screaming, etc. In fact, my experience has been that there will generally be a *lot* of screaming. We're not allowed to scream in a classroom and the permission can be liberating. But after these first two rounds, re-read the rules with special emphasis on:

- Looking for patterns you can repeat.
- Looking for relationships you can continue throughout.
- Continuing to do whatever you end up doing . . . on and on . . . until it evolves into something else on its own. Base that change on interaction with someone else, even if that person is across the square from you. If you sense someone suddenly running, run.

What's hard for a performer to give up is the sense that the performance is about *him*. And that he has to be interesting. What he eventually comes to observe in this exercise when he's watching others perform it, however, is that if he's not alert to what's going on around him and how he fits in, if he's not aware of the choices others are making and his ability to reinforce those choices, the theatrical result is chaos and boring to watch.

Do another round, this time fifteen minutes long. (If there's still a lot of screaming, I suggest you stop the exercise and limit everyone to three screams in total. Screaming is exciting, but it's alarming and tends to shatter the event if it's continual.)

When this exercise was first introduced to us, I didn't know what was going on. As a performer, I kept trying to make sense of it. I couldn't understand it in the beginning. But I came to realize that I was learning a new sense of perception that my psyche was previously unfamiliar with. I think you'll find that after doing it *and* watching it a few times, a whole new sense of theatrical event and stage picture will become clearer to everyone. And you'll find that some of the scenes are haunting, some are frightening, and some are hysterical.

Union Jack: Second Game

If you have the time and want to continue, here's a variation:

Sit each individual in a chair and ask him to describe a favorite relative of his. Let him go on for a minute and watch for a short phrase and a gesture. For example, he might say, "My brother is a hermit," and roll his eyes as he tilts his head back. Or, "My aunt is a fabulous cook," and splay his hands. The gesture could come at the same time as the phrase or be unrelated. He might throw his arms in the air, or shrug, etc.

The performer now has two new elements . . . this phrase and this gesture . . . to add to his repertoire of movements and sound in Union Jack.

Now do another round of Union Jack and have the performers add these elements, each performer adding only his own two. The phrase and gesture can be used as many times as he wants; they can occur simultaneously or occur separately. For example, the performer with the shrug gesture may shrug over and over and never say the phrase.

Union Jack: Third Game

Have each performer choose a prop and come up with three ways to use it that aren't ways you would normally use the object. A self-opening umbrella could be a bazooka, a telescope and, when it opens, an explosive device. Add these three choices to the performance vocabulary. These scenes can last as long as thirty minutes. Don't let the prop take over your work, just as you shouldn't scream all the time just because you can. And avoid semi-dangerous props or those that are cumbersome.

Conclusion

Union Jack is an exercise that emphasizes *Make your partner look good* and *Say Yes! And . . . to all of your partner's offers*. It is about subsuming your ego to the common good, giving up control in the creative effort, resonating with and reinforcing your partner's choices, and surrendering yourself to the unknown future. In solo art forms, like painting and stand-up comedy, this isn't always necessary. However, in communal art forms like theater and improvisation, this attitude is essential.

Whether you are reinforcing an uncertain Expert in the Expert's Game by nodding and smiling, or picking up on offers in Union Jack, the effect of *Making your partner look good* and *Say Yes! And . . . to all of your partner's offers* is to surrender yourself to a larger communal good, and to create a theatrical event that is bigger than all of you. Audiences flock to watch this happen. And directors hire performers who can do it.

Class

[18] Mock Auditions

Auditions can be highly stressful events. Unlike performances in a play—where you can gradually lose yourself in the surroundings, the other characters, and the story you involve yourself in—at auditions, you're fundamentally marketing yourself from the moment you walk in to the moment you walk out.

Part of the challenge of auditions is finding material that shows you off at your best. Then there's the added confusion of having to enter as a charming person, switch to the pathos of your character as you perform it in a space you're not familiar with, and then exit as a charming person after tentatively cross-examining those present for pertinent information—which you then try to remember. All in five minutes. Every aspect of it can make huge demands on your sense of confidence and self-worth.

Part of the purpose of this class is not only to come into the unique voice in the arts that you already are, but also to present that voice with confidence and conviction, on stage and off. So as an exercise in reinforcing this unique voice, we're going to re-examine this daunting thing called the audition and what you may feel is the right way to approach it. Using the skills we've developed so far in this class, we're going to spoof auditions. And in the process of making fun, you're going to write your own audition material. It's another way of exercising the storytelling skills we've been developing. And you may end up with a monologue that solves that first challenge—finding appropriate material—one that gives those who are holding the audition what they're looking for: you, unique and clear.

Before the Class

As the students are waiting for class to begin, the instructor should listen in on conversations and write down next to each student's name one sentence he hears him say.

Bill: "I had the worst subway ride this morning."

Jane: "Like my new sneakers?"

Sue: "Yuk!"

Set these aside once class begins. You'll get to them later.

Warm-up

- Physical Warm-up
- I Am Superman/Superwoman! (See Appendix 1: Warm-up Games)

The Four-Part Story

As a review of the Four-Part Story, repeat Exercise 1 in Class 15: Story Structure. Moving one student at a time around the circle for one round, have each person describe which part he's relating, and then add to the story.

Audition Monologues

There is a big difference between doing a monologue in a play and doing that same monologue for an audition.

When you're doing a monologue in a play, the purpose is to convey the playwright's intention as clearly and efficiently as possible. This usually means altering who you are. And it certainly means ignoring your own personal needs from the audience to such an extent that if you're playing a bad guy, one sure sign of your success is lack of applause when you take a curtain call. They *should* be thinking, "Yuk. There's that creep."

When you're doing the same monologue at an audition, however, the purpose is different. You're there to show yourself at your best, and in this case the monologue is a tool, not an end. Your relationship with your audience—the auditioners in this case—is paramount. Finding monologues that fit you and show you at your best, as the unique voice in the arts that you are, is essential. Tweaking that monologue, even though it may not be exactly what the playwright intends, is in fact recommended if it shows you to your best advantage.

I've been using a monologue for years at auditions that I actually constructed myself by pasting together from various parts in a play. No one I've ever done it for has heard of the play. And depending on what they're looking for, I've done it with a British accent, a Southern accent, as a farce, as pathetic realism, even as a Restoration comedy. Of course you can't do this with a monologue from *Glass Menagerie*. Everyone knows the play and if you make Tom a Restoration hero, they'll just think you're a bad actor.

"How dare you do that?!" you may be thinking. Because it got me the parts. Again, the purpose of an audition monologue is to show you at your best.

In any event, we all know how difficult it is to find the perfect audition monologue that fills all the criteria: two minutes in length, with a beginning, middle, and end; one for Shakespeare auditions, another one for comedies, another for realism, etc.; all of which show you off at your absolute best.

I've offered one solution above: take an obscure play and paste a monologue together. Another?

Write your own monologue.

Now pay attention to the way you feel at this moment. *That's not playwrighting!* you may be thinking. Why not? You're an artist. And at this moment, without effort, you are a unique voice in the arts. Why would you feel that what you write is in any way inferior to anyone else?

But they don't want to see you do your own material! Why not? If the purpose of an audition is to show yourself off to your best advantage, a) what difference does it make *who* wrote it, and b) what could show you off in all your uniqueness better than something you've written yourself? I *will* admit that for some strange reason, some auditioners balk when they find out it's your own material. I don't know why. The solution? Tell them Robert Gilligan wrote it. *Who's that?* I just made that name up and you probably believed me. They will too.

I want to take a moment to point out very strongly that this is the *only* thing you should *ever* lie about at an audition. Never lie on a resume. They may find out or ask questions about people you've said you've worked with, and you'll probably be pretty thoroughly dismissed if they catch you.

But this particular lie is in fact harmless when you focus on the purpose of an audition: to show yourself off to your best advantage. And, again, what could reveal you and your unique voice more than something you've written?

That said, you're now going to write a monologue, and whether you actually use the results of this exercise or not at auditions, have fun with this exercise. It's easy, hysterical and terribly revealing. And at this point in the course, I hope that all of you are comfortable enough with each other to celebrate what flies out.

Writing a Monologue

The instructor should now reveal to each student the phrase he overheard him say before class began. This is the opening line of that student's monologue.

Everyone now has ten minutes to write a monologue. It should take the shape of the Four-Sentence Story. That is, shortly after it begins there should be an ". . . and every day . . ." platform statement followed by detail. Then a "one day . . ." event statement with detail; then a Resolution, then a closing platform, "Ever since then . . ."

Exaggerate the emotions and/or violence of these stories. They usually end up being about over-the-top wackos. The event must reach such an emotional out-of-control peak that the character has to slap his hand over his mouth to contain himself before moving into part four.

Outside of following this four-part shape, don't edit, just spew onto the page. And use plenty of detail: be specific about locations you're in or products or holidays you use, etc.

Here's an example: At the beginning of class, I overheard a student say, "I know you're cute." In ten minutes, she wrote:

"I know you're cute but every day you flirt with me and I can't do it anymore. I used to know a guy just like you. He was real cute. But one day he just came right out and kissed me. Well, nobody kisses me and gets away with it. So I grabbed him by the hair and started banging his head against the piano, and he was screaming and howling in pain and I just started laughing. I mean it was so funny. Well, the next thing I know the police show up. They asked me to release my victim and I was, like, 'Victim!? *I'm* the fucking victim here!' And I shoved the jackass into the police. So, yeah, I was arrested. I'm on parole now and seeing one of those therapists. She says I'm ready for human contact again. So what are you doing Friday?"

The teacher should let the students know when they have five minutes left, then two minutes, etc. When you're done writing your monologue, make up a title for the play that this monologue is from and a playwright: e.g., *American Singles* by Clarence Beuford. This was the first thing that came to her head.

The Audition

You are now going to hold a mock audition. All the students should leave the room and prepare their auditions by going over their monologues. As they're leaving, the teacher should sit behind an audition table and let the class know who will audition first. Then as each one leaves his audition, the teacher tells him who to send in next.

Again, this is a mock audition. *Make fun* of the audition process. Each student should enter with exaggerated, pleasant high status. Fill the space with your presence. Go over the top, gushy. Introduce yourself and invade the teacher/producer's space by bee-lining in to shake hands. (Don't shake hands at a real audition unless the auditioners offer theirs, which they seldom do; they see many people and this is a fast way to spread germs. But this class is an exercise in high status, so take over.)

The teacher/producer should ask for the name of the play and the playwright. Then read the monologue, getting as emotionally and physically involved as possible. Don't worry about looking silly, this is an unfinished work, dashed off in ten minutes. Play! After each monologue, the teacher/producer (like the interviewer in the Expert's Game), should gush with enthusiasm, nodding at and thanking the auditioner. And ask him to send in the next auditioner.

I usually take a few notes while students are auditioning to help in the following step.

Reviewing Auditions

When all the auditions are over, the teacher should call everyone back in and review: the next assignment is to re-shape these monologues. It seldom takes much. Here are some suggestions:

With each monologue, decide who the character is addressing. In the vast majority of cases, the characters are so over the top that the best imaginary situations are where hidden feelings suddenly have permission to explode: a psychiatrist's office; a therapy group; a witness stand; a party where everyone is stoned/drunk, etc. *Don't* try to be clever with this location. I had one class where everyone was talking to their psychiatrist. Great! The location isn't important, as long as it allows the unique kind of explosive revelation each character experiences.

If the monologue moves into science fiction, e.g. "And then a gorilla ate the house!" either change it to something possible, "And then the earth opened and swallowed the house!" or make it a dream sequence. You can do that usually in one sentence.

If there is something unclear, clarify it quickly. We had one monologue where I thought the character "Cheryl" was the actor's daughter. It was her roommate. So when she first mentioned her, she just added "My roommate, Cheryl." Bingo.

Choose a prop or costume piece that's appropriate to bring back to next class. One item. It could be a pair of glasses, or putting your hair in pigtails if you've decided your character is twelve-years old, or a security blanket if your character is sick all the time, a bandana if you're militant, or just pull your hair into your face if you're a street bum. Memorize the monologues and present them in the next class.

Editing the Monologues

Look at the monologue above. I suggested to the student that it might be a girl in a singles bar, sitting at the bar talking to the guy next to her. I saw her sitting on a stool with a drink and a cigarette. And with discussion, she re-wrote it like this:

"(*Turning to the guy on her right*) I know you're cute but every day you flirt with me and I can't do it anymore. (*She drags on her cigarette*) I used to know a guy just like you. He was real cute. But one day he just came right out and kissed me. Well, nobody kisses me and gets away with it. So I grabbed him by the hair and started banging his head against the bar (*originally "on the piano," but now she can demonstrate, where she's sitting, as she bangs this imaginary head over and over onto the bar*) and he was screaming and howling in pain and I just started laughing. I mean it was so funny. Well, the next thing I know the bartender shows up (*this was originally the police, but now she can face downstage and talk to the imaginary bartender*). He asked me to release my victim and I was, like, 'Victim!? *I'm* the fucking victim here!' And I shoved the jackass backward onto the floor (*originally, "into the police"–again, she can enact this by shoving the imaginary guy backwards*). So yeah, I was arrested. I'm on parole now and seeing one of those therapists. She says I'm ready for human contact again. So, what are you doing Friday?"

My feeling is, this is a very usable audition piece for an appropriate audition. You can't use it for Shakespeare or *Glass Menagerie*. But if the theater is looking for this kind of character, this performer couldn't do a better piece.

Another Example

At the beginning of class, I'd overheard this student say, "I wouldn't count going out with your dad as a date."

"I wouldn't count going out with your dad as a date, but what you might call an engagement . . . a meeting? Y'see, last year, the 'Toot Your Horn' samba dance was being held at Long Shore Funeral Home. It was the biggest event of the year here in Paddlewood, Mississippi. I searched everyday for a date! I asked Billy Bob, Joe, and Chris Lyllelner and ever one of the O'Farrely brothers. They all said no . . . they each had dates from the big industrial town due east that makes rubber tires. All their girls were planning on wearing gowns made out of rubber. They're so cool.

"So one day I just got so upset that I couldn't get a date that I went home crying to my mom kicking and screaming and wailin' like our pet pig, Jasper. She said 'I have a great idea. Why don't you go over to pappy's trailer and see if he'll go with you.' I admit it sounded a little incestuous, but it is deep Mississippi, so what doesn't sound incestuous?

"To make a long story short, my dad went. He showed up in a bright blue tux, red bow tie, patent-leather green shoes, and a top hat. He was the most handsome man at the dance. We danced the night away.

"All the girls from the mills were so jealous. The anger fueled inside them like a barbecue pit. They came over and ripped my yellow taffeta dress to pieces. They started yelling names and it looked like a canary bird had blown up in the funeral hall. I stood there in shreds and my father had tears in his eyes. It was the most humiliating experience of my life.

"Then my father said, 'Sugar, I still love you.' and we re-enacted the whole finale to *Dirty Dancing*, with the swan leap and everything.

Lucky for me, the producer of *Dirty Dancing/The Musical* was there and now I'm going to be a big star in New York City!"

Preparing for the Next Class

Leave ten to fifteen minutes at the end of this class to assign the Neutral Scenes required for the next class and to read them through together. Read the next chapter for an explanation.

Class

[19] Using Improv Skills in Scripted Scenes

Again, one of the purposes of this course is to give you improvisation skills that you can carry directly into scripted theater.

When you're playing Juliet in *Romeo and Juliet*, no matter how many thousands of productions there have been before, you have to believe that Shakespeare wrote this part for you. The unique, voice-in-the-arts that you are and the unique life experiences that you bring to the part will result in a unique creation. The exercises in this course have been designed to help reinforce this uniqueness and your confidence in it.

Yet when you're doing a play, there you are, facing a script that you can't change. And it might seem at first glance that this rigid adherence to the words in a script, and the blocking you've arrived at in rehearsal limit your ability to use improvisational skills.

However, it's those very skills summed up in the three rules of improvisation that result in that unique Juliet: Trust your own spontaneous emotional impulses, and the relationships to your partners that result (*Say the first thing that comes into your head*). At the same time, stay in the moment and be changed by your partner's impulses (*Say "Yes! And . . ." to all of your partner's offers*). And foster a sense of communal support that liberates your partner to create a Romeo that is just as uniquely his (*Make your partner look good*).

We're now going to use these improvisational techniques to experiment with some neutral two-person scenes. As part of this exercise, I encourage the instructor to assign each scene to at least two different couples. Doing so will help highlight the purpose of your work in this course so far: Four actors using improvisational techniques on the same material—whether it's Romeo and Juliet or neutral scenes like these—will create something that is a unique expression of the four people involved. For example, I've seen one of the scenes included in Appendix 5: Neutral Scenes take place in an apartment and in a subway men's room, and the same scene be about a birthday party and a serial killer.

Warm-up

- Physical Warm-up
- Poison Peepers (See Appendix 1: Warm-up Games)

Neutral Scenes

There are several neutral scenes in Appendix 5. The teacher should assign these scenes in the previous class and read through them to see if there's anything that needs clarification; but there shouldn't be a discussion of location, relationship, etc. Students, memorize the scenes before this exercise begins. If you choose to memorize them with your scene partner, don't make any decisions about the script while you're doing so. Simply run the lines.

Up until this class, the scenes you've done and all the elements in them—character, location, lines, environment—have been completely improvised. But as you bring these skills you've developed to scripted scenes, adjustments have to be made. These adjustments may feel like encroachments now that you've gotten used to and have perhaps begun to enjoy making *everything* up as you go along.

However, your career will be filled with adjustments like these, considerations that seem at first glance to cramp your artistic expression. I was recently in a play directed by an Armenian who spoke no

English; the entire rehearsal period was done through a translator. The director had been directing this particular play for twenty-four years and he insisted that lines be memorized by the first day of rehearsal, a rehearsal that was held in full costume with sound and lights. I'd never worked this way before and the adjustment was very difficult.

But that's my job. If you choose a career as an actor, you will leave classes with skills you've developed in common with your fellow students, only to be faced with people who don't work the way you do. When I first left school and worked with strangers it took me a while to understand that there are as many different acting techniques as there are actors. You find the skills that work for you and use them to the best of your abilities, adjusting to the skills of others. Because in a communal art form like theater, where the product is an expression of all the collaborators contributing and adapting to each other's contributions, adjusting is not only essential—it's your job.

Honoring the Script

To begin exploring this transition, start by honoring the script. Your lines in these scenes and in any play you're in must be memorized verbatim. Your role as a member of a cast is to deliver the playwright's intentions using the words he intended. Changing the lines or throwing in idiomatic expressions such as "like" and "I mean" may make it more comfortable and organic to you. But you have no more right to alter the script of a modern play to make it more "like you" than you have altering Shakespeare. But, you may argue, Shakespeare is literature. Every script you're handed should be treated as literature. Your job is to interpret the part, not rewrite the play. In fact, this is so important that actors can be—and have been—fired for changing their lines.

Therefore, I recommend that the teacher hand out these scenes one or two classes ahead of time, and then have each couple do a line run at the beginning of this class. If you're grading the class, make it clear that grade points will be deducted if lines aren't down (see Appendix 5: Grades). Having lines memorized before doing the following scene work keeps the work from getting bogged down by people struggling with lines or working with scripts in their hands. And it makes it easier for your partner to do the work he needs to do, thus making him look good.

Getting the Facts

These scenes are neutral scenes; they are deliberately vague. Like all scenes, however, there is a certain amount of information about the characters in the script. When you're doing scenes from full-length plays, it's important to know the whole play and then to make choices about relationships, locations, actions, costume, etc., that don't violate this information or the playwright's intentions; e.g., you don't turn a Pinter scene into a broad farce, or do the rape scene in *Tartuffe* realistically.

The information in these neutral scenes, however, is minimal. So first, review the facts that you do know from the script: We know I have a mother because she's mentioned. We know one of us is leaving, but the script doesn't say which one. We know we have at least a two-room dwelling because a bedroom is mentioned and we're not in it in this scene.

Just state the bare facts. Don't project anything yet or draw any conclusions.

Exercise: Setting the Scene

Now decide where the scene takes place. Don't try to be clever about this; take whatever occurs to you or seems obvious from the script. It could be a living room, a park, an airline terminal, etc. Then start pushing furniture around to create a set without consulting one another. You're going to discover with the following exercise what this set is.

The instructor begins by asking character A to point to something in the space and tell him what it is. Character A may say "That's a sofa."

He then asks character B to go over to the sofa and as he touches it, to describe it physically. Make sure he makes the dimensions of the sofa clear by the way he touches and handles it. Prompt him for physical information as he describes it: "What's the fabric?" "What does it feel like when you sit on it?" "Does it smell like anything?" Also add embellishments to the sofa that lead to an open-ended question: "There's a stain on the arm. What kind of stain is it?" "Reach under the sofa. What do you find?" "Lift up the cushions. What does the label say?" "There's something you really hate/love about this sofa. What is it?" At this point, keep all responses to these questions in the physical realm. That is, the something he hates is the lump right in the middle of it, or the arm protectors that keep falling off. For this step in the exercise avoid answers like, "The fact that it's from her mom." "The lousy night's sleep that I associate it with after we fight." These are relationship or historical answers, which we're coming up to next.

After character B has described the sofa, return to character A and ask him to tell you an anecdote about the sofa that involves him or his scene partner or both of them. If you're character A, you can tell this anecdote in the four-part story mode if you want. What we're looking for is a detailed description of a story from your past.

When A is done, repeat this exercise three more times. Next time begin with character B and ask him to point to something else in the room, then ask character A to show its dimensions and describe it physically and B to relate an anecdote involving himself, his partner, or both of them. As you do, if you find you need to rearrange the furniture to make it more theatrical (e.g., move the sofa so that it's facing downstage; moving a "refrigerator" because it's blocking the audience's view, etc.), do so.

Once you've done this four times, both actors will have a great visual sense of the room. And if their minds wander while doing the scene, this sense memory can be relied on to help bring them back into this imaginary world.

Equally importantly, it will give them a rich history to fall back on. One that is a unique expression of the two of them. And one that, in the course of inventing, will give them major clues as to their characters, and choices they can expand on with these neutral figures to create with ease something truly original.

Honoring Your Professional Commitment

I began this book with an explanation of the three rules, underscoring the fact that, simple as these rules sound, everything that life has taught you discourages you from following them. We don't want to "Yes! And . . ." a partner's offer, because it means giving up control of the future. And we certainly don't want to say the first thing that comes into our head, because we're afraid that, among other things, we may reveal ourselves.

You will. And here's where the entire class—as professionals who agree to honor the "sacred" space that is this room—must commit themselves to the third rule, making their partners look good.

This exercise is a culmination of everything we've dealt with so far in this course: the spontaneity fostered in decision-making (Say the first thing that comes into your head.); the incorporation of every offer from your partner (Say "Yes! And . . ." to all of your partner's offers.); and, finally, the willingness on each partner's part, as well as the entire class's, to e-duco each participant—to lead them out as they reveal more and more of themselves (Make your partner look good.) It is this last attitude throughout each class, and in this exercise in particular—both on stage and as audience—that defines a sense of professional commitment.

I've taught at a college level for many years. My students are young, and not far from the high school years where *every* moment was a social event. That is, they were and still are acutely sensitive to the opinions of others, both in and out of the exercises. But at the same time, I have also found that they are generous and eager, and simply need to be reminded of this commitment.

For example, in the dialogue below taken from one of my classes, I illustrate the kinds of questions the instructor should use to encourage more and more "motormouth" from the scene partners as they define the set, their relationship, and their history. Now, at one point in this particular class, you'll notice that someone in the audience groaned at something a performer said, something that clearly revealed the performer spontaneously and that I assumed reinforced a poor opinion the audience member had of him.

And the performer flinched.

Catch this when it happens. Remind everyone of their commitment: the performer's commitment to trusting that what they have to say spontaneously is worth saying, *and* the audience's commitment to accept, support, and lead out whatever that performer has to say. I have encouraged you to begin each class with a warm-up that includes this reminder: to let everything go and make the commitment to be here for these people for the length of this class period: that is your job. This final exercise gives you an opportunity to not only experiment with the three rules and status, but also to monitor this sense of commitment and generosity as well. There's nothing wrong with your impulse to censor what another performer may utter spontaneously. You can't help your feelings. However, your job is to catch these impulses during any class-room/rehearsal period of creativity and protect that fellow performer from them.

Note on Setting the Scene

In some neutral scenes, one of the characters may be new to the environment. For instance, he may be visiting someone's apartment for the first time, seeing furniture and props he's never encountered before. As a result, when it's his turn to tell an anecdote about the sofa, he'll have no common history with this sofa. In that case, he can spin off and tell a story that involves the two of them and *any* sofa. If a bar has been described on the set that he has never seen before, he can tell a drinking story about the two of them, etc. It makes no difference if the bar or sofa in his story are on stage or off; they are just offers you make to trigger anecdotes of any kind, giving your actors richer and richer history and background.

Objectives

Now have one of the performers leave the room. Ask the other for an objective for his character so that the class hears it, but the partner doesn't. Then switch. You're going to vary and adjust these objectives each time you do the scene, so for right now don't worry about getting them right.

At the same time, however, choose a powerful objective. Keep in mind that theater is about extraordinary moments in people's lives, not ordinary moments. The purpose of this exercise is to make each of these scenes an epiphany for both characters involved.

But, you may be thinking, these scenes sound so ordinary. Yes, they are, and this is the point of neutral scene work: By using the skills you've developed, allowing yourself to improvise rich histories for these characters, making choices that raise the stakes and looking for moments of status transfer, your job is to make these scenes—and every scene you ever do—as dramatically interesting as possible. In most plays you are both guided and limited by the facts in the play that you can't deny. In these scenes of little information, however, you have the freedom to go anywhere you want.

Finally, have one character leave the playing area to make an entrance (if it's appropriate in the scene that he should), and begin the scene.

In order to make this exercise clear, including the kinds of questions that should be asked and where they should lead, I'm including a transcription of one of our class sessions. Read Scene 1 in Appendix 5: Neutral Scenes that begins "The plane leaves in an hour. . . ."

Example B: The Facts

Me:	What facts do we know from the script?
Character B:	I've called a taxi.
Character A:	And I'm leaving.
Character B:	I have a mom. She speaks Italian and she has a pair of my baby booties.
Character A:	I saw her this morning at church.
Me:	What were you doing there?
Character A:	I was dropping off some albums. There was a Vic Damone album in them and she recognized it.
Character B:	She lights candles for me at church.
Character A:	We slept in the same bed last night.
Me:	What else do we know about your space?
Character B:	It has at least two rooms because we talk about a bedroom. The bedroom has shelves, which are now empty and there used to be some macramé hanging in it that's hers.
Me:	Are we in the apartment now?
Character A:	Not necessarily. I mean, we could be in a park since there's nothing in the script that identifies where we are.
Character B:	When she asked me what was up last night, I ignored her.

Continue doing this with every scene until you've sifted out all the facts, i.e., information in the script that you can't contradict. Make sure at the same time that you're not projecting new facts that aren't given.

Example: Creating Character, History, and Environment

Now that the facts are defined, we start creating character and history as we describe the environment.

Me:	Where does this scene take place? Make an obvious choice—you can't get it wrong.
Character A:	Our apartment.
Me:	Good. (*to Character B*) Point to something in this apartment and tell me what it is.
Character B:	(*pointing to a chair*) That's a recliner.
Me:	(*switching to Character A*) Go over and touch the recliner showing us how big it is and describe to me.
Character A:	(*shows with her hands the dimensions of the recliner*) It's this big and it's made of corduroy.
Me:	What color is it?
Character A:	Brown.
Me:	There's a stain right here. What color is the stain?
Character A:	Purple.
Me:	Lift up the cushion. What do you find?
Character A:	Coins.
Me:	How many coins?
Character A:	Four.
Me:	What are they?
Character A:	Two pennies, a dime, and a nickel.
Me:	On the back of the recliner here there's a label. What does it say?
Character A:	Barcalounger.
Me:	Good. Underneath the footrest that flips up there's something on the floor. What is it?

Character A:	A dog chewy.
Me:	A dog chewy! Good, good, good. Is it, like, a fresh dog chewy?
Character A:	It's chewed a little.
Me:	It's chewed a little. So I'm assuming we've got a dog someplace in the play. Okay. Great! (*switching to Character B*) Okay, now tell me an anecdote about the recliner that involves you or her or both of you.
Character B:	Um . . . I gave it to her for her birthday because she complained how she was never comfortable sitting in the living room. And we got in a big fight because I told her I bought it at Art Van, and I actually bought it at a garage sale.
Me:	And "Art Van" is what?
Character B:	It's a Midwest thing . . . a furniture store . . .
Me:	Good. So you led her to believe that it was bought at furniture store. And she was pissed off.
Character B:	Well, she found out later when she found that there were coins and stuff already under the cushion. And it smelled kind of bad too. Even though I'd Febreze'd the hell out of it.
Me:	Sure, sure, sure. Why did this make her angry?
Character B:	Well, because I told her that I had bought something really nice from Art Van, so she was expecting something really nice. And when she got this she said, "Okay, well, it's not that bad," but then she flipped over the cushions and found that I'd lied to her, so . . . but we kept it anyhow.
Me:	So it was a breach of trust?
Character B:	Yeah.
Me:	That was a big issue . . . that you'd lied? Is there a history of this?
Character B:	Yeah. I'm a jerk and when I get into a tight corner, I make something up. I think it's funny and no big deal, but it means a hell of a lot to her.
Me:	Has she ever done the same thing to you?
Character B:	Yeah. She cheated on me once . . .

Me: With . . .

Character B: Some guy . . .

Me: Raise the stakes. Make it more important.

Character B: My dad.

Me: Wow! What's his name?

Character B: Dad. Bill.

Me: How did you feel about that?

Character B: She said fucking behind my back and lying about it was the same as me lying to her. And now I know how she feels.

Me: How did you feel?

Character B: I hit her.

Me: Have you hit her before?

Character B: Yeah. A lot. But only recently.

Me: Good. (*switching to Character A*) Point to something else and tell me what it is.

Character A: (*pointing to a box on stage*) A TV.

Me: Okay, come over here and point to it specifically because we don't know where it is. Good. (*switching to Character B*) Come over here and touch the TV and describe it to me.

Character B: It's a top-of-the-line RCA. It's pretty small. It's color. We have cable but we only get, like, four channels because we never pay our bills on time.

Me: Good, good.

Character B: It's got wood on the top. It's got a black frame. It's got bunny ears, here. And it's not plugged in.

Me: Is it actually this big?

Character B: Yeah.

Me: What's it doing on the floor?

Character B: Uh, we never could afford a coffee table.

Me: Good. So you guys don't have much money.

Character B: No. We go to garage sales to buy recliners and stuff.

Me: (*switching to Character A*) Tell me an anecdote about the TV that involves you or him or both of you.

Character A:	We've been wanting to get a TV but we couldn't afford it; we were going to wait until he'd saved up enough money. So then one day when I got home from work it was there. And I found out that his mom had bought it for us.
Me:	The Italian mother.
Character A:	Yeah. And I wasn't particularly happy because I wanted us to get it ourselves.
Me:	Okay. So, what's your relationship with his mother?
Character A:	She's an evil woman.
Me:	Good, good. What has she done besides this that makes her an evil woman? Keep going.
Character A:	She thinks that he's her little boy and doesn't want him to find another woman. She's the only woman in his life.
Me:	That's right. So you're not good enough for her son. Tell me specifically one thing she did that was just horrible to you.
Character A:	I don't know . . .
Me:	Yes you do! You can say anything at all! Look at the floor. What do you see?
Character A:	Lint?
Me:	Good! So tell me about the lint thing, the lint episode.
Character A:	She comes over and cleans.
Me:	Yes!
Character A:	She says that I don't keep a tidy enough house.
Me:	That's right! And how does she say that? Do her voice for us? When she's yelling at you?
Character A:	(*in a wonderful, bad Italian accent*) American women!
Me:	Excellent! Go! This is the imitation you do for him that pisses him off.
Character A:	You're not good enough for my son! I wish he had never met you!
Me:	Good! And what do you do when she does this?
Character A:	I cry.
Me:	. . . and . . .

Character A: I run into the bedroom and slam the door.

Me: . . . and . . .

Character A: I make something out of macramé.

Me: Good. (*switching to Character B*) Point to something else in this space and tell me what it is.

Character B: Okay . . . I'm seeing a shelf of, like, random knick-knacks.

Me: (*switching to Character A*) Okay, go over there and touch the shelf and describe it to me physically. You can describe the knick-knacks, too.

Character A: It's a long wooden shelf against the wall. There's a piggy bank that I had from when I was a little kid.

Me: (*pointing to a random area on the shelf*) And what's this right here?

Character A: A clock. It's silver and little and it belongs to him.

Me: And there are pictures up there. Point to two of them and tell me what they are.

Character A: That's the two of us when we went on vacation to Atlantic City.

Me: What's the background? Be obvious.

Character A: The beach.

Me: And what are you wearing?

Character A: Bathing suits.

Me: And what are you doing in the picture.

Character A: Holding some beers.

Me: Point to the other picture and tell me what it is.

Character A: That's him and his mother.

Me: Yes! And what's in the background? Where was this picture taken? Be obvious.

Character A: In her backyard.

Me: And what's the backyard like there?

Character A: It has statues of St. Anthony.

Me: More than one! Plural? Statues of St. Anthony. Good! Bingo! And what are they doing in the picture?

Character A: Praying!

Me:	Yes! Yes! How are they praying? Look at the picture and tell me.
Character A:	They're kneeling on the grass.
Me:	And who took the picture?
Character A:	Me.
Me:	Yes! (*switching to Character B*) Tell me an anecdote about this shelf. You can choose anything you want there and tell me a story that involves you, her, or both of you.
Character B:	There's a . . . well, because we don't clean too much there's a couple of empty cans of beer up there. We just kind of tossed them up there and forgot they were there. And that shelf just kind of became less of a place to store valuable things and more of a storage space.
Me:	Good. Tell me about the piggy bank, the silver clock, or one of the two pictures.
Character B:	Well, the picture of us praying—mom and I are both real big on our heritage. And she's from Sicily and so we're real big with our religion. So whenever we go over to the house my mother always insists that we take some kind of picture praying in different places and different conditions. We went to Disneyland and she insisted that we get down in front of Mickey and pray. And we did the same thing at Vegas. So, she's always the one that takes the pictures. And mom won't take them unless she's there to take them. She won't let anybody else take the pictures.
Me:	Okay. Are there any pictures of her (*pointing to Character A*) praying at all?
Character B:	None.
Me:	What's your last name?
Character B:	Corleone.
Me:	That's right. You're Corleone. Good, good, good. How did you feel about the *Godfather* movies?
Character B:	Oh, I love them. But my mother thinks they're the devil.
Me:	I mean there he is with the same last name as you.

Character B: You know a lot of people thought that was based on the actual Corleone family and I said "No! It's fake!"

Me: And then what would you do.

Character B: Punch them out.

Me: So it sounds like you are, or you've recently become, an extremely violent guy with a short fuse.

Character B: Yeah.

At this point, someone in the class groaned, and I could see the performer wince. I immediately jumped in and congratulated him for revealing something spontaneous that could cause this kind of visceral reaction from an audience. It's what they come to the theater for. Then I asked the audience member why she'd groaned. She said the actor's name and shook her head, implying her disapproval of him and this kind of violence. I pointed out to her that I felt the same way about violence, but that it's this kind of inappropriate *expression* of that feeling from the audience that can shut down a performer, reducing classes and rehearsals to social events.

Again, the instructor should catch these reactions and, without shaming the audience member, remind everyone of their commitment. As performers, we are all capable of a wide range of human behavior—from the pleasant to the abominable. Audiences turn to us to see this reflected. And in order to do our job, we need the freedom to uncover those aspects within ourselves without fear of peer censorship.

Finishing the Exercise

We did a final round of this exercise, this time with Character A pointing out a window, B describing it and the view, and A telling an anecdote.

Then I had Character A leave the room and asked Character B for his opening objective. His choice was, "To cold-shoulder her out of the apartment and my life." He then stepped outside, Character A returned and her objective, she decided, was, "To get the stupid idiot to admit that I'm the woman who made his life begin." Keep in mind that these are opening objectives. They don't have to be maintained throughout the scene and can be altered at any moment.

Then Character A stepped outside to begin the scene. Character B sat down and began watching TV with the remote. I said, "Curtain going up. Lights!" and the scene began.

Incorporating the Three Rules

A communal endeavor like scene work—and all rehearsals—works most successfully when everyone involved is playing by the three rules. As you work on these neutral scenes, choose an objective, and then, based on your partner's reactions at that moment, improvise a tactic (*Say the first thing that comes into your head*) When your partner reacts, no matter how unexpectedly, "Yes! And . . ." his offer. And when the scene is over, however it went, process the event with mutual support (*Make your partner look good*).

To practice this mutual support and cooperation, do the scene several times, each time with a new approach (as I'll describe below) that you haven't discussed with your partner. The goal is to surprise each other and then, with your objectives in mind, to react honestly to what you're given.

Again, each of you should leave the room while the other discusses the new approach with the instructor so that the rest of the class can hear. These discussions can and should be brief, two minutes at the most. They're not meant to be in-depth scene analyses, but playful attempts to make the scenes more interesting both dramatically and theatrically.

By dramatically I mean: How can you make this day different than any other day in the lives of these two people? And more than just different—how can you make them extraordinary, an epiphany in these characters' lives? The instructor should ask each character how he or she could raise the stakes. For Character A in the above scene: "I'm pregnant and I haven't told him." "To prepare myself for leaving, I've been sleeping around. But it's never, never any good because I can't get him out of my head and I *hate* him for it." Character B: "She was the first person I've ever had sex with and she doesn't know. It blew me away the first time—it always does—and it validates me every time we do it. And I'm afraid that if she leaves, my mother will inhale me once again." "Anticipating her leaving has been so depressing that for the last week when she's not around I've been putting this loaded revolver (opens a drawer) into my mouth."

In a real production, the audience never has to know these things. What we're doing here is fueling the scenes—making them dramatically more interesting.

And theatrically more interesting as well. By that I mean, as you make riskier character choices, make a few decisions about the staging and presentation as well that underscore what's happening and help communicate your dramatic choices as efficiently as possible. The instructor as an outside eye, as a director, should give input here. If there's an imaginary full-length mirror on stage, for example, you may want to move it to the downstage wall so that the audience can see the character full front when she's looking at herself. In the middle of the scene there may be a moment where it felt appropriate for one character to simply walk out of the room, and then re-enter, slamming the door against the wall. One character may be doing something the other doesn't notice and a pause here may be appropriate so the audience can take it in. Don't be too heavy handed with this kind of staging. But if something seems obviously appropriate to make the presentation of the scene more successful theatrically, do it.

Here are some examples of how we investigated raising the stakes in the above scene using the status work we'd learned earlier in the class.

The next time we did the above scene in our class, we had Character A enter low status, shrinking from space and maintaining that posture throughout. Character B began high and also maintained that status throughout. The next time through, we switched: Character A entered high and Character B remained low. And, finally, I asked Character A to begin low, Character B to begin high, and to look for an opportunity to do a status transfer. As it worked out, when Character A in her low-status posture suddenly said, "Shut up. You're leaving. Fuck Italy!," she turned on B like a buzz saw, raising her status dramatically. B suddenly collapsed and ended up with his head in her lap. And when the scene was over and he was looking up at her, she simply rose and walked out on him.

Keep in mind, you're not trying to get this scene "right." You're being playful. Make a game out of it, enjoy yourselves. Encourage each other as you invent new approaches. You are creating events that are unique expressions of the two of you, and ultimately a scene that galvanizes the entire room for the moment and is bigger than both of you.

Conclusion

Throughout this course, it has been the instructor's job to support and encourage each participant's development. Everything in life tells you not to follow these three rules, yet audiences will flock to watch you play by them. The instructor's role has been to keep you on course as you've struggled to incorporate these rules in your work. And he or she does this by gentle and positive affirmation and, with side-coaching, by prompting you through a successful execution of each exercise.

However, as I mentioned before, once you leave the classroom, you will be continually thrown into professional situations with people who don't work the same way you do. And there will be no instructor. Your job is to incorporate these three rules and the same kind of gentle, positive affirmation into the moment-to-moment choices both you and your partner make in every "sacred" space in which you find yourself, be it rehearsal or performance.

Everyone is a critic, from the fellow student who groans in class at choices you make to the people who write about you and are printed in newspapers. And over and over again, this criticism can reinforce the messages: guard what you say, stay in control, and don't trust people—each message a denial of the three rules.

But if you choose a career in a communal art form such as theater, the three-way combination of personal courage, acceptance, and generosity embodied in these rules will help you to assert the best of yourself. In his book *Impro: Improvisation and the Theatre*, Keith Johnstone points out that despite the fairly universal education available in most modern cities, there is a far lower percentage of the kind of creative geniuses that seemed to flourish in Elizabethan London. Contemporary society, education, advertising, etc., tend to reward us for our level of conformity: to be "as smart as" or "as cool as." We realize ourselves—they imply—by joining the crowd.

Releasing yourself from these restraints is a daily commitment. And this commitment is the heart of these three rules as you continue to uncover both you and your partner and share the unique voice in the arts that you already are.

Part III
Appendixes

[1] Warm-up Games

As I explain in Class 2, the purpose of any opening warm-up game is to be silly and have fun in the process. A class in improvisation is high risk for a lot of people. The purpose of being silly and having fun is to make sure that everyone "loses face" and lowers his status so that no individual is perceived by the others as "cooler" than they or detached; in short, a possible threat or critic.

It's also important that everyone focus on the game to make it work. As in all communal art forms, you must bond as a group in mutual cooperation as best you can before you can create communally.

In the class descriptions I've suggested when to introduce each of the games below. But feel free to introduce these games whenever you like. "Whoosh!" is a great game for beginning improvisers and can be played for several classes as you add the variations described below. But as soon as a class gets either bored with a game or so highly skilled that they're no longer screwing it up, introduce a new one.

Remember, the purpose of these games is to excite the class, get them working as much as possible as a group. There should always be a risk of failure in all these games. That is "the moment of theater," when we see someone in trouble, risking failure, and yet they choose to move forward and solve it. One of the purposes of this course is to get students comfortable with being uncomfortable. Doing so, facing these new risks and stepping forward, should excite them, just as it excites an audience to watch them. So, again, when a game gets too easy, introduce a new one.

Variations on the Basic, Physical Warm-up

During the physical warm-up I've described in chapter 2 I've suggested introducing yourself to your partners on your right and left while making faces. Here are some alternatives to be substituted whenever you're "comfortable" with the current warm-up:

- Introduce yourself to your partner on your right and left as if you had speech impediments.
- Later in the course when you're comfortable with each other, ask your partners on your right and left for permission to rub your butts together. Give permission, do it, then face each other again, put your hands on each other's shoulders and say, "Thank you!"

"Whoosh!"

See Class 2 for the description of this game. The following are additional moves. Remember, this game should go as fast as possible, and everyone should get slightly ahead of himself and a little "out of control."

- "Groovalicious!" When it's your turn, yell out "Groovalicious!" Everyone repeats, "Groovalicious!" and dances like they're cool and groovy until the caller resumes the game with "Whoosh!" or "Zap!" or another "Groovalicious!"
- "Freak out!" Yell "Freak out!" Everyone screams, waves their arms in the air, and changes places in the circle as fast as they can. Caller then resumes by yelling "Whoosh!" or "Zap!," etc.
- Caller assigns a task to three people standing next to each other. This can be anything: "Sing opera in gibberish." Ask

three guys to act like girls; ask three girls to act like guys. "Find out who farted." "Worship Linda." "Speak Swedish." If somebody completely screws up in the game (great!), later you might have three people imitate him screwing up. This should last no longer than five seconds. Caller then resumes game. It's important that you ask three people to do this because there's safety in numbers—asking just one to do this is potentially embarrassing.

Blind Offers

This is a great game to substitute for "Whoosh!" It can also be used in the Physical Warm-up in place of introducing yourselves and making faces.

The leader pairs everyone up. If there's an odd number, he can participate. All together, each member of the pair takes a turn putting out his hands to the other and says enthusiastically, "This is for *you*!" The receiver immediately identifies the "gift," saying the first thing that comes into his head. "Oh! It's a dog! And *this* is for you!" extending his arms and offering a blind gift in return. Again, like all responses in this class, this is not about saying something clever. It should go so fast that there's no time to think, and I highly recommend glancing at your partner or around the room to get an idea for the gift you're receiving. "Oh! It's an eyeball!" "Oh! It's a light switch!" What's important here is a *rapid* response and *enthusiasm*.

Later, as you get better at this game, once you've identified the gift, use it physically and say one sentence about it. "Oh! It's a dog! (*Walk the dog.*) Now I have a friend!" "Oh! It's an eyeball. (*Eat it.*) Now I'm not hungry!" You can use it the "correct" way . . . "Oh! It's a comb! Now I can fix my hair." Or any way that comes to you without thinking. "Oh! It's a comb! (*Fling it.*) Now I have something to throw out the window." Finally, feel free to repeat anything if that's the first thing that comes into your head. If you've accepted a dog, you can receive a gift and say, "Oh, wow! Another dog!" Just do it fast, without thinking. It's an exercise both in saying the first thing that comes into your head and in making your partner's offer look good.

Kitty Wants a Corner

- Class stands in a circle, spreading out as far as the room allows.
- Whoever is "it" steps into the circle, approaches someone, and says "Kitty wants a corner." That persons responds, "See my neighbor." The person who's "it" then moves to the next person, left or right, and repeats the question, gets the response, and continues to move around the circle, changing direction at will.
- Meanwhile, everyone else in the circle should be looking around, and if they make eye contact with someone and they both nod, they should race across the circle and change places as fast as they can.
- However, if the Kitty sees an empty space and jumps into it before one of the pair gets there, that person whose place has been taken is the new Kitty.
- Emphasize that being the Kitty isn't a *bad thing.* You are a community making a game. Running across the circle makes the game work by taking risks; being the Kitty makes the game work by raising the stakes.

Poison Peepers

- Stand in a circle with your head lowered.
- The leader, also with his head lowered, says, "One, two, three . . . look!"
- Everyone snaps his head up and looks directly at someone else.
- If the person you're looking at is looking at you, you both scream.
- If there's a scream, everyone drops his head again and the leader repeats, "One, two, three . . . look!"
- This goes on until no one screams—that is, until everyone is looking at someone who is looking at someone else.
- At this point, everyone should think of the first word that comes into his or her head. When you have it, raise your hand. When all hands are up, drop them in the order they were raised and announce your word as if you're in a Greek theater, projecting to the back row, creating a fake "Haiku" poem.
- When all words are announced, everyone should nod their heads very seriously and say, "Oh . . . wow!"
- Repeat.

Bunny

- Stand in a circle.
- The leader puts his hands to the sides of his head, palms forward, and waggles them like ears, saying "Bunny, bunny, bunny . . ."
- At the same time, the person to his right leans into him, places his right hand to the right side of his own head, and waggles it, also saying, "Bunny, bunny, bunny. . . ." The person on his left side does likewise, waggling his left hand.
- When all three are coordinated, the leader flings his hands forward, throwing the "bunny" to someone across the circle, shouting, "BUNNY!"
- That person then becomes the center of the new trio and the people flanking him have to adjust accordingly as quickly as possible, right person leaning in and waggling right hand, echoing "Bunny, bunny, bunny . . .," left person doing same.
- Toss the "bunny" around the circle as fast as you can.

Sound Ball

- Stand in a circle.
- The leader takes an imaginary ball and flings it to someone across the circle making a noise: "Whack!" "Blagga, blagga, blagga." "WooOOOoooOOOooo!"—anything that immediately comes out of his mouth. Don't use actual English words, and make sure it's crystal clear who you're throwing it to.
- The receiver catches this imaginary ball making the same sound as the thrower (or as close an approximation as he can). Then he immediately flings the ball to someone else, making a new noise. Don't think about it; open your mouth and make the first noise that comes into your head. The receiver imitates that noise as he receives the ball, etc.
- Do this as fast as you can.

Variations on Sound Ball

1. Add a second, and then a third, sound ball, all tossed simultaneously. Just like Slap Pass it's the thrower's job to make sure his ball is received successfully. If his partner doesn't see him throw

it, he must continue to throw and make the noise over and over until his partner does.

2. When you receive the sound ball, spin 360 degrees before throwing it.

3. After receiving the ball, throw it with a different body part. Throw it with your head, your feet, your butt, etc. Whoever receives it must use the same body part.

4. This is one of my favorites, which you can introduce after everyone's been playing Sound Ball for a while. Three people in unison must throw the sound ball, making an identical noise and using the same body part without discussing it ahead of time. Any number of people on the other side of the circle can receive it, again making the same noise and using the same body part as the throwers. Then, without discussion, they must wind up a different body part and throw the ball with it, making an identical sound. It will take a couple of seconds to coordinate.

Wrong Names

Everyone walks around the room at the same time, pointing emphatically at things and shouting out their wrong names. For example, point to a chair and shout, "Dog!" Point to a fire extinguisher and shout, "Mom!" Do this for about 30 seconds.

"I Am Superman/Superwoman!"

Stand in a circle. One by one, at random, every one takes a turn jumping into the middle of the circle and shouting, "I am Superman (Superwoman) because . . . !" and fills in the blank. Everyone else jumps up and down and cheers. Each person makes three successive announcements like this before leaving the center of the circle. "I am Superman because I got my paper done last night!" Cheers! "I am Superman because I didn't want to jump into the middle of this circle and I just did!" Cheers! "I am Superman because I can waggle my head like this!" Cheers!

Appendix

[2] Lists for Jump-Starting Games

Below are two lists of suggestions for beginning exercises.

The first is a list of fields of expertise to use in the "I Love You" Scenes with Expertise (Class 4). The second is a list of assignments for the King Game (Class 9).

The class instructor is certainly welcome to invent his own suggestions. But I strongly recommend that the suggestions for these games should never come from the students. This can quickly reduce itself to a cleverness competition, as they invent wilder and wilder suggestions, putting their partners on the spot, and then sit back and leave them to struggle. This is an element of gag improv and contrary to the spirit of *Make Your Partner Look Good*.

Students may argue that coming up with suggestions is just innocent fun. But watch closely: as this kind of competition develops, you will see those who aren't involved visibly shrinking.

Something should already be clear when you've finished playing the earlier Expert's Game: it isn't the cleverness of the suggestion that makes the scene funny. It's the character's *passionate commitment* to the suggestion, *whatever* it is, that makes us laugh. In short, the humor is character humor, not joke humor. In fact, I think you'll find that an extremely clever suggestion often works against a scene. If the suggestions are terribly funny, the scene is often an exercise in performers trying to match the humorous suggestion.

"I Love You" Scenes with Expertise Suggestions

Sticking your tongue in electrical outlets
Kissing bricks
Singing through your nose
Smacking old ladies
Teaching penguins to dance
Throwing cats
Stomping on soup cans
Burping in libraries
Tipping cows over
Spitting on cars
Licking lamb chops
Making faces at children
Eating Vaseline
Tying up grandmothers
Sucking light bulbs
Pinching nuns
Gargling with Lysol
Painting dead bodies
Tossing puppies over waterfalls
Sticking cigars in your ear
Dancing down the aisle in church
Kicking fire hydrants
Repairing nose jobs
Teaching watermelons how to surf
Eating bugs
Slaughtering dogs
Tickling zebras
Singing Swedish opera
Greasing peas
Teaching plastic gloves how to whistle
Eating Nerf balls
Sleeping with mice
Slapping immigrants
Singing with your mouth full

Using your mom as a punching bag
Heating golf balls
Using pianos as mouthwash
Shooting cats with erasers
Climbing walls upside down
Smacking your lips
Playing violin with a cobra
Teaching small children to poke elephants
Grinding old cars into paste
Hanging from your feet over Christians
Opening beer bottles with babies
Coating old women with plastic
Combing your hair with dirt
Teaching dead monkeys to fly
Performing surgery on dust balls
Shaving with a chain saw
Swimming in Jell-O
Flapping your arms like a chicken
Farting
Crawling into classrooms on your belly
Playing the tuba with your nose
Kissing fire hydrants
Throwing toddlers in the lake
Smelling cheese
Burning fish
Playing the cello under water
Spraying people with Jell-O
Drinking nasal spray

King Game Assignments

Teach the king how to summersault
Examine the king's throat
Teach the king to dance
Teach the king to fly
Teach the king to whistle
Wash the king's hair
Read the king's palm
Aerobics instructor

Hairdresser
Voice coach
Massage the king
Measure for clothes
Meditation instructor
Guitar instructor
Manicure
Apply toenail polish
Clean the throne
Serve tea
Feed the king
Apply makeup on the king
Dentist
Eye doctor
Paint king's picture
Take king's photograph
Seduce the king
Change the king's clothes
Peel a banana for the king

Appendix

[3] Grades

It's very difficult to assign grades to a class in the arts. For example, the student may in fact be making remarkable progress in his own growth, but that progress may seem small in comparison to others to whom improvisation comes easily; and he may be graded accordingly. For some students, simply showing up for a class they perceive as high risk takes remarkable commitment, the kind of courage and determination that makes a successful artist; but this, too, may not be perceived by an instructor. In addition, this is a class that promotes risking failure, which is intimidating enough. To hang a letter grade over the students' heads makes potential failure even more daunting.

However, a school's credibility and its financial health—in short, it's existence—depends on standards and grades. And while a good grade won't get you a part in a play, it can do two things: If you have a scholarship, it will help you maintain it. And if you like to act and teach like I do, thanks to your degree, people will pay you to do both.

If you're a teacher and you feel the same difficulty with grades that I do, I suggest this policy. It's one that I feel is fair to students and respectful of an institution's need for standards.

I feel that grades in this course should *not* be a reflection of talent. I feel my students are all talented, if for no other reason than they've been accepted into this course. Anyone of them could take their talent and start a career. I assume that they've chosen instead to come here to *improve* that talent. And to improve their sense of professional discipline. No one wants to work with an undisciplined actor; they don't pay you enough.

So grades can be figured in the following manner as a reflection of this desire for improvement and self-discipline:

Everyone starts with an A (100 percent). In the twenty-eight-class course I teach, for every absence, I take off two grade points (from 100% to 98%). For every tardy up to twenty minutes, I take off one grade point. (You can adjust this deduction and what constitutes being "late" to fit your class.)

If there are assignments, they are all pass/fail. Assignments can include writing papers on the class or selected reading material; memorizing lines for a line run by a certain date for neutral scenes; showing up for class on days their scene is due. If they pass, their grades remain unaltered. If they fail, points are deducted. The amount is established when the assignment is given. For instance, if a paper isn't turned in, I'll deduct six points; if lines aren't memorized for a line run, I'll deduct two grade points, etc. And if a student fails to show up for a scene, leaving his partner in the lurch—which I consider pretty unforgivable—I'll deduct as many as ten points.

And I make it clear that there is no way to raise grades in this class. This is a class about doing the work and getting it into your bodies. You have to be present in class to do that. Coming to an acting teacher and saying, "I missed class. Can I do a paper?" is no different as far as I'm concerned, than going to a director and saying, "I missed rehearsal. Can I do a paper?"

What I like about this policy is that the grade is entirely in the student's hands. I make it very clear right from the start that they can do terrible work in the class and it will not affect their grades. They can see other students doing "better" work, and if they wonder if those students will get better grades, the answer is no. They can even dislike me and the course and it will not affect their grade. This takes the onus of making grading judgments off of me as well as taking the pressure of doing "good" improv off the students.

And what I've found at the end of the course is that the grades that students end up with are in fact pretty much what I would have given them if I'd had to make one up. With this method, however, there is no argument. If a student doesn't like his grade, you can point to the attendance sheet.

This is more than just making it easy for the teacher, by the way, and I hope that's understood. The purpose is to take the pressure of grades off of the students while they're taking the kind of creative risks, failing and succeeding, that a course in improvisation demands.

Appendix

[4] Side-Coaching

This chapter is for the instructor.

As I was preparing to write this book, I recorded an entire semester of classes to use as a reference. I've always been aware that I do a certain amount of side-coaching during scenes. And as I've listened to these tapes, the importance of side-coaching has been reinforced.

Certainly one of the skills required to teach this or any course that encourages taking risks and breaking barriers is the ability to create a sense of safety. Throughout the course I've mentioned dealing with safety issues: getting the class to agree to let everything that happens in the class remain in the class; checking in with students after particularly exaggerated exercises to make sure that they're OK and not shutting down. In the "Whoosh!" game, for example, if you assign someone to act like a monkey or sing opera in gibberish, have three people do it together. Don't ever make someone do it alone. Your role is one of pleasant, compassionate high status.

A lot of the exercises in this course have rules, some more complicated than others. And as I mention in the introduction, I have deliberately limited the number of games in the course, choosing games as much as possible that build on the rules and skills developed in previous games, so that students don't spend their performance time in their heads trying to remember everything. This course is about trying to get them *out* of their heads.

This is where side-coaching comes in. Like the Interviewer in the Expert's Game, your job is to both urge them on to take greater and greater risks and to gently nudge them along the path of the game's intentions by reminding them from "off stage" what to do, to correct them if they get off course.

If you've never side-coached before, it's fairly simple. Here are some suggestions to help you get started.

How to Side-Coach

It's easy to get caught up in how entertaining a scene is, particularly when students are on a roll. But new improvisers tend to gravitate toward the easy laugh, and they feel validated in this choice if the instructor simply joins in the hilarity, singling out particularly funny lines afterward. Gradually, "make the teacher laugh" becomes the focus of the class, students begin to compete to do so, and you're into gag improv. Again, the skills strengthened in gag improv, which include competition, focusing on the audience, etc., don't translate readily into scripted theater.

Narrative improv skills do, however: cooperation; passionate attachment to your objective; staying in the moment by "Yes! And . . ."-ing your partner's offers, however unexpected they may be. And as instructor, it's important to stay slightly objective about what's going on, side-coaching on the fly to keep the exercise on track.

If you're new to side-coaching, there are two criteria when it's appropriate, which I think are fairly easy to keep in mind.

First, of course: are the performers following the rules of this particular exercise? If the scene is about a status transfer, for example, and one student is clearly raising his status, is the other lowering it accordingly? If not, urging "Bill, go down" is often all he needs to hear. And if he's clearly trying to go down but not succeeding, simply remind him of the tactics that he's already familiar with from the previous class work: "Bill, start crying." "Beg for forgiveness." "Crawl on the floor." Name the student's name when you're coaching so that another participant doesn't think the coaching's for him.

The second criteria is very simple and may sound like a contradiction of what I've said above: Is the narrative story they're

unfolding entertaining you? This is different than just being enter-
tained. The focus here is on the narrative aspects of the exercise.
Are the performers telling a good story? Gags, jokes, partner put-
downs can all get laughs and are entertaining in the moment, but
they stop the through-line of a good narrative story, one with a
plot, suspense, sudden twists—in short, characters who are in trouble, advancing into an unknown future and working it through.
Are you personally excited by the story unfolding before you? Are
you held in suspense, concerned about the outcome? Do you *care*
about the lovers falling in love? Are you laughing because Bill's
always such a funny guy and knows it (gag improv)—or because
his character is so absurd in his serious passion about pancakes
that his outrageousness and the turmoil this puts his new wife in
are what's making you laugh? (narrative improv). A good rule of
thumb: Would the performers feel rewarded by laughter—a sign of
gag improv—or would their characters be annoyed because they
take their passion seriously?

As you side-coach, your voice should be just loud enough to
be heard. Imagine you're sitting on the performer's shoulder
planting these thoughts in his ear. Your tone of voice should be
pleasant and encouraging; be very careful of using a tone that
sounds in any way shaming or corrective. Imply by your tone that
you're a best friend with the performer's best interests in mind,
and you want to see him do his best. If you don't know how to do
this, simply smile when you side-coach. It pretty much guarantees
the right tone of voice. Try it.

Side-coaching is particularly important early in the course; for
example, during the Gift-Giving game and the Expert's Game.
Every time an expert "Yes! And . . ."-s a question, every time an
interviewer bases a question on something the expert is wearing
or doing rather than going into his head for inspiration, every
time the expert answers with enthusiasm before he has any
idea what he's going to say, muttering "Good!" is like a pat on
the back in the middle of their confusion. It congratulates the performer for his choices, encourages him, and tells him he's on the
right path.

And when a he's on a roll and way ahead of himself, shouting
"Go! Go!" is often just the kind of validation he needs as he finds
himself in new places, flailing for a handhold and not knowing if
he's doing the right thing. You are parenting at this point, just as

a child looks at a parent when it falls, to see if it should laugh or cry. As you keep the game's intentions in mind, this kind of compassionate enthusiasm is often exactly what he needs to expand into new and appropriate territory. Later, I've found that he'll discover that in fact he's just walked into the something that is more his true self than anything he's been acculturated into believing. You are giving him permission to go there.

Appendix

[5] Neutral Scenes

Below is a collection of Neutral Scenes to use in the last chapter on scene work.

There is some discussion as to what actually constitutes a "neutral scene" in an acting class, some people feeling that the dialogue should be completely devoid of content. The scenes below, on the other hand, do imply a minimum of historical background. Whatever your understanding, the information has been deliberately included in these scenes to trigger the kind of discussion described in the chapter.

Scene 1

A: The plane leaves in an hour.
B: I've called a taxi.
A: Will you miss me?
B: Will you?
A: Not especially.
B: (shrugs)
A: It's your fault.
B: Here we go!

A: I'll stop.

B: Damn straight.

A: I saw your mom this morning. I stopped by the church to drop off your records. She was kneeling down praying . . .

B: . . . lighting candles for me . . .

A: . . . holding a pair of baby booties.

B: Oh, my god.

A: I told her we were doing fine but she recognized her old Vic Damone album and started crying. She called me a lot of things in Italian. And you know, I just stood there and took it. I stood there holding your albums while she flailed your baby booties at me yelling at me in some third-world language . . .

B: Italy isn't . . .

A: Shut up. You're leaving. Fuck Italy!

B: I love you. I love you so much. I woke up next to you last night, looked at you and I was so happy I started crying. I couldn't remember why the bedroom shelves were empty, but I laughed when I saw your macramé was gone.

A: I started laughing too.

B: And then I remembered why.

A: And I asked you what was up.

B: I ignored you.

Scene 2

A: It's only me.

B: Hi.

A: I brought you something.

B: What.

A: Here. Open it.

B: Oh, my god.

A: Do you like it?

B: What do you think?

A: I've been thinking about you a lot lately. Obviously. I saw this and thought, "Yep, this is it. This is just perfect."

B: I have something to tell you.

A: You're leaving.

B: Uh huh. When I opened this I thought . . . Well, never mind. Um. Can I make a suggestion?

A: What?

B: Stop that. Stop it now. If you know what's best for you, you'll stop that. Please. Please.

A: I have something to tell you. I've been waiting to do this for a long time. You probably didn't think I was capable of it, or, if you did, you didn't think I'd ever have the nerve to say it.

B: It won't make any difference.

A: I love you.

B: You're one of the best friends I've ever had.

A: Good bye.

B: Good bye.

Scene 3

A: Wow! What a place!

B: Yeah . . . well, it's . . . yeah.

A: You've done well!

B: Yeah. Surprise, surprise.

A: And you look . . . amazing!

B: You really hate this, don't you?

A: What?

B: Sit down. I'll get you something.

A: What do you mean, "I hate this"?

B: How have you been?

A: The same. Worse. Look at me.

B: Look at you.

A: This is all happening so fast. Wow. What is this?

B: Look on the bottom.

A: I gave you this.

B: Take it.

A: Oh, god . . . It's been . . .

B: Take it. Shut up and take it. I was doing fine. For five years I've lived alone, not terribly happy but getting on. Then this morning my coffeemaker broke. I went to the mini-storage to get my old one . . . thrifty me . . . and found that. Fuck. I love you. I always have. There.

I'm clear. Take it and get out. Maintenance is arriving in fifteen minutes to fix my sink.

A: Shut up. Shut up. I'm married. I don't want this. I was so happy to get your call that I left my suburban dump this morning and petted three dogs on the way here. Your doorman was rude and it made no difference. I knew it wasn't you. I love you. Too.

B: Now what.

A: This coffee sucks.

Scene 4

A: Hi.

B: Thanks for coming over.

A: Uh . . .

B: What?

A: I've never been in love before.

B: Are you now?

A: Yes.

B: How do you know?

A: I can't explain it . . .

B: Oh.

A: Can you?

B: Explain about being in love?

A: Yes.

B: Yeah, I guess.

A: Heh heh heh.

B: Love songs suddenly make sense. You hear one, and it's like running into a brick wall that you didn't see was in front of you.

A: I feel like I'm treading water.

B: Like I'm treading air. I've got to get this done.

A: Are you in love with somebody?

B: [Robert/Jill]'s coming over tomorrow and I've got to get the place straightened. Help me with this.

A: Oh, my god.

B: No. It's not what you think.

A: Oh.

B: His/Her parents are going to Cleveland and I said he/she could crash here until they got back. Here.

A: You know . . .

B: What?

A: I'm sorry.

B: That's OK. You don't have anything to be sorry about. Really. Are you listening to me? What's wrong.

A: I'll just put this right here.

B: Thanks.

A: You're welcome.

Scene 5

A: Hi!

B: Hi.

A: What a great surprise! I didn't expect to find anyone here.

B: Yeah.

A: Is something wrong?

B: I just lost my job, my parents have kicked me out of the house, my girlfriend/boyfriend just told me that kissing me revolts her/him since I have acne, and on the way out of my parents' garage, I backed over my dog.

A: Is he dead?

B: No.

A: You must be really upset.

B: Will you knock it off! Where do you get this goody-goody act? I can't believe anybody is as naive as you.

A: I can't believe anybody is as dumb as you.

B: Shut up!

A: I'm serious. You've got everything everyone wants. You're popular, you have a car, for God's sake, your grades are always great and you never even study. You have two VCRs.

B: You have a refrigerator in your room.

A: No, I don't.

B: I was there.

A: When?

B: Friday night.

A: Were you hiding under the bed?

B: What do you mean?

A: I was alone in my room all Friday night studying. Wait. Who do you think I am?

B: Jean/Joe Maldanado.

A: I'm Sue/Bill Trent. We sit next to each other in Communications.

B: Oh.

Scene 6

(A is packing a suitcase. B is sitting watching.)

A: So I said, "Look, I'm an employee at Burger King. I don't belong to Burger King. We have a working agreement that you pay me hourly to serve this stuff. If you want me to stay overtime, you pay me overtime. Otherwise, I don't care who's celebrating their third birthday 'the Burger King way,' find someone else to wipe this shit off those little snots' faces. He bit me!"

B: What did she say?

A: "Young lady/man, you march right out of here." Young lady/man. Jesus. Where did she learn human relations? Nun school?

B: So what are you doing?

A: Packing.

B: You're leaving?

A: San Bernadino here I come!

B: I was in San Bernadino once. They had this train engine made out of plaster and you went inside it and ordered burgers. You never saw the guy. The food arrived at your place on a Lionel train.

A: Don't talk to me about burgers. I've never eaten alfalfa sprouts, but I think I'm developin' a hankerin'.

B: (pause) I'll miss you.

A: (pause) What?

B: I'll miss you.

A: Aaaaah, no, don't. . . . .

B: Sorry. I was walking through the "No Nonsense" mall the other day and another shop had closed. That unisex barber shop "Clip Joint." I looked in and someone had knocked all the stools over. There was a police sticker sealing the door. The bakery next door still had those same stupid wedding cakes in the window with the groom tilted sideways. And I thought . . . I really did think this . . . bad as it looks and bad as it makes me feel, we'll laugh about it tonight.

A: (continues packing . . . finishes) Good bye.

B: (they hug) Will you . . .

A: What?

B: Good bye.

Scene 7

A: Do you mind?

B: Go ahead.

A: Jesus! Pat?

B: Yes.

A: Jean! (Gene) Jean Stark!

B: Well!

A: You still wear Lagerfeld.

B: This is embarrassing.

A: You haven't changed!

B: Neither one of us has apparently.

A: Goddamn! (sings) "When You Wish Upon a Star . . ."

B: Don't.

A: "Makes No Difference Who You Are . . ." You were walking across campus wearing what I can only describe as a "come fuck me" outfit . . .

B: I'd come from the gym.

A: . . . and—sproing! My twelve years of Catholic education down the tubes. I followed you . . .

B: You chased me.

A: . . . into the Ratskellar and drank six beers before I could even look at your table. You were gone. Oh my god! So I turned, and—ta da!

B: You gave me a nose bleed.

A: Pat, Pat, Pat. (They embrace.)

B: I hate you. I hate you, I hate you, I hate you. I was collected; on a career path . . .

A: . . . in library science. Pfft!

B: I had my own room. I had privacy for the first time in my life and was in shape, loved my hair, bought my first full-length mirror . . .

A: . . . and were lonely as bat shit. And there I was with my new nursing degree bandaging your nose and Tony Bennett was singing, "Fate Is Kind. It Brings to Those Who Love . . ."

B: Sproing! was right.

Appendix

[6] Source Materials

Books for Inspiration

When teaching academically, I always have my students read out-side material for inspiration. The following are three of my favorites.

All of the work I've done both as an improviser and as a teacher was initially inspired by:

Johnstone, Keith. *Impro: Improvisation and the Theatre.* New York: Routledge, 1981.

I've worked with Keith and feel that he's one of the few geniuses I've ever met. His work has inspired me, disturbed me, awakened me, and radically changed my perceptions of life in general and theater in particular. Keith invented the TheatreSports format: Improvisation as a Competitive Sport. This format is played around the world and has made it to television.

The book is extremely provocative. As a class assignment, I have students take three quotes from each chapter that inspire them, make them laugh, or that they disagree with, and write about each one, using stories from their own lives to illustrate their point. This assignment not only exposes them to a remarkable man, it encour-ages them to say the first thing that comes into their heads by telling obvious stories from their own lives, reinforcing the unique voice in the arts they already are.

Another powerful source of inspiration is:

Ueland, Brenda. *If You Want to Write: A Book about Art, Independence and Spirit*. St. Paul, MN: Graywolf Press, 1987.

It's not so much a book on writing technique. Ms. Ueland is a cheerleader for self-expression and my students have loved this book. I re-read it myself every few years.

And finally:

Nachmanovitch, Stephen. *Free Play: The Power of Improvisation in Life and the Arts*. New York: Putnam, 1990.

This is a rich, thought-provoking book on the process of creativity.

Source Material for Improvisation Games

With all the improvisation companies currently in existence, your best and most up-to-date method of finding games for both rehearsal and performance is to go to the Internet. Games are always changing, and new ones are constantly being invented.

An excellent general source for improv information, including listings of events across the country, articles, books and publications, etc., is the website *Yes And: The Improv Information Source That Cannot Be Denied: www.yesand.com/*

In addition, I put "improv games description" into a search engine and came up with the following sites at the time of this book's publication. If they no longer exist, you're sure to find similar sites using the same method.

Improv Encyclopedia: *www.humanpingpongball.com*

Improv Games: *www.fuzzyco.com/improv/games.html*

Improv Games: *www.nicoth.com/articles/improv_games.htm*

Improv Games at Improvland: *www.improvland.com/magazine/columns/games/*

Improv Games for Rehearsal and Performance: *http://mosaics.org/resources/improv_games.html*

TOAS Improvisation Games: *www.upstagereview.org/improvartsindex.html*

Index

Books from Allworth Press

Allworth Press is an imprint of Allworth Communications, Inc. Selected titles are listed below.

Making It on Broadway: Actors' Tales of Climbing to the Top
by David Wienir and Jodie Langel (paperback, 6 × 9, 288 pages, $19.95)

The Perfect Stage Crew: The Compleat Technical Guide for High School, College, and Community Theater
by John Kaluta (paperback, 6 × 9, 256 pages, $19.95)

Business and Legal Forms for Theater
by Charles Grippo (paperback with CD-ROM, $8\frac{1}{2}$ × 11, 192 pages, $29.95)

Movement for Actors
edited by Nicole Potter (paperback, 6 × 9, 288 pages, $19.95)

Acting for Film
by Cathy Haase (paperback, 6 × 9, 224 pages, $19.95)

Creating Your Own Monologue
by Glenn Alterman (paperback, 6 × 9, 192 pages, $14.95)

Promoting Your Acting Career
by Glenn Alterman (paperback, 6 × 9, 224 pages, $18.95)

An Actor's Guide—Making It in New York City
by Glenn Alterman (paperback, 6 × 9, 288 pages, $19.95)

Career Solutions for Creative People
by Dr. Rhonda Ormont (paperback, 6 × 9, 320 pages, $19.95)

Building the Successful Theater Company
by Lisa Mulcahy (paperback, 6 × 9, 240 pages, $19.95)

Please write to request our free catalog. To order by credit card, call 1-800-491-2808 or send a check or money order to Allworth Press, 10 East 23rd Street, Suite 510, New York, NY 10010. Include $5 for shipping and handling for the first book ordered and $1 for each additional book. Ten dollars plus $1 for each additional book if ordering from Canada. New York State residents must add sales tax.

To see our complete catalog on the World Wide Web, or to order online, you can find us at ***www.allworth.com.***